Torah, Service, Deeds

Jewish Ethics in Transdenominational Perspectives

Edited by
Jonathan L. Friedmann and Joel Gereboff

Ben Yehuda Press
Teaneck, New Jersey

TORAH, SERVICE, DEEDS: JEWISH ETHICS IN TRANSDENOMINATIONAL PERSPECTIVES ©2023 by the authors. All rights reserved. No part of this book may be used or reproduced in any manner whatsoever without written permission except in the case of brief quotations embodied in critical articles and reviews.

Published by Ben Yehuda Press
122 Ayers Court #1B
Teaneck, NJ 07666

http://www.BenYehudaPress.com

To subscribe to our monthly book club and support independent Jewish publishing, visit https://www.patreon.com/BenYehudaPress

Ben Yehuda Press books may be purchased at a discount by synagogues, book clubs, and other institutions buying in bulk. For information, please email markets@BenYehudaPress.com

ISBN13 978-1-953829-44-3

23 24 25 / 10 9 8 7 6 5 4 3 2   202230421

Contents

Preface — v

Introduction — vii
    Jonathan L. Friedmann and Joel Gereboff

Mitzvot and Human Dignity — 1
    Art Levine

Set One

Principled Indignity Leading to Principled Reparation:
Microcosmic Injuries and Recovering from Them — 11
    Rochelle Robins

Intellectual Honesty: An Ethical Approach to Adult Jewish Education — 25
    Revital Somekh-Goldreich

Set Two

Spirituality and Ethics in Transdenominational Jewish Pedagogy — 49
    Stephen Robbins

Interpersonal Ethics: Our Partner in Digital Citizenship — 59
    Corinne Copnick

Set Three

The Human Covenant: Toward an Ethic of Jewish Political Engagement — 79
    Shaiya Rothberg

Fear of Sin and of One's Teacher in Early Rabbinic Judaism — 97
    Joel Gereboff

Set Four

Growing from Interfaith Environmental Conversations   123
    Nina Perlmutter

A Difference of Degree: Toward a Post-Anthropocentric Judaism   139
    Jonathan L. Friedmann

Set Five

The Ethical and Religious Duty for Jewish Clergy:
Speak Out, Warn, and Take Action
Against All Injustice and Threats to Inclusive American Democracy   159
    Stan Levy

White-Designated Jews Are Obligated to Fight White Supremacy   171
    Robin Podolsky

Set Six

The 13 Principles of Ethics
at the Academy for Jewish Religion California   195
    Mel Gottlieb

Spiritual Ethics: Rachamim   203
    Susan Goldberg

About the Contributors   225

Preface

The title of this collection, *Torah, Service, Deeds*, derives from *Pirkei Avot* 1:2: "Shimon the Righteous was one of the last of the members of the Great Assembly. He used to say: 'On three things the world stands: on Torah, on service (*avodah*), and on deeds of lovingkindness (*gemilut hasadim*).'" These three facets are at the core of the Academy for Jewish Religion California (AJRCA), a transdenominational seminary founded in 2000 to train rabbis, cantors, chaplains, and other Jewish communal leaders. They comprise AJRCA's institutional learning outcomes; all curricular and co-curricular requirements stem from and connect back to them. As the student catalog states: "All our programs share basic overall objectives of education for Jewish leadership. We affirm the Jewish tradition that our life, collectively and individually, rests on three pillars: Torah, *avodah*, and *gemilut hasadim*."

The third pillar, in particular, guides the school and its students in living out the trifold adage. It is also a working definition for how the term "ethics" is used in this book. The catalog describes it thus:

GEMILUT HASADIM (acts of lovingkindness) represents the ability to contribute to the enhancement of Jewish life through service, education, leadership development, an exemplary personal lifestyle, and ethical behavior. It includes supporting and guiding individuals and groups toward positive change and enabling them to discover their own potentials for service. In achieving this outcome, the AJRCA student is expected to acquire the following core competencies:

- Skill in helping individuals and groups develop healthy responses to life issues, deeper spirituality, and positive connections to community.
- Ability to contribute to productive work environments, work in teams, and communicate with people of diverse backgrounds and needs, both in the Jewish world and in interfaith contexts.
- Practical understanding of the role of the rabbi, cantor, chaplain, or community leader in relation to various institutions and resources in the Jewish community, including synagogues and their internal structures, schools, professional organizations, and charitable institutions.

This book is the second in a series exploring the unique vision, purpose, and contributions of AJRCA and the individuals who teach and learn in its programs. The first book, *Nondenominational Judaism: Perspectives on Pluralism and Inclusion in 21st-Century Jewish Professional Education* (2020), collected essays from faculty, administrators, and alumni from AJRCA and other institutions engaged in pluralistic higher Jewish educations. Those essays explored the "what:" personal, academic, and philosophical reflections on learning, teaching, administrating, and leading in transdenominational Jewish settings; the unique roles of pluralism *vis-à-vis* denominational models; and the benefits and challenges of nondenominational Jewish education. The present volume addresses the "how:" practical applications and aspirations that actionize, in diverse and meaningful ways, AJRCA's mission to "transform the Jewish world" and beyond.

Introduction

Jonathan L. Friedmann and Joel Gereboff

> Judaism is an organism; the fabric of its weaving is alive.
> —Rabbi Milton Steinberg[1]

Founded in 2000 as a transdenominational Jewish seminary, the Academy for Jewish Religion California (AJRCA) brings together faculty, students, ideas, and practices from the range of Jewish approaches without adhering to any one movement, branch, or denomination. AJRCA acknowledges that "Judaism is not monolithic—sages from different centuries add to its profound wisdom as it adapts to new circumstances while maintaining its eternal principles and values while evolving through time."[2] Program curricula explore the wide corpus of Jewish law, literature, ritual, and lore, studying ancient and modern insights in search of truth (or, really, numerous truths)—all with the aim of developing Jewish leaders who transform the communities they serve into places where individuals grow toward spiritual wholeness and wellbeing. As the twenty-first century continues to bring rapid changes to Judaism and Jewish affiliation, and as major challenges continue to mount within and well beyond the Jewish world, effective leadership increasingly requires familiarity with and dexterity in various ethical areas: interpersonal, social, political, environmental, medical, and business.

Training rabbis, cantors, chaplains, and other Jewish community leaders in AJRCA's eclectic environment is at the same time innovative and organic. In truth, Judaism has never been a single, inflexible entity, but has existed as an array of "Judaisms"—a plural understanding that caught on in the late twentieth century, but was used a hundred years earlier by English author and cultural Zionist Israel Zangwill: "So many Jews, so many Judaisms."[3] A recent textbook by Aaron J. Hahn Tapper, *Judaisms: A Twenty-First-Century Introduction to Jews and Jewish Identities*, foregrounds this polyphony.[4] Each of the book's chapters takes a plural heading: Narratives, Sinais, Zions,

---

[1] Milton Steinberg, *Basic Judaism* (New York: Harcourt, Brace & World, 1947), 4.
[2] "Our Philosophy," Academy for Jewish Religion California, https://ajrca.edu/about/our-philosophy/.
[3] Israel Zangwill, "English Judaism: A Criticism and a Classification," *Jewish Quarterly Review* (1889): 377.
[4] Aaron J. Hahn Tapper, *Judaisms: A Twenty-First-Century Introduction to Jews and Jewish Identities* (Berkeley: University of California Press, 2016).

Messiahs, Laws, Mysticisms, Cultures, Movements, Genocides, Powers, Borders, and Futures.

It turns out that Jewish tradition is actually Jewish *traditions*, Jewish thought is Jewish *thoughts*, Jewish practice is Jewish *practices*, Jewish community is Jewish *communities*; this is the way it has always been, from proto-Jewish biblical times to the postmodern present. For every purported Jewish mainstream, there are many tributaries. At certain times and places, tributaries can become mainstreams and vice versa, and new rivers and streams emerge as well. Implicit in the terms *k'lal Yisrael* (all Jews), *am Yisrael* (people of Israel), and *amiut Yehudit* (Jewish peoplehood) is a recognition of multi-layered variety: geographical, political, cultural, generational, ideological, linguistic, ritualistic, and otherwise. The Jewish people's "collective soul" comprises a complex assortment of individual souls—and even the concept of "soul" (*nefesh*) is interpreted in variegated ways.

So, how can there be something called "Jewish ethics" when both halves of the construct exist in the plural? In many ways, impediments to defining Jewish ethics—or deciphering what constitutes such a category—is part of a larger conceptual challenge: the imprecision of labelling *any* aspect of Jewish thought and practice. Philosopher Zachary Braiterman of Syracuse University is skeptical about the possibility and utility of labelling Jewish ethics, noting that, prior to the 1970s, the term appears only episodically:

> Jewish ethics is a mythical beast that slips the net the moment one thinks one has it trapped, which is not to say that this chimerical creature has no indigenous habitat in the sources of Judaism. The tradition is not without its own peculiar moralities, but the tradition is "unethical," which is to say morally inconsistent, complicated by extra-moral aspects not theorized as such.[5]

Tracing a range of factors that call into question the meaningful use of the term "ethics"—particularly in relation to the diversity of modes of Jewish expression and tensions between laws and other values—Braiterman concludes his essay by observing:

> Jewish ethics had to be invented in the 1970s because it did not exist in the first place, not being an "independent thing," not unambiguously backed up by God at the foun-

---

[5] Zachary Braiterman, "Ethics ex Nihilo: The Invention of Jewish Ethics," *The Journal of Jewish Ethics* 7:1 (2021): 83.

dational center of a continuous group of teachings stretched across the tradition. Submerged into theology, ritual, law, ethos, and ethnos, it is not clear that the Jewish ethical tradition exists apart from its retrospective consecration as a more or less profound work of the modern moral imagination.[6]

Ronald M. Green, emeritus religion and ethics professor at Dartmouth College, touches on this conundrum in his essay, "Foundations of Jewish Ethics." Green contends that Jewish ethics is an inadequate term when discussing behavioral standards and expectations of the Jews:

> The lesser place given to systemic ethical reflection in Jewish thought stems from the fact that Judaism developed independently of the two traditions that shaped Western approaches to ethics: the Greco-Roman tradition of moral philosophy, and the Christian tradition of ethical teaching. The philosophers of Greece and Rome imparted to the field of ethics a commitment to the rational analysis and reasoned justification of moral norms in terms of their impact on human well-being.[7]

In contrast, argues Green, the Jewish impulse for law (*halakhah*) reflects a conviction that moral requirements must be *embodied*, not intellectualized. As such, Euthyphro's famous dilemma, derived from Plato's dialogue *Euthyphro*, is not quite the puzzle for Jews as it is for many theists: "Is it morally good because the gods [or God] will it, or do the gods [or God] will it because it is morally good?" In the action-orientated framework of Jewish life, whether theistically rooted or not, ethical commandments (*mitzvot*) are felt to be both inherently good *and* commanded because they are inherently good: they are inter-human requirements with divine approval. As *Pirkei Avot* 3:10 relates: "Anyone who is liked by their fellow human beings is liked by God; anyone who is not liked by human beings is not liked by God."[8] This is why, for instance, the "golden rule" remains golden with or without the theistic formula used in Leviticus 19:18: "Love your

---

[6] Ibid., 105.
[7] Ronald M. Green, "Foundations of Jewish Ethics," in *The Blackwell Companion to Religious Ethics*, ed. William Schweiker (Malden, MA: Blackwell, 2005), 166.
[8] Translation from Irving (Yitz) Greenberg, *Sage Advice: Pirkei Avot with Translation and Commentary* (New Milford, CT: Maggid, 2016), 133

fellow as yourself: I am God." As a collection of embodied actions, Jewish ethics is simultaneously authoritative (obedient to the most powerful) and consequentialist (judged to be right based on their consequences). While the Talmudic sages distinguished between ritual (human-divine) and ethical (inter-human) *mitzvot*, ethics did not become an independent category. Instead, inter-human commandments were placed within the larger covenantal relationship to God.[9]

This dual grounding helps explain how Polish-born rabbi Abraham Joshua Heschel, a refugee from Nazi Europe and a descendent of rabbis on both sides of his family, could frame his involvement in the American Civil Rights Movement in theological terms, drawing lessons from the biblical prophets, whereas the predominantly secular Jewish student activists, who disproportionately filled the ranks of "white" civil rights campaigners, gave little thought to theology. Among the young activists was Jacob Schlitt, a New York-born native Yiddish speaker, who remarked: "Trying to find in your religious upbringing a sense of social justice I think is a stretch. I think, by and large, if you're a good person—Jewish or not Jewish—you're going to have a concern for the weaker and the oppressed and people whose lives are harder."[10] Another young activist, Michael Steinlauf, now a professor of history and director of the Holocaust and Genocide Studies Program at Gratz College, recalled: "Little did I know how many Jews were involved in this. It didn't matter to me. But, of course, large numbers of Jews were involved, and I've thought quite a bit about it. This was our largely unconscious answer to 'never again.'"[11] Erich Fromm, a Jewish humanistic psychologist who fled Nazi Germany for the U.S. in 1933, observed during the civil rights era that because Jews were "among the suffering and despised, they were able to develop and uphold a tradition of humanism."[12] Like Heschel, Fromm saw the prophets as ethical role models; however, he downplayed the need for theology after the prophetic period:

> [The prophets] developed their thought to the point where God ceases to be definable by any positive attributes of essence, and where the right way of living—for individuals and for nations—takes the place of theology. Although

---

[9] Shaul Magid, "Ethics Differentiated from Law," in *The Blackwell Companion to Religious Ethics*, ed. William Schweiker (Malden, MA: Blackwell, 2005), 176.
[10] "Jews and Activism in the 1960s," Wexler Oral History Project, Yiddish Book Center, January 17, 2012, https://www.youtube.com/watch?v=n3u2_8LJtSI&t=219s.
[11] Ibid.
[12] Erich Fromm, *You Shall Be as Gods: A Radical Interpretation of the Old Testament and Its Tradition* (New York: Fawcett, 1966), 16.

logically the next step in the Jewish development would be a system without "God," it is impossible for a theistic-religious system to take this step without losing its identity.[13]

While these positions—theological, secular, and somewhere in between (Fromm called himself a "nontheistic mystic")—are intellectually interesting, what truly matters is that they led to shared concerns and engagements, namely what is variously called *tzedek* (justice), *tikkun olam* (healing the world), prophetic Judaism, and social justice.

But what about the southern Jews who resented northern Jews coming to their cities and "stirring up trouble"? Fearing antisemitic backlash, were they not justified—perhaps even *ethically* justified—in wanting to navigate the status quo? Some opposed oppression on moral grounds but believed the fight for racial equality was potentially "bad for the Jews." This might be described as situational ethics, where decision-making is contextually dependent on a specific set of circumstances. Such decisions are *halakhically* frowned upon under ordinary conditions, but are generally accepted when a situation's unusualness or complexity puts it "beyond the line of the law" (*lifnim mishurat ha-din*).[14] To be sure, hindsight paints southern Jewish objectors in a negative light, especially as some southern Jewish leaders took a proactive stance against segregation.[15] Still, the messiness of the moment can often put our better angels on hold.

As this example shows, not all conceptions of Jewish ethics are the same. Given Judaism's multi-vocal nature, how could they be? The guiding philosophy of AJRCA, cited above, is instructive: adhering to Judaism's "profound principles and values while evolving through time." The core of such principles—what social psychologists call "prosocial behaviors"—do not fundamentally change. Yet, how they are interpreted, reinterpreted, emphasized, deemphasized, limited, or expanded can vary subtly or drastically from community to community. Such malleability is a byproduct of evolving, adapting, and situationally informed Jewish experiences. Harold M. Schulweis, the late spiritual leader of Valley Beth Shalom in Encino, California, observed in his aptly titled essay, "The Single Mirror of Jewish Images: The Pluralistic Character of Jewish Ethics":

---

[13] Ibid., 44.
[14] See Shmuel Shilo, "On One Aspect of Law and Morals in Jewish Law: *Lifnim Mishurat Hadin*," *Israel Law Review* 13:3 (1978): 359–390.
[15] Chris Webb, *Fight Against Fear: Southern Jews and Black Civil Rights* (Athens: University of Georgia Press, 2003).

> Liberal authors characterize Jewish ethics as idealistic, universal, this-worldly, optimistic, rational, anti-ascetic, humanistic. Writers of the orthodox school depict the same subject matter quite differently. To them it appears other-worldly, particularistic, largely concerned with ritual, law and obedience to Divine Will.[16]

Notwithstanding the many shades of gray on both the liberal and orthodox sides, Schulweis rightly highlights how conservative and progressive tendencies, changing zeitgeists, and differing schema (authoritative or consequentialist) can yield contrasting views. Yet, at the end of the day, both are authentic variations of the thing called "Jewish ethics." Schulweis continues:

> To appreciate the wholistic character of Jewish ethics, it is better to abandon these partisan, single-strained characterizations which lay exclusive claim to represent the authentic tradition. We have before us two principal sources to draw upon in portraying the nature of Jewish ethics: the maxims and epigrams aphoristically strewn throughout the entire body of the literature; and the ethics, both implied and articulated, in the codes of law and ritual practice. We cannot produce without distortion an undiversified Jewish system of ethics out of this civilizational complexity. A truer picture will portray a gamut of pluralistic moods and dialectical exchanges reflecting the richness of the Jewish experience.[17]

Proving his claim, Schulweis pulls from a number of ostensibly contradictory ethical sayings, such as: "Every person will be held accountable before God for all the permitted things he beheld in life and did not enjoy"[18] and "In order to be holy it is necessary to abstain even from things that are permitted."[19] We can imagine these opposing views being appropriate for particular moments and, as such, being equally valid and true. This is not unlike the fabled pockets of Rebbe Simcha Bunim of Peshischa. In one pocket was a piece of paper stating, "I am only dust and ashes," to be read when feeling too proud or self-centered. In the other pocket was a paper

---

[16] Harold M. Schulweis, "The Single Mirror of Jewish Images: The Pluralistic Character of Jewish Ethics," *University Papers* (University of Judaism) (Jan. 1982): 2.
[17] Ibid., 3.
[18] y. *Kiddushin* 4:12.
[19] b. *Yevamot* 20a.

stating, "For my sake was the world created," to be read when feeling low or disheartened. One of the benefits of the unsystematic nature of Jewish ethics—and Judaism more broadly—is the possibility of holding many truths in our pockets, each of them at once eternal and flexible.

While it may well be true that the category of ethics is not native to Jewish vocabulary throughout the ages, it is clear that Jewish ethics, like many other terms, has achieved a level of acceptance in both Jewish and broader academic and general communities. This evolving understanding is consistent with the ideology of AJRCA, as well as efforts like the *Oxford Handbook of Jewish Ethics and Morality*,[20] the *Journal of Jewish Ethics*, and the Society of Jewish Ethics which publishes that journal. These reflect a deepening and expanding field. Although not all the contributors to this volume have studied in depth the concerns raised by Braiterman, Green, Schulweis, and others, or have attended graduate programs in ethics, they skillfully draw from different aspects of Jewish traditions and their own experiences to advance insightful analyses and illuminating assertions.

A final note: While the term "ethics" is used throughout this book, we are cognizant of a further challenge that can be raised. Academically trained philosophers and ethicists often distinguish between the words ethics (ethical) and morals (morality). Whereas morality applies to discussions of specific issues, such as whether to discontinue medical intervention with regard to a dying patient or to provide subsidies to the poor—and is therefore called "first-order" discourse—ethics refers to more abstract debates about theoretical matters, such as whether moral judgement ought to be made based on overall effects (consequentialist) or if the morality of an action is based on whether the action itself is right or wrong, regardless of the consequences (deontological). Thus, ethics is a "second-order" level of conversation. However, in popular parlance, the terms are frequently used interchangeably. Following that practice, this book employs "ethics" or "ethical" in reference to both laying out positions on specific actions and making decisions in relation to more general principles and approaches.[21]

*****

Torah, Service, Deeds collects essays on diverse approaches to a spectrum of ethical issues. Written by faculty and alumni of AJRCA, the chapters

---

[20] Elliot N. Dorff and Jonathan K. Krane, *Oxford Handbook of Jewish Ethics and Morality* (New York: Oxford University Press, 2012).
[21] Ibid. Dorff and Crane discuss these points in their collection of essays, which are divided into two sections: one tracing the history of Jewish ethical theories, and the other looking at Jewish views on specific issues, such as biomedicine and poverty.

demonstrate that a shared and genuine commitment to values and concerns can be expressed through varied lenses and applications. Each author has been paired with another who has written on related themes. Following their essays, the two authors respond to one another, modeling pluralistic Jewish dialogue. It is our hope that this "simulated *chavruta*" (study pair) inspires readers to reach out to people of other stripes, Jews and non-Jews, to productively engage the issues of today. Examining our similarities and differences can yield positive growth and renewed commitment to healing our world: "As iron sharpens iron, so does a person sharpen the wit of their friend" (Prov. 27:17).

The chapters open with Rabbi Dr. Art Levine, z"l, a brilliant lawyer, historian, and alumnus of AJRCA's Rabbinical School, who sadly died in October 2021 after a long bout with cancer. His essay is compiled from blog entries published on his still-active website, rabbiartlevine.com. Rabbi Levine examines the relationship between *mitzvot* and human dignity, both in terms of self and others. This is a starting point for all discussions of Jewish ethics.

Rabbi Rochelle Robins, AJRCA's vice president and academic dean of the Chaplaincy and Rabbinical Schools, follows with an essay on "microcosmic injury," or "the phenomenon of our own suffering when we contribute to the suffering of others as the result of supporting misaligned authority structures." Rabbi Robins explains that while these moral injuries might be construed as "microscopic," as they occur between individuals, seem minor, and are easily overlooked, they are in fact "cosmic" in that they are part of a universal problem of interpersonal relationships. Her examination is anchored in a reappraisal of Miriam's leprosy and her brother Aaron's response (Num. 12), and how that episode mirrors our own unacknowledged culpability in the suffering of others. Revital Somekh-Goldreich, a visual artist, alumna of AJRCA's Master of Jewish Studies Program, and a professor of biblical studies and Jewish history at AJRCA, similarly stresses the importance of intellectual honesty in reading biblical texts. She advocates for wrestling with received tradition, classical commentaries, and modern biblical criticism as a way to deepen our connection with texts that, all too often, are subject to whitewashing or apologetics. This is crucial in adult education, where withholding academic textual criticism, in particular, can be considered unethical in that it forecloses the student's ability to grow spiritually through tension and doubt.

Rabbi Dr. Stephen Robbins, co-founder of AJRCA, articulates the unity of spirituality and ethics in Jewish thought and practice, stressing that all forms of spirituality have an ethical component and demand to be actualized in behavior. This "unified theory" of Jewish life, in which spirituality, ethics, and morality are intertwined, transcends denominational distinctions and, according to Rabbi Robbins, must be centered in transdenominational education. AJRCA alumna Rabbi Corrine Copnick, a *dayan* and governor of the Sandra Caplan Community Bet Din and founding rabbi of Beit Kulam, both in Los Angeles, looks to the Torah for a "biblical blueprint" for positive interpersonal communication. In our digital age, when interpersonal interactions can be far from ethical—and often far from personal—enacting these fundamental teachings is a practical way of unifying the spiritual, moral, and ethical in our daily lives.

Dr. Shaiya Rothberg, a Jerusalem-based scholar and activist and AJRCA visiting faculty member, writes that politics, "the realm of social justice and injustice," requires our active participation. Drawing together Jewish teachings and insights from the 1948 Universal Declaration of Human Rights, Dr. Rothberg argues for a textually and contextually informed Jewish political engagement, especially as we witness the erosion of global democratic and human rights ideals of the post-World War II era. Dr. Joel Gereboff, AJRCA professor of Bible and Jewish history, looks at two uses of "fear" in early rabbinic literature: fear of sin (*yirat chet*) and fear of one's teacher (*morat rabbo*). Exploring what role, if any, emotion plays in these conceptions and considering what role fear should play in Jewish life, Dr. Gereboff shows that behaviors and relationships based on rabbinic ideas of fear can be a constructive aspect of ethical living.

AJRCA alumna Nina Perlmutter, rabbi of Congregation Lev Shalom in Flagstaff, Arizona, and faculty emerita at Yavapai Community College, reflects on her experiences teaching Jewish environmental ethics in interfaith settings. Discussing key differences between how Jews and non-Jews (esp. Christians) read sacred texts, Rabbi Perlmutter highlights ecological teachings sprouting from the covenantal, theocentric soil of Jewish religious thought. Cantor Dr. Jonathan L. Friedmann, an AJRCA alumnus and professor of Jewish music history and academic dean of the Academy's Master of Jewish Studies Program and Rabbinical School, critiques Judaism's anthropocentric tendencies and how the special status given to humans in all strands of Judaism—from orthodox to humanistic—ignores similarities we share with non-human animals. Cantor Friedmann proposes expanding interpersonal ethical ideals, such as creation in God's image and loving one's neighbor, to include non-human animals as well.

AJRCA co-founder Rabbi Stan Levy shares lessons from decades of work in social justice, both as a rabbi and as a civil rights and public interest lawyer. His urgent message, born from years on the ground and study of

Jewish texts, and inspired by courageous Jewish and non-Jewish leaders, is that all Jews—and Jewish leaders most of all—have a duty to combat racism, bigotry, and oppression in the U.S. and in Israel. Rabbi Robin Podolsky, an educator, activist, writer, and AJRCA alumna who serves on the board of governors of the Sandra Caplan Community Bet Din, concurs that American Jews must oppose institutional racism and "all its ideological and functional props, including antisemitism." Rather than finding false comfort in tenuously ascribed "whiteness" and the perceived privileges it affords, Rabbi Podolsky insists that white-designated Jews must actively confront white supremacy, as well as those who downplay or dismiss the long history of systemic racism and its lasting impacts.

AJRCA president emeritus Rabbi Dr. Mel Gottlieb lays out thirteen ethical principles for the school, following Maimonides' template of thirteen principles of Jewish faith. Rabbi Gottlieb's formulation, rooted in his long involvement with Mussar—a Jewish spiritual practice offering concrete instructions for ethical and meaningful living—is applicable in all collaborative Jewish settings: listening; lovingkindness; consistency; concentrated study; humility; pursuit of justice; universal love; individual uniqueness; joy of acceptance; learning from others; strength in discipline; honoring others; and the interconnection of all Jews. AJRCA alumna Rabbi Susan Goldberg, founder of the Nefesh community in Los Angeles' east side, focuses on compassion—*rachamim*—a central *middah* (value) of Mussar. Rabbi Goldberg reminds us that compassion is not merely a feeling, but an action to be carried out in our relationships with ourselves, others in our community, and the broader world. Achieving this requires discipline, practice, exterior feedback, and interior work.

As rich as these essays and the authors' responses to them are, they can only scratch the surface of a topic as hugely important, always evolving, as ever-relevant as Jewish ethics. Readers are encouraged to put this modest volume to practical use, applying the teachings and techniques herein to encounters with self, others, and the Earth.

Mitzvot and Human Dignity

Art Levine

By tradition, there are 613 *mitzvot*, or commandments, in the Torah. None of them explicitly states that we must preserve the dignity of another person or oneself. But these obligations are deeply and widely suffused among the *mitzvot*. They are also a very high priority among the rabbinic rulings that interpret and apply the *mitzvot*. This chapter examines this important aspect of Torah commandments, its elucidation in rabbinic literature, and its significance for us today.

Protecting Others' Dignity

When the offering of the first fruits (*bikkurim*) was brought to the Temple, a number of verses had to be read with the offering. Initially, those who could not read repeated the words that were pronounced for them by a reader. The rabbis then instituted a rule that permanent readers should read for everyone, to avoid embarrassing those who could not read.[1] This is the practice adopted today in most American synagogues for Torah reading. Since most people today cannot chant the Torah with the proper melody, a Torah reader reads for everyone, even those who can read, in order to avoid embarrassment.

Similarly, it was the custom to bring food to a *shiva* house of mourning. However, the poor used to bring food in plain baskets while the rich brought food in fancier baskets or on trays, which caused embarrassment to the poor. Therefore, the rabbis instituted a custom whereby everyone had to bring food in a plain basket to the house of mourning. Likewise, rich mourners would serve wine in clear glasses and the poor in colored glasses; to protect the dignity of the poor, the rabbis ordered that all must use colored glasses.[2]

Sometimes, the Torah's concern for human dignity is not so obvious, although it is no less real or important. For example, *parashat Tzav* (Lev. 6:1–8:36) sets forth the circumstances and procedures by which sacrificial offerings were to be brought. During the days of the Temple, some sacrifices were obligatory, some were voluntary donations of thanksgiving, and some were brought to atone for sin. In this last category were the *chatta'ah* (sin-offering), brought for an unintentional transgression; the *asham* (guilt-offering), brought, for example, for the sin of swearing falsely;

---

[1] m. *Bikkurim* 3:7.
[2] b. *Moed Katan* 27a.

and the *olah* (burnt-offering), sometimes brought for improper thoughts, although it could be brought for other reasons as well, unrelated to sin.

If different locations at the Temple had been designated for bringing the various sacrifices, or if this had been left to the priests to decide, spectators would know the nature of a person's sacrifice. The Temple would become a place of public humiliation. To prevent this, the rabbis observed that the Torah specifically commands: "In the place where the *olah* is slaughtered shall the *chatta'ah* be slaughtered" (Lev. 6:18) and "In the place where they slaughter the *olah* shall they slaughter the *asham*" (Lev. 7:2).[3] Under this system, spectators would never know whether a particular sacrifice was a voluntary offering or something obligatory in expiation of a sin. This is one way the Torah sought to protect dignity and esteem, even of the sinner.

Have you ever wondered why we say most of the *Amidah* (standing prayer) silently? The rabbis used these Torah verses about sin offerings as their source for a regulation that the *Amidah* is to be recited quietly in order not to embarrass people who confess their sins.[4]

Maimonides ruled that a person may violate any rabbinic (although not biblical) injunction in order to preserve human dignity.[5] Since most of Jewish practice is rabbinic, rather than biblical, most practices in Judaism can be violated if doing the *mitzvah* would necessitate violating a person's dignity.

Of the many instances in the Torah which depict preservation of an individual's dignity, two stand out for me. Tamar was willing to be burned to death rather than reveal that Judah had impregnated her (Gen. 39). And God changed his account to Abraham regarding what Sarah had said rather than embarrass Abraham with her actual statement (Gen 18:12-13). These certainly demonstrate that one of our most important responsibilities is to save others from public embarrassment. This includes making our criticisms in private and stopping others from causing embarrassment, even when the target has indeed misbehaved. It also includes protecting others from potentially embarrassing situations, even if we must inconvenience ourselves to do so. Rabbi Joseph Telushkin relates the following incident:

> For many decades, Rabbi Joseph Soloveitchik [1903–1993] taught the *shiur* (class) in Talmud at Yeshiva University. His lessons generally lasted two or three hours. One year, one of his students, Ezra Lightman, was diagnosed with Hodgkin's disease, for which he was receiving chemothera-

---

[3] b. *Sotah* 32b; y. *Yevomot* 8:3.
[4] b. *Sotah* 32b.
[5] Moses Maimonides, *Mishneh Torah, Hilchot Kelayim* 10:29.

py treatments. In those days, people kept such information to themselves. Rabbi Soloveitchik was a family friend and therefore knew of the illness, although none of the students in the class was aware of it. Rachel Wiederkehr, Mr. Lightman's sister, recalls, "Once a chemotherapy appointment meant that Ezra would have to leave the *shiur* early. Aware that my brother's departure would arouse the curiosity of his classmates, Rabbi Soloveitchik dismissed the entire class early that day so that Ezra would not feel conspicuous and so that his secret would remain safe."[6]

Promoting Self-Dignity

Why should we observe the Torah's commandments? The traditional rationale could not be simpler: because God, our Creator, said so. But over thousands of years, many Jewish scholars have offered additional or alternative reasons. These include honoring our covenant at Sinai; societal preservation and welfare; personal health; furthering Jewish tradition, continuity and distinctiveness; and, of course, maintaining Jewish values and standards, such as preserving life and the ethical treatment of others.

Without discounting or minimizing any of these or other reasons, I find the role of *mitzvot* in promoting character development to be especially appealing. For example, the prohibition against gossiping aids humility, and the prohibition against recreational hunting reduces the affinity for violence. Positive commandments such as "Love your neighbor as yourself" (Lev 19:18) and giving *tzedakah* also build character, as well as helping others.

Parshat Tetzaveh, "You will command" (Exod. 27:20–30:10), provides at least two examples of *mitzvot* which have been interpreted for character development. The first mandates that when Aaron, the High Priest, officiated in the sanctuary, he would wear a robe hemmed with bells of gold, so that their sound would be heard when he entered and when he left (vv. 28:31–35). This would seem a straightforward and limited *mitzvah* that would have no application today, and certainly not affect the rank-and-file Jew's required behavior. But that is not how the rabbinic commentators viewed it.

According to the *midrash*, when Rabbi Yochanan was about to go in to inquire about the welfare of Rabbi Hanina, he would first clear his throat, in keeping with the Torah verse, "And [the sound]—his voice—shall be

---

[6] Joseph Telushkin, *A Code of Jewish Ethics*, vol. 1 (New York: Bell Tower, 2006), 289–290.

heard when he goes in."⁷ The Talmud also teaches us, from this verse, that we must knock before entering a room.⁸ Rabbi Yochanan learned from this the practice of always knocking on the door of his *own* house before entering, and this was one of the seven directives that Rabbi Akiva gave to his son Rabbi Yehoshua: "Do not enter your own house suddenly [that is, without knocking]; all the more so, the house of your neighbor."⁹

In the second example from this Torah portion, the priests were commanded to wear linen breeches from the hips to the thighs to "cover their nakedness" when they approached the altar or entered the Tent of Meeting (Exodus 28:42–43). We can easily imagine that if they had ascended steps without any "underwear," their strides would have been lengthened and their "nakedness" exposed. Yet we know from Exodus 20:22 that the altar did not have steps, it had a gradual incline. Rashi, citing the *Mekhilta*, explains:

> Had there been steps, the priests would have widened their paces; and although it is not an actual uncovering of nakedness, for the priests wore breeches, nevertheless the widening of one's paces in ascending and descending steps is akin to uncovering nakedness and this would be considered acting toward the altar in a disrespectful manner. From here we have a *kal vechomer* [a rule of interpretation]: "The stones of the altar have no understanding or sensitivity to shame, nevertheless the Torah says that since they fulfill a need you must not act toward them in a disrespectful manner. How much more so should you not act disrespectfully towards your fellow man who is an image of your Creator and is sensitive to his shame."¹⁰

About this, Rabbi Zelig Pliskin commented:

> This statement speaks volumes on the Torah's attitude toward man. We must treat our fellow man with more respect than we would the altar in the *Bais Hamikdosh*. Anyone visiting the *Kosel Hamaaravi* (Western Wall), which has less sanctity than the altar, will have a glimpse of this level of respect. If someone were to sling mud at the *Kosel*, ev-

---

⁷ *Leviticus Rabbah* 21:8.
⁸ b. *Pesachim* 112a.
⁹ Ibid.
¹⁰ Rashi on Exodus 20:23; *Mekhilta d'Rabbi Yishmael* 20:23:1.

eryone present would run to stop him. How much greater is our obligation to prevent someone from slinging verbal mud at another person![11]

Thus, the rabbis extrapolated from a commandment about priests wearing breeches when officiating to everyone respecting each other through their speech.

There are many other *mitzvot* that seem impractical, unnecessary, or even ridiculous when taken only at face value. Why should we knock before entering our own home; be forbidden from cursing the deaf, who cannot hear us do so; be obliged to thank inanimate objects (such as our car when we arrive safely or the automated voice on our cell phones when it answers a question)? Because we are creatures of habit. The *mitzvot* train us to be considerate, respectful, humble, and grateful.

As noted, *Tetzaveh* means "You will command." God commanded Moses to bring clear oil made from beaten olives for lighting and to keep burning the *ner tamid*, the eternal light. The great nineteenth-century Torah scholar Yehudah Aryeh Leib Alter, known by his work as the S'fat Emet, interpreted this as a command to "bring the *mitzvah* into the souls of Israel so that they themselves become *mitzvot*."[12] This seems to follow Deuteronomy 10:13, which states, "Keeping the Lord's commandments and laws, which I enjoin upon you today, *for your good*."

I am not suggesting that we look only inward for reasons to observe the *mitzvot*, but if we do, we will certainly find them—character development and spiritual refinement. Things for which I hope we all strive.

"You Shall Not Oppress the Stranger": Preserving Human Dignity
Some of the Torah's *mitzvot* imply a unity of the other's dignity and one's own. This is perhaps best illustrated by the repeated command to not oppress the stranger. I have not counted them to confirm this number, but the Torah evidently has 304,805 letters.[13] According to a principle of rabbinic exegesis (scriptural interpretation), not even one of these 304,805 letters is superfluous. Each has meaning. Therefore, whenever there is repetition, such as the

---

[11] Zelig Pliskin, quoted in "Parshas Yisro," Weekly Torah Portion, JEP Queens, https://www.jepqueens.com/weekly-torah-portion/parshas-yisro/parshas-yisro-would-you-throw-mud-at-the-kosel/.
[12] Cited in Amy Scheinerman, "The Meaning of Mitzvah for Reform Jews," in *Fragile Dialogue: New Voices of Liberal Zionism*, ed. Stanley M. Davids and Lawrence A. Englander (New York: CCAR Press, 2017), 140.
[13] This number is repeated in several scholarly and popular sources, including Arthur Kurzweil's primer, *The Torah for Dummies* (Hoboken, NJ: Wiley, 2007), 236.

famous verse in Deuteronomy 16:20, "Justice, justice you shall pursue," the rabbis assign diverse interpretations to each of the repeated words.

What, then, are we to make of the extreme repetition of one of the verses in Torah, "You shall not wrong a stranger"? It appears twice in *Parshat Mishpatim*, at Exodus 22:20 and again at 23:9, and an incredible thirty-six times in Torah. The ostensible reason for this *mitzvah* is usually stated right along with it: You know the soul of the stranger because you were strangers in Egypt. You know how it feels to be ostracized, marginalized, hated, and oppressed. Empathy is therefore required of you.

However, this does not explain why this admonition is repeated over and over, three dozen times (and some say forty-six times).[14] After all, there are many other very important *mitzvot* that are not repeated even once in Torah, and others only twice, such as the so-called "Ten Commandments."

Perhaps this extraordinary repetition is intended to emphasize a dark aspect of our nature. Many of us do *not* learn from our own suffering not to inflict suffering on others. The last people we would expect to abuse their children are those who themselves were abused as children, but, in fact, they are far more likely to do so than adults who were not abused.

Similarly, historians have often explained the widespread German support for Nazism as a response, in part, to the severe terms the Allies imposed on the Germans at the end of World War I. In short, suffering is often not an ennobling teacher. But that is exactly what the Torah demanded of the Israelites, and continues to demand of Jews today: Learn from the bad treatment you have experienced at the hands of others not to treat others in the same way.

Rabbi Jonathan Sacks pointed out that even the most universal of religions, founded on principles of love and compassion, have often seen those outside the faith as Satan, the infidel, the antichrist, a child of darkness, the unredeemed.[15] They have committed unspeakable acts of brutality in the name of God. The great crimes of humanity have been committed against the stranger, the outsider, the one-not-like-us. Rabbi Sacks taught us that recognizing the humanity of the stranger has been a historic weak link in most cultures. Even with the Statute of Liberty lifting her lamp beside the golden door, in the words of Jewish poet and activist Emma Lazarus, we know that strangers and minorities in our own country have been and still are subject to discrimination and many other misfortunes.

And so, perhaps the reason that "You shall not oppress the stranger"

---

[14] b. *Bava Metzia* 59b.
[15] Jonathan Sacks, *Not in God's Name: Confronting Religious Violence* (New York: Schocken, 2017).

is repeated over and over and over in Torah is to emphasize that we must constantly fight to overcome our ingrained bias against, and even revulsion toward, those who are different than we are.

To accomplish this, I believe, more is required of us than merely refraining from acts of overt oppression. Benign neglect—if neglect can ever actually be benign—is also a form of oppression, especially when we are also commanded to *pursue* justice. Not just to *do* justice, but to *actively pursue* it.

In our polarized society, anyone who does not share our physical or virtual "bubble" constitutes a "stranger." Anyone who does not share our political views is not only a "stranger" but is too often regarded as a threat—to ourselves, our values, our nation. These attitudes are the seeds of oppression of the stranger. We must demonstrate that, to use the vernacular of our time, "strangers' lives matter."

What can we do, then, from within our bubble, to obey the Torah's incessant and insistent command not to oppress the stranger—who can be our next-door neighbor? The first step, I believe, is to try harder to understand what others believe and why.

We can subscribe to newspapers of different editorial viewpoints. We can watch television stations and Internet websites of differing political orientations. We can train ourselves—force ourselves, if necessary—to listen to earnest, knowledgeable, good-faith spokespersons of other views.

We can discuss religion with friends and followers of other faiths. We can join groups that advocate for minorities or the poor, and we can donate to worthy charities that do so. We can refuse to "stand idly by"—or simply sit at our computers—and instead actively object to discriminatory, hateful, and xenophobic comments whenever we read or hear them. The Torah also obligates us not to listen to *lashon hara*—evil speech—or to accept it when we do hear or read it. And, of course, when we personally encounter a stranger, or hear of strangers in our community, who need help, we are obligated to provide or arrange for that help.

That "You shall not oppress the stranger" is stated three dozen times in the Torah should make this *mitzvah* a continuous priority in our lives. Doing so will not only help us to "Do the right and the good," but to inspire others to do likewise. In the process, we will not only elevate our own dignity, but also protect the dignity of others.[16]

---

[16] For a history of the notion of "dignity," especially among modern religious thinkers, see Gaymon Bennett, *Technicians of Human Dignity: Bodies, Souls, and the Making of Intrinsic Worth* (New York: Fordham University Press, 2015).

Set One

Principled Indignity Leading to Principled Reparation: Microcosmic Injuries and Recovering from Them

Rochelle Robins

Intellectual Honesty: An Ethical Approach to Adult Jewish Education

Revital Somekh-Goldreich

Principled Indignity Leading to Principled Reparation: Microcosmic Injuries and Recovering from Them

Rochelle Robins

Biblical Relevance as a Beginning

This chapter discusses the damages of microcosmic moral injury: the phenomenon of our own suffering when we contribute to the suffering of others as the result of supporting misaligned authority structures. Analysis of microcosmic moral injury centered in Torah will serve as a springboard for further exploration and questioning, and as a means of approaching larger issues of contemporary relevance. By elucidating the concept through an account of the story of Miriam's skin affliction (Num. 12:10), Aaron's role, and possibilities of interpretation, and applying those lessons to ourselves, we can come to appreciate our roles as participants in and potential repairers of microcosmic moral injury.

Prophetic Visionary

Moses, Aaron, and Miriam lead the people Israel from slavery to an arduous freedom in the wilderness. Within their triumvirate sibling prophetic team, Miriam stands out as a particularly influential and vocal contributor. For instance, rabbinic texts acknowledge Miriam's unique prophetic vision to work to reunite her parents' marriage so that Moses could be born to lead the Hebrews.[1] Additionally, according to the rabbis, it is Miriam's vision, courage, and even her audacity and insolence to speak truth (as exhibited in her reprimand of Pharaoh himself after learning about the edicts against the Hebrews to throw their infant boys into the Nile)[2] that shifts her family's consciousness towards what they are compelled to do to save lives and gain freedom.

Miriam is the prophetic visionary and connector to water,[3] without

---

[1] This idea is mentioned in a number of Talmudic and Midrashic texts, including but not limited to b. *Megillah* 14a.
[2] *Shemot Rabbah* 1:13.
[3] *Targum Pseudo-Yonatan*, Numbers 21:17 and *Tosephta Sotah* 11:1 offer examples of writings that refer to Miriam and water.

which all would perish. Her voice in the Torah and rabbinic commentaries is perhaps the earliest one of utmost strength and conviction. It is not uncommon for those who speak out with right-minded conviction, especially when of less privileged social status, to experience suffering as the result. Miriam's personage in the Torah is one of brilliant color. Her strength and prophesying seem evident. Yet, we know very little about her personal suffering.

We celebrate her contribution to the Song of the Sea (Exod. 15:1-18) and meritorious water-well[4]—her life-giving influences. But while it is important to consider rabbinic commentaries, we may not want to be so accepting of their assertion that her brief leprous ailment in the desert was due to *lashon hara*—idle gossip; unwarranted complaints; jealousy over Moses' leadership status; or envy over his direct communication with God. As layers of Torah meaning increase with human consciousness and relationship with one another, it is reasonable to reconsider God, Moses, and Aaron's pact and privilege against and over Miriam.

Rethinking Miriam's Leprosy

The rabbinic explanation for Miriam's *tzara'at* can be perplexing. Why did God give Miriam leprosy at all, and why didn't Aaron also contract it if both of them approach Moses with concerns about his behaviors? Here are the main points of the narrative from Numbers 12:1–16: Miriam and Aaron confront Moses about the Cushite woman he had married. They remind Moses that he is not the only one whom God speaks through—that God speaks through them as well.[5] At this point, God becomes incensed that Miriam and Aaron would speak against Moses and, after chastising them both in Moses' presence, God departs from them (most likely out of anger)[6] and Miriam becomes stricken with what is commonly understood as leprosy. Literally, Miriam contracts "snow-white scales" (Num. 12:10). Aaron recognizes his sister's malady and pleads with Moses that she not be as a stillborn child with half-worn flesh; essentially that she not be left to die. Moses then utters the well-known prayer on Miriam's behalf, "*El na r'fa na*

---

[4] b. *Taanit* 9a. This text is an example of one that merits Miriam with Israelite access to water during her lifetime.

[5] It is difficult to determine which complaint over the two, concern about the Cushite woman or their envy, was the primary motivation for Miriam and Aaron instigating confrontation. Another rebellion is found after this section in the story of Korach, who challenges Moses' authority in Numbers 16:31–33.

[6] The biblical text does not explicitly state that God was angry upon exacting Miriam's affliction, though this is often seen as implied by the events in the narrative. One could argue against this, but for the sake of this essay, ascribing anger to God is reasonable but measured.

la"—"Please God, please heal her!" (Num. 12:13).[7] God agrees to Miriam's healing, but only after she undergoes a seven-day period apart from the rest of the camp; implying quarantine or, more colloquially, a "time out."[8] The snow-white-scales appear to reduce Miriam to the state of *tzara'at*, affliction, that would presumably require an individual to be quarantined until pronounced clean or fit by the priest to return to the community. In this case, God allots the required amount of time that Miriam needs to be away from the main camp before returning. The text tells us that the Israelites did not travel onward without her. They waited until she returned and then journeyed on to their next encampment.

Textual Grappling

The rabbis wonder, as we do, who is this Cushite woman? The ample rabbinic debates include identifying her as none other than Tzipporah, the wife of Moses who is named in the Torah, the term Cushite being an indication of Tzipporah's fine qualities.[9] According to this *midrash*, Miriam knew that Moses was not honoring his matrimonial obligations to Tzipporah, and Miriam, in familial support of Tzipporah and with Aaron's backing, complains to Moses about this.[10]

Another possibility is that Moses took a second nameless, silent wife. The term Cushite is thought to stem from the land of Cush or Cusu, referring to a region in Africa, perhaps in the areas within or near today's Ethiopia.[11] Was Miriam and Aaron's dissent of the Cushite woman due to the darkness of her skin color? Bible scholar David Adamo contends that this argument cannot be true because, unlike our world today, where racism due to skin

---

[7] The entire verse reads, "And Moses cried out to Adonai, saying, please God, please heal her."
[8] The use of the term "time out" is a colloquialism, yet its originator is behavioral psychologist Arthur Staats, who held firm to the belief that briefly isolating a child for a period of time is more effective than punishing either physically or verbally. Art Staats, *Child Learning, Intelligence, and Personality: Principles of a Behavioral Interaction Approach*, 1st ed. (New York: Harper and Row, 1971).
[9] *Tanhuma, Zav* 13.
[10] Ibid. While it is debated that the text is one about skin color and specifically about the darkness of the Cushite woman's skin, God's punishment of Miriam is to turn her skin into snow-white scales. This observation is interpretive in nature and does not provide a definitive response to the question about prejudice in the text. However, if Miriam's articulated complaint is centered on skin color, God punishes her with an affliction that is diametrically opposite to the complaint.
[11] There are many sources where Cush is explained as a location in Africa/Ethiopia, though its precise location is not definitive. A late nineteenth-century citation for this can be found in *Encyclopedia Britannica: A Dictionary of Arts, Sciences, and General Literature* (New York: Scribner and Sons, 1878), 729. See also James Strong, *Strong's Exhaustive Concordance of the Bible, Updated Edition* (Peabody, MA: Hendrickson 2007).

color pervades, "black people were highly respected in the ancient time."[12] He also argues that during biblical times, the African nations served as dependable if not salvific allies to ancient Israel due to their military might.[13] Questioning racism and prejudice is an important aspect of contemporary Torah exploration. It is imperative to raise such questions. At the same time, we cannot be certain that our perspectives on current societal issues can lead to a definite indication of racism in biblical literature.[14]

To be sure, brushing aside possible instances of racism and other prejudices is ill-advised, especially as this chapter examines ways in which we suffer as the result of injurious behaviors towards others based on social status. The topic of using caution when applying contemporary understandings to long-standing norms and customs will be addressed later.

Another area of rabbinic and scholarly struggle is the question of why Miriam was struck with snow-white scales while Aaron's suffering had no sign of physical manifestation. Two of the most common justifications are:

1. Miriam was the speaker as indicated by the Hebrew in Numbers 12:10, where it says: "Miriam and Aaron spoke against Moses because of the Cushite woman he had married." The operative word in question is "spoke," *va'tedaber*, which grammatically is in the first person feminine singular, thus indicating to the rabbis that Miriam was the speaker and Aaron simply went along with her in passive, speechless support.[15]
2. Miriam was commiserating with Tzipporah over Moses' lack of marital attention, either because he married a second wife, or the primary *midrashic* reason being that Moses was no longer paying conjugal attention to Tzipporah.[16]

Aaron's Microcosmic Moral Injury: An Interpretive Leap

In exploring this *parasha*, Rabbi Rachel Biale contends that Miriam is "speaking truth to power." Her commentary focuses on "Miriam and Aaron's respective roles in challenging Moses' prophetic authority and the disparity

---

[12] David Adamo, "A Silent Unheard Voice in the Old Testament: The Cushite Woman whom Moses Married in Numbers 12:1–10," *In die Skriflig* 52:1 (2018): 6.
[13] Ibid.
[14] Further explorations on the complex topic of prejudice and "racism" in antiquity can found in Jillian Stinchcomb, "Race, Racism, and the Hebrew Bible: The Case of the Queen of Sheba," *Religions* 12 (2021): 795.
[15] *Sifrei Bamidbar* 99.
[16] Ibid.

[between them] in the consequences."[17] This section of Torah might be read to show that, even when an individual from a marginalized group—female, LGBTQ+, person of color, etc.—reaches close to the top, being removed from it can create significant and painful disparities of power, especially when "those in dominant roles [are not] willing to diminish their power to accommodate justice."[18] Initially, Aaron did not seem ready or willing to accommodate justice. Yet, to his credit, he immediately sees his mistake and shows regret.

Aaron, a persecutor through complicity in this particular reading of the text, instigates his own suffering, as he plays a role in originating the anguish of another. He becomes his own victim, which draws the reader into a sense of compassion for him. Instead of speaking out, he watches passively as Miriam challenge Moses' authority. Implicitly she is speaking up to, not necessarily against, God as well. Immediately when Aaron observes Miriam's skin turning scaled and snowy-white, he begs Moses—in a manner that is also requesting the same of God—not to punish her for their shared sin; to release Miriam from her illness: "And Aaron said to Moses, 'O my lord account not to us the sin which we committed in our folly'" (Num. 12:11). The word lord, "*adoni*," in the verse indicates Aaron's deference to Moses' authority and higher status. Whether or not Aaron believed he and Miriam truly sinned, he confesses that they did because of the ensuing suffering. How many times have human beings asked for forgiveness not because we thought we were wrong, but because we feared the outcome of our actions? We may have also feared the shame, humiliation, and rejection that can surface when authority castigates us for critiquing those presumed to be "untouchable."

In the biblical account, Aaron's reckoning with his mistake is instantaneous and he wants to help Miriam. Perhaps had Miriam not appeared to be in physical distress so immediately, Aaron's capitulation to the circumstance would not have been instantaneous; perhaps it would not have taken place at all. It could be that he immediately sees the damage he caused not from approaching Moses while standing at Miriam's side, but from allowing her to do the heavy lifting alone. In fact, it is quite possible that the biblical text itself implies, in a small and almost undetectable way, that the voiced concerns of Miriam were accurate.

---

[17] Rachel Biale, "Miriam: Speaking Truth to Power (*Parashat Be'Ha'alotekha*)," *Keshet*, June 2, 2007, https://www.keshetonline.org/resources/miriam-speaking-truth-to-power-parashat-behaaealotekha/.
[18] Ibid.

The only other time in the Chumash,[19] the Five Books of Moses, that the term for snow-white scales (*metzora'at k'sheleg*) appears is in Exodus 4:6, when God is coaching Moses to confront and speak truth to Pharaoh: "And Adonai said furthermore to him, 'Put your hand to your chest.' He put his hand to his chest; and when he brought it out, his hand was evident with snow-white scales." In this section of the Torah, God is stating an imperative that Moses travel to Egypt to confront Pharaoh, to use his voice, to begin the process of proclaiming God's power to free the Hebrews from bondage.

Would it not then be possible, as the only other mentioning of *metzora'at k'sheleg*, that Miriam, too, was speaking truth? Just because God apparently disapproves does not mean there is not truth being spoken. The position here is that the Torah itself reveals what often happens in human discourse and interactions. That is, Aaron harms Miriam by leaving it to her alone to speak truth to authority. Thereafter, a microcosmic moral injury results within Aaron as he sees the impact of his privileged choice and begs for Moses' mercy. Whether or not he views his actions against Moses by Miriam's side as wrongful, he pleads with Moses for the sake of her well-being. Perhaps if he spoke alongside her in the strength of his voice rather than allowing her to express the singularity of her lone female voice, the outcome for Miriam would have been more favorable. Conceivably he knows this and he panics and begs forgiveness out of regret and guilt.

While the microcosmic injurious (most if not all of us have fallen or can fall into this category) may not always be aware of the pain they are causing to themselves, living within structures of unbounded authority takes its toll even on those who benefit from them. This is why instead of naming the phenomenon microscopic moral injury, which connotes "small," a better term is *microcosmic*, which signifies the injuries that may appear to be insignificant due to their one-on-one interpersonal context, but are nevertheless connected to a much larger universal problem.

Accommodating Justice

The Academy for Jewish Religion California (AJRCA) is a trans-Jewish[20] graduate school that educates rabbis, cantors, chaplains, and community leaders. Its primary philosophy, though phrased in the author's terms, is to accommodate justice and bring people together—Jewish spiritual leaders-in-training, faculty, and interfaith colleagues and friends from all

---

[19] The only other mention of the condition in biblical literature is in 2 Kings 5:27, where the term does refer to a punishment. This does not necessarily weaken the parallel in the Torah itself in relation the Moses, Miriam, and Aaron story.

[20] The term "trans-Jewish" is one that I prefer over transdenominational. Judaism, Jewish experiences, and identities are vaster than the religious movements.

backgrounds—to collaborate and build intrareligious, interreligious, and cross-cultural relationships. AJRCA bridges unnecessary divides to create deeper and more connected relationships among people and communities. Accommodating justice necessitates inviting and making room for new and once-silenced voices, opinions, and realities to add to a more truthful picture of what Jews, Judaism, and the world contain. We attempt to travel beyond old stereotypes of male dominance, heterosexism, authority structures, attitudes, and practices. AJRCA is committed to both historical and innovative ways of interpreting text and tradition to increase the visibility of those once invisible and on the margins—to bring all of us into the center of Jewish experiences. The task is not simple, but it is worthy and valuable.

One way we accommodate justice is through allowing sacred texts to reveal new insights according to our evolving understandings. It is unfortunate that those who seek to implement biblical hermeneutics for less righteous means, such as ideas that promote racism and hatred of any kind, also possess a vast array of options that promote injury of all kinds. When we accommodate justice, there is a letting go of past ideas that stifle. We have the opportunity to step out of the garden into an intricate panoply of understanding, thus ultimately shifting our behaviors for the betterment of those who are suffering. Confronting moral injury and this newly presented idea of microcosmic moral injury requires methodical analysis, brave and even insolent conversation (like Miriam's), and letting go of privilege/power to improve relationships.

The microcosmic morally injurious person often functions sub- or unconsciously under the rule of regimes dictating outcomes. They are hurt, we hurt, under the peril of un-confronted and unquestioned privilege.

We are living during a painful time in which old establishments are attempting to strangle new life and creativity. Yet new life and creativity continue to burgeon. Not all regimes are authoritarian or totalitarian. However, even as establishments can appear flexible and open, when placed under a magnifying glass, it is a façade of benevolence hiding unbalanced levels of power. Other institutions can be well-intended but lack the skill to truly see themselves and enact change. They can also be open-hearted, like AJRCA, not entirely bereft of topics of privilege due to social location, but boldly accepting of the conversations, encouraging growth, while still maintaining that strong leadership is not the same as undue power and authority. We are at the forefront of shaping and reshaping memory, including voices that are vying to be heard. This can be as messy, frightening, and chaotic as it is exhilarating.

Reshaping Memory and History

Who shapes memory and history? Comparative religious ethicist Diedre Butler states that "certain memories have been privileged at the expense of others." She writes that a "thick" description of Jewish feminist ethics "allows us to open up the discourse to include other experiences that have been marginalized or silenced."[21] The word "thick" refers to an ethic that intertwines and weaves diversity, multiplicity, and multi-vocal considerations into its foundation. Based on the work and terminology of anthropologist Clifford Geertz, Butler asks "what might a 'thick' account of Jewish feminist ethics—that can integrate compound layers of meaning and interpretation of several cognate disciplines and multiple experiences and perspectives—look like?"[22]

What would it look like? Most of us in the trans-Jewish world agree with the general concept and value of multi-vocal, diverse, and layered considerations. As a general concept it is held close to the heart as the critical ethic of our era. On a more specific level, it requires practice, skill, and a willingness to invite the age-old reality of diversity to reshape memory and history. For the teachers sometimes trapped in our ways, views, and disciplines, it requires consultation and precious time to open up new conversations and methods within old frameworks. Students, who bring their own wisdom, can both respect the old language/terms and theories, while also assisting faculty members to improve their own andragogic approaches. A combination of courage, kindness, and audacity is needed to risk educating an authority figure.

The Disappointment of Education Might Be Ideal

Studying biblical literary criticism, biblical history, and the documentary hypothesis[23] can unearth, disorient, disenchant, and challenge a once-held divine approach to the study of sacred text. Illusions are broken. Enrichment is gained. Grief can also occur as something more innocent is lost. Perhaps disappointment itself is of a spiritually sacred nature. The way we care for one another within it is also a determining factor of how relationships will transpire and build. A more secular approach to the process of disillusion-

---

[21] Deidre Butler, "Disturbing Boundaries: Developing Jewish Feminist Ethics with Buber, Levinas and Fackenheim," *Journal of Modern Jewish Studies* 10:3 (2011): 340.
[22] Ibid., 320.
[23] Innumerable resources exist on the documentary hypothesis that explore biblical and sacred literature from the perspective of literary redaction, which necessitates human intervention. This can be shocking for students who have not yet gained awareness of historical and literary analysis of texts. One of the most widely used resources on the hypothesis is Richard Elliot Friedman, *Who Wrote the Bible?* (New York: Simon & Schuster, 1987).

ment, anger, and re-acclimation can be presented through people's responses to the Thanksgiving holiday in the United States.

When an individual's joy for Thanksgiving is placed in peril by learning that the holiday is inherently connected to the incalculable loss of Indigenous American lives, sovereignty, land, and heritage, grief might ensue. An unbounded joy becomes constrained and tainted by knowledge and anger at an original myth. A perceived Garden of Eden becomes relocated to a deeper understanding of the knowledge of good and evil. Among other influences, Dee Brown's book, *Bury My Heart at Wounded Knee*,[24] shifted the consciousness of open souls who began to understand that the place of their home, their residence in a nation, and the celebration of a holiday is centered in annihilation and thievery. Many of us have experienced the movement of college students and enlightened individuals of all ages who, after being exposed to the historical and current realities of Indigenous plight, rebel against family Thanksgiving celebrations in one way or another—mostly by mentioning concern at the table, which may not be accepted or appreciated. It can be a veritable bummer if not an all-out strain for families to be served a side of truth during a customarily festive time.

The theological presumption of manifest destiny—the nineteenth-century doctrinal position that American land acquisition by Christian colonialists was determined by God—is an oppressive tyrannical construct that also led to the mass freedom of immigrants around the world. You and I are likely among those who benefitted from the upside of the doctrinal views of the colonialist. Throughout history, countless individuals and cultures bury their hearts in the wounds of others' presumptions and privilege. Sometimes we bury our own hearts after gaining awareness of our own privilege. Is it possible to be a victim of our own privilege?

Few of us ever possess the knowledge or relationships to understand if and how this is reconciled in Indigenous American culture. Most Jewish citizens of the United States happily dine with their families and do not think of protesting or observing a national day of mourning, similar to Tisha B'Av, which has become a practice in many tribal communities. It is probably more than somewhat analogous to our protests in the Babylonian empire in the sixth century BCE. Yet it is difficult to hurt and dishonor our parents, grandparents, and relatives we want to honor and offer thanksgiving.

We can teach each other and our children to embrace an ethic and assumption of disappointment through dismantled stories as a path to transformation of history, stories, celebrations, and ritual. It can be a spiritual experience to grasp onto what is true as we negotiate the joy, the suffering,

---

[24] Dee Brown, *Bury My Heart at Wounded Knee* (New York: Holt, Rinehart & Winston, 1970).

and everything in between. Included in our ethic of disappointment is a responsibility to endure disappointment that the world is not precisely as we were told or as we saw it—that someone or many have been left out. The ethic includes preparing one another to gain knowledge, joy, and recognition through the shattering of one-sided tales. When we perpetuate such one-sided tales, we risk microcosmic moral injury to ourselves and larger injuries to others.

Microcosmic Moral Injury: We Are All Capable and Culpable

Moral injury is a term originally created by psychiatrist Jonathan Shay, who studied and treated the impacts of war on veterans.[25] While this is still the term's primary area of use, as treatments, social awareness, and categories of human transgression continue to be understood in relation to dominant systems of control and privilege, the spectrum of moral injury and its inheritors broadens. "Moral injury involves an act of transgression that creates dissonance and conflict because it violates assumptions and beliefs about right and wrong and personal goodness."[26] The Veterans Administration defines moral injury as "when one feels they have violated their conscience or moral compass when they take part in, witness or fail to prevent an act that disobeys their own moral values or personal principles."[27] In clinical treatment for moral injury, moral repair is a term used to define a corrective approach to emotional and psychological healing within trusted relationships.

This chapter is not presuming that every time someone has consciously or unconsciously wronged someone else, it fits the category of moral injury. Terms that are defining and diagnostic can become all-encompassing for ranges of nuanced phenomena. For progress to take place, we would do well to remember that both overt and subtle, even well-intended, conscious and unconscious demonstrations of assumed power and privilege are inescapable. Thus, our participation in microcosmic moral injury is practically inevitable. Embracing this, accepting it, and finding tools to negotiate it is both frightening and essential. Leaning into it and assessing our own choices and behaviors is Mussar[28] on steroids. It can be as simple as acknowledging

---

[25] Jonathan Shay, "Moral Injury," *Psychoanalytic Psychology* 31:2 (2014): 182–191.
[26] Brett T. Litz, Nathan Stein, Eileen Delaney, Leslie Lebowitz et al., "Moral Injury and Moral Repair in War Veterans: A Preliminary Model and Intervention Strategy," *Clinical Psychology Review* 29 (2009): 696.
[27] "What is Moral Injury," Disabled American Veterans, https://www.dav.org/veterans/resources/moral-injury/.
[28] Mussar is a daily Jewish practice centered in living according to Jewish values, virtues, and ethics.

that we are not aware of our biases and that we can and do hurt others because of this.

Earlier we discussed the importance of an ethic of disappointment, that is, knowing there will be times when history and privilege let us down. We learn that we are treading on others even when we are celebrating something historically joyful to us. An ethic of disappointment urges us to accept new knowledge in all of its loss, navigate it, and hold the tension respectfully to rebuild the proverbial house with as much kindness as possible toward all parties. Another ethic is to reflect on our own lack of awareness, prejudice, and indignities; yet we can only do this if we accept that we possess them.

Reciprocal Injurious Effect

It is possible for microcosmic moral injury to have a reciprocal injurious effect. For instance, if an individual in authority uses an expired or outdated term to discuss a social issue or identity, the term might be offensive to others. The insensitivity of the offender might be the result of an innocent lack of exposure or an unwillingness to gain a broader perspective. The latter I propose can be classified as a less innocent principled indignity (*avel ekroni*). Principled indignity is an attempt to avoid shame and responsibility through justifying long-standing privilege that upholds roadblocks to change. On the other hand, if the offender, either right away or down the road, following a period of reflection, is open to removing obstructions to their own awareness, education, language, and sensitivity, and engage in dialogue with the offended, this can be classified as principled reparation (*tikkun ekroni*). Principled reparation is an opening up of the heart to the other through the removal of unnecessarily placed obstacles due to privilege.

In contrast, reciprocal injurious effect occurs when the offended is not open to exploring their own biases, expressions of anger (though sometimes appropriate), and roadblocks to relational conversation about being affronted. This in itself can be a form of principled indignity. For instance, it is not uncommon for ageism to exist among those who are confronting old systems and the people within them. It is also not uncommon for legitimate new waves of reformist enlightenment to undermine what others have been through in their own time to combat inequalities. Here too, the originally offended, following a period of reflection, can return to their offender—even if this person is in a role of authority—with a gesture of principled reparation, opening up doorways of understanding that initially appeared closed.

Within the framework of AJRCA's educational and trans-Jewish purposes, principled indignity can begin to heal by the remedy of principled reparation.

Intrinsic Natural Forces

We inspire one another at AJRCA. We work together to grow in community. AJRCA colleagues and students, our board members, alumni, and community affiliations inspire growth beyond our own biases and essentialist thinking. Even when we know how to encounter one another in appropriate and accepting ways socially, it is inevitable that we are consistently ironing out internal barriers and assumptions about others to perform *mitzvot*[29] and *tikkunim* in the world—acts of goodness (*chesed*) and reparation. There are times when we harm each other unknowingly. And there are other moments when stubbornness or pain clouds our ability to come through for one another to accept each other's alterity. As much as we strive to behave virtuously, we are not always able to accomplish it. Our rabbinic texts tell us numerous times that repentance was created before the world itself. Repentance/*teshuva*, the thorough, inward revolutions to do and be solidly good was created before the firmament, the land on which we solidly stand, and our very selves.[30]

The idea that *teshuva* is older than the creation story signifies an intrinsic natural force placed within us to evolve. It also signifies another intrinsic impulse to stray away and devolve. AJRCA's trans-Jewish philosophy embraces these competing elements of humanity. The rejection of a person over an idea or belief in our actual or virtual hallways, though we may vehemently or lightly disagree with them, is not within the scope of options. We are invited to enter the *ma'avak* (lit. "battle" or "struggle"), the fray of discourse for the sake of authentic, multi-vocal, trans-Jewish relationship and community.

Cautious Justice and Restoring Relationships

Derick Bell, the founder of what is known as critical race theory (CRT), claimed that "diversity is not the same as redress," since it can "provide the appearance of equality while leaving the underlying machinery of inequality untouched."[31] While Bell propelled a revolutionary legal and theoretical lens with which to instigate social change and civil rights, as most founders of schools of thought, he was impacted by how the masses used and viewed CRT—for the knowledge and enactment of good, evil, and anything in between. Efforts towards justice enforced from reactionary responses can cause more harm and inequity.

---

[29] The word *mitzvah* may be defined as "attach" or "join" in the Aramaic. The word is being used in this colloquial manner to illustrate the importance of removing barriers for connectedness, rather than in the literal sense of "commandments."

[30] Selected texts that present this idea include but are not limited to: b. *Pesachim* 54a:9, b. *Nedarim* 39b:6, *Pirkei DeRabbi Eliezer* 3:2.

[31] Jelani Cobb, "The Man Behind Critical Race Theory," *The New Yorker*, September 13, 2021.

How do we redress and compensate for the machinery of inequality and privilege that is often unknown to its possessors? There is no easy answer here, though philosophical frameworks within modern Jewish thought may assist us in our redress. Buber's I/Thou approach to authentic connection,[32] the embracing of otherness in Levinas' work,[33] and the *tikkun olam* premise in Fackenheim's writings[34] are modern tools for us to continue to use. However, even here there is microcosmic moral injury to confront based on the limitations of these great thinkers, due in part to the era of their proliferation.

Butler contends that Buber "does not disrupt existing power inequalities,"[35] and Levinas emphasizes alterity without including women as participants in and contributors to the highest purpose of human existence. Yet as a Jewish feminist philosopher, with appropriate critique as part of the creation of an evolving set of ethics, Butler recognizes their foundational contributions to Jewish feminist ethics. Questioning the thinkers we admire, whether still living or not, is part of the process of redress. We admire them and are disappointed enough with their limits to build upon their work. Refusing opportunities to make excuses for the microcosmic or grand moral injuries of any time or person is honorable, especially if we continue to grow through and with them.

Aaron in the Now

Biblical Aaron in the now, with the knowledge and wisdom of our current faculty and student body, might not stand idly by. His silence would not instigate Miriam's snow-white appearance. Perhaps her sudden illness was the liminal space of social abandonment, spiritual distress, and castigation when he allowed her to speak the truth unsupported. He left her on her own to contest unchallenged privilege and authority. The text brings attention to Moses, stating that he is the most humble of human beings (Num. 12:3). Yet even humble human beings, especially ones with power, should ideally be—and want to be—held accountable by the Miriams among us. In the biblical account we see that Aaron also suffers. In frantic desperation and immediate regret, he pleads with Moses to do something on Miriam's behalf.

Perhaps the heroes in this story are not the authority figures: God, Moses, Aaron, or even Miriam. Rather, they are the people who hear and see her— the souls of the entire people who will not move camp without Miriam,

---

[32] Butler, "Disturbing Boundaries," 332.
[33] Ibid., 334.
[34] Ibid., 338.
[35] Ibid., 329.

their prophetic visionary, assessor of balances and imbalances, and knower of the ebb and flow of the waters of justice.

As we move through our own waters of life, we are accountable for our transgressions and reparations, our *avel ekroni* and our *tikkun ekroni*. We are living in a time when even the smallest of injuries towards another or within oneself is of great cosmic and universal significance. Finally, the time has arrived.

Intellectual Honesty: An Ethical Approach to Adult Jewish Education

Revital Somekh-Goldreich

I. Standing on the Shoulders of Giants

In 1993, Tikvah Frymer-Kensky, professor of Bible studies, published a groundbreaking book that not only explored the role of goddesses in Ancient Near Eastern religious systems, but also aimed to "remedy the results of millennia of misogyny and marginalization in the monotheist religions."[1]

On Passover 2001, Rabbi David Wolpe, spiritual leader of the Conservative Sinai Temple in Los Angeles, shocked his congregation. He told them that "the way the Bible describes the Exodus is not the way it happened, if it happened at all!"[2]

In 2004, Jacob Neusner, the late professor of Jewish studies and Conservative rabbi, wrote that what actually happened in 586 BCE does not entirely correspond to the paradigm fabricated by priests in Jerusalem. Only a minority of the people had in fact been exiled and only a fraction of those returned to Zion. The priests, through the Pentateuch, turned a minority report into the only paradigm of Jewish experience. They ignored the Jews who chose to remain in Babylon, failed to acknowledge the large Jewish community in Egypt, and positively rejected those who stayed in the land and did not experience exile.[3]

In 2005, Marc Zvi Brettler, a biblical scholar and co-founder of the website thetorah.com, wrote, "I am an observant Jew, yet I am aware of the composite nature of the Hebrew Bible...that it is a human rather than divine work and—based on the latest scholarship—I know that the beginning of Genesis is a 'myth'; that the Exodus did not happen as described in the Hebrew Bible; that King David composed none of the psalms; and that Song of Songs is a secular work."[4]

---

[1] Tikvah Frymer-Kensky, *In the Wake of the Goddesses: Women, Culture and the Biblical Transformation of Pagan Myth* (New York: The Free Press, 1992), viii.
[2] Teresa Watanabe, "Doubting the Story of Exodus," *The Los Angeles Times*, April 13, 2001.
[3] Jacob Neusner, *Transformations in Ancient Judaism: Textual Evidence for Creative Responses in Crisis* (Peabody, MA.: Hendrickson, 2004), 18–22.
[4] Marc Zvi Brettler, *How to Read the Bible* (Philadelphia: Jewish Publication Society, 2005), 279–282.

In 2016, Ariel Picard, a research fellow at Shalom Hartman Institute and a rabbi ordained by Israel's chief rabbinate, while acknowledging that "the sea of traditional sources is infinite," emphasized that we should adopt and adapt meaningful and relevant interpretations, and that our choices should be grounded in our contemporary reality. He added, "The realization that the belief in the eternity of Torah does not mandate belief in the eternity of *the concrete reality to which Torah refers* requires a comprehensive and brave hermeneutics…hermeneutics that deals with the meaning of the text and its implications for life. Such hermeneutics enables *the transition* from studying traditional texts in order to understand the texts themselves *to studying these texts in order to understand ourselves.*"[5]

In 2019, Dalia Marx, a professor of liturgy and *midrash* and Reform rabbi, discussing the political dimensions of religious behavior in the Bible, suggested that King Jeroboam I (who reigned c. 930–910 BCE)—despite being maligned by biblical authors and commentators alike—might have been a social and religious reformer; a reading that is "admittedly incompatible with traditional interpretations of the biblical text. But to those willing to take a fresh look at the story, this subversive reading and its model of ritual pluralism in ancient Israel are not unreasonable."[6]

And yet! Most Jews are unaware of these and other facets of our vast body of traditions and texts. It is our responsibility, as clergy and educators, to teach biblical texts transparently, thereby enhancing the depth and meaning of Bible study for our congregants and students. It is as if too many of us do not trust our congregants or students—or ourselves—to be able to process, appreciate, celebrate, and enjoy the wonderful richness and complexity that would be revealed by engaging with the texts as part of an ongoing process of evolution, revolution, and revelation. Teaching the Bible either as literally true or as if its views (and those expressed by traditional interpreters) have aged well—when many are obsolete, one-dimensional, homophobic, xenophobic, androcentric, constricting, or otherwise offensive to modern sensibilities and identities—causes too many Jews to give up on any attempt to (re)connect with their Jewish roots and communities.[7]

---

[5] Ariel Picard, *Seeing the Voices* (Tel Aviv: Miskal-Yedi`ot 'Ahronot and Hemed, 2016), 287–288. [Hebrew; translation and emphases mine.]

[6] Dalia Marx, "Jeroboam: A Sinner or a Social Leader and Religious Reformer?" *CCAR Journal: The Reform Jewish Quarterly* (Spring 2019): 39.

[7] According to a 2020 report of the Pew Research Center, 27% of Jewish adults in the U.S. "do not identify with the Jewish religion: They consider themselves to be Jewish ethnically, culturally or by family background and have a Jewish parent or were raised Jewish, but they answer a question about their current religion by describing themselves as atheist, agnostic or 'nothing in particular' rather than as Jewish. Among Jewish adults under 30, four-in-ten

Most contemporary Jewish religious leaders are aware of what they are hiding. Jewish seminaries across the United States expose students to the various approaches of biblical criticism. According to a recent study by Joel Gereboff, "All non-Orthodox denominational institutions treat the Bible as having a history to its formulation, as reflective of developments of ancient Israel set within the broader Ancient Near East....All share the conviction that the Bible, including the Chumash, has a history to its formation and that source and literary critical approaches are essential to understanding the various units of the Bible."[8] So why, despite the few and far between instances, don't we teach it that way to the general public? Why, for the most part, do we continue to keep this liberating and potently empowering aspect of biblical studies to ourselves?

II. The Risks and Rewards of Embracing Intellectual Honesty in Adult Education

This essay claims that it is possible, beneficial, and ethically imperative to study and assess the role humans played in the creation of the Hebrew Bible (Tanakh) and its vast body of interpretation. Adult students deserve to be treated as adults and to be trusted, empowered, and invited to take part in an ongoing dynamic of revelation and evolution of Jewish traditions. Ongoing revelation should encompass an earnest attempt to separate narratives and rules that are time-bound, politically motivated, and socially outmoded from those that help further the development of values and practices toward the just, life-affirming, and spiritually meaningful culture envisioned by our Torah(s) and prophets. As evidenced by a change in attitudes of my own students, such an approach to adult Jewish education brings about re-enchantment with and recommitment to Jewish texts and traditions in many who have been offended by the obsolete aspects of some biblical studies and interpretations.

At the same time, this writer acknowledges the limited importance and

---

describe themselves this way." Additionally, this appears to be a growing trend as the same document reports that "There were some signs of this divergence in Pew Research Center's previous survey of Jewish Americans, conducted in 2013. But it is especially evident in the 2020 survey, conducted during a polarizing election campaign." "Jewish Americans in 2020," Pew Research Center, May 11, 2021, https://www.pewforum.org/2021/05/11/jewish-americans-in-2020/.

[8] Joel Gereboff, "Denominational, Nondenominational, Transdenominational, Post-denominational or Pluralistic: Does the Nature of the Institution Really Matter When Teaching Certain Courses?" in *Nondenominational Judaism: Perspectives on Pluralism and Inclusion in 21st-Century Jewish Professional Education*, eds. Jonathan L. Friedmann, Joel Gereboff, and Stephen Robbins (Teaneck, NJ: Ben Yehuda, 2020), 123, 125.

utility of historical accuracy as a vehicle for instilling and strengthening Jewish values and identity. In other words, myths that elucidate timeless Jewish values and promote the just, life-affirming, and spiritually meaningful culture mentioned above should not necessarily be invalidated by intellectual integrity, but rather studied and passed on to future generations as brilliant yet imaginative illustrations of those values. Rabbi Wolpe, in his 2001 Passover sermon and subsequent talks in his synagogue, exemplified this approach. Despite being the subject of responses from all over the world, many of them critical, he persevered and repeatedly emphasized that "fundamental spiritual truths" can exist quite apart from historical facts, and that this, for Jews, can be found in what the Bible tells about the Exodus;[9] a minor historical event, which may not have actually happened.

Incidentally, Wolpe was not the first to make this point to a non-academic audience. Not long after the emergence of Zionist movements, Ahad Ha'am, a Hebrew essayist and founder of Cultural Zionism, wrote:

> I care not whether this man Moses really existed; whether his life and his activity really corresponded to our traditional account of him; whether he was really the savior of Israel and gave his people the Law in the form in which it is preserved; and so forth. I have one short and simple answer for all these conundrums. This Moses, I say, this man of old time, whose existence and character you are trying to elucidate, matters to nobody but scholars like you. We have another Moses of our own, whose image has been enshrined in the hearts of the Jewish people for generations, and whose influence on our national life has never ceased from ancient times till the present day. The existence of this Moses, as a historical fact, depends in no way on your investigations. For even if you succeeded in demonstrating conclusively that the man Moses never existed, or that he was not such a man as we supposed, you would not thereby detract one jot from the historical reality of the ideal Moses—the Moses who has been our leader not only for forty years in the wilderness of Sinai, but for thousands of years in all the wildernesses in which we have wandered since the Exodus.[10]

---

[9] Gustav Niebuhr, "Religion Journal; A Rabbi's Look at Archaeology Touches a Nerve," *The New York Times*, June 2, 2001.
[10] Asher Zvi Hirsch Ginsberg (aka Ahad Ha'am), "Moses," in *Selected Essays* (Philadelphia:

The scope of the discussion here is restricted to adult education in academic, seminarian,[11] and lay settings. While differentiating education from indoctrination should occur before students reach adulthood, it is never too late to make this distinction. Having said that, issues related to raising students who are able to fearlessly face and practice intellectual honesty—while not losing their sanity, identity, and faith in the process—are beyond the scope of this chapter. Additionally, despite the applicability of the approach proposed here to other areas of Jewish studies, the examples are limited to the study of biblical texts and commentaries thereon.

The milestones marking the path toward intellectual honesty in education are ancient and have served as guideposts in the evolution of both biblical and rabbinic Judaism since antiquity. In the search for meaningful and relevant interpretations, we should start by questioning answers rather than by answering questions. As heirs to a widely dialogical culture, we should be comfortable by now with having more than one answer to each question, and with the Jewish paradox of somehow ending up with more questions than answers.

What might look like a paradigm shift from a so-called scientific approach of either/or to a more holistic approach of both/and has its roots in our *midrashic* literature, by which I mean both the *aggadic* and *halakhic* portions of that endeavor.[12] One needs only to open a tractate of Talmud to be swept away by a storm of disputes that acknowledge the validity of opposing arguments and that often lack a clear-cut directive or narrative conclusion. Similarly, throughout the ages and across the world, Jewish communities have produced tomes of commentary and responsa which belie claims that the vast body of our traditions and texts could yield just one unanimous, indisputable answer, valid for all times, to any *halakhic* or theological question.

Speaking of questions, with each passing generation, it is becoming ever clearer that asking, "What does Judaism say about...?"—or even, "What does the Tanakh say about...?"—is the wrong question. No amount of

---

Jewish Publication Society, 1912). I am grateful to Cantor Jonathan Friedmann for bringing this article to my attention.

[11] Comments from my students at AJRCA and the American Jewish University have led me to conclude that encouragement to take an intellectually honest approach to Bible study in congregational adult education is the exception rather than the rule.

[12] The terms *aggadic/aggadah*, literally meaning legendary/legend, refer to narratives that embellish biblical stories, fill in gaps, provide clarification, and/or attempt to resolve or harmonize contradictions. The terms *halakhic/halakhah*, literally meaning legalistic/law, refer to a similarly creative endeavor that results in rules and regulations for the practice of Judaism. At times, both types of *midrash* are found to comprise support for a debated rule or practice.

fervent harmonizing or creative interpreting or explaining of lacunae could solve, once and for all, the numerous contradictions in the vastly varied body of texts and traditions that are currently defined as "Jewish." Suffice it to point out just two luminous examples: The very different approaches to Bible study and *midrash* introduced by the rationalist Maimonides and the mystical Zohar not only exist side-by-side under the category of *classic* Jewish texts, but also, and possibly more importantly, were both initially met with suspicion, criticism, and controversy.

When I speak of a both/and approach, I am referring not only to the preservation of minority opinions, but also to accepting and even embracing what is now a fact on the ground. Namely, that there is more than one way to be Jewish; that there is more than one Judaism (including the cultural, humanistic, or secular types); and that our traditions and practices are a mixture of history and myth.

Consequently, a both/and approach calls for a balancing act. Namely, the mature and expansive ability to hold onto multiple—and at times contradictory—interpretations. It celebrates the fruits and rewards of such ability and finds a place at the table for all types of Judaisms. Such fruits and rewards, despite the occasional frustration, are many—though not easily produced and harvested.

Such a balancing act calls into question the same full disclosure and intellectual honesty mentioned above. How do we open ourselves up to a certain measure of indeterminacy without losing our sanity, identity, and faith? What about "Who is a Jew?"; a question that has been paramount in the minds of rabbinic courts and the Ministries of Immigration and Interior Affairs in Israel since its inception.[13] Who is authorized to sift through the various interpretations and serve as gate keepers, tasked with the mandate to decide and enforce who and what is "in" or "out"?

Our history is rife with examples of internecine tensions and even wars. Sadly, the competition for hegemony in Judaism, which some claim was the cause of the destruction of the Second Temple, is far from a thing of the past. Tribalism continues to infect and rage in our midst, both in Israel and in the Jewish diaspora.

Against this backdrop of competition, alienation, and excessive particularity exist phenomena such as membership in more than one synagogue, radical inclusivity, and sensitivity to the intersectional nature of our commu-

---

[13] In Israel, the battle of "Who is a Jew?" (*Mihu Yehudi*) began in the 1950s, when Prime Minister David Ben Gurion sought the opinions of leading rabbis from Israel, Europe, and America and Jewish secular scholars, jurists, and essayists on the matter. See Baruch Litvin, comp., *Jewish Identity: Who is a Jew? David Ben Gurion's Query to Leaders of World Jewry and Their Responses*, ed. Sidney B. Hoenig and Jeanne Litvin, 2nd ed. (New York: KTAV, 2012).

nal and individual identities. This is where transdenominationality comes in, with its mission to find a seat at the table for all types of Jews. It promotes the exchange of views and ideas without coercion or expectation that anyone denounce, renounce, or modify one's point of view. More importantly, it opens the door to acknowledging ways in which aspects of our identities, such as race, gender, class, geographic origin, or sexual orientation were neglected, vilified, or otherwise unfairly treated by biblical authors, editors, and interpreters. Such acknowledgement will hopefully lead to revised interpretations and self-understandings that will correct some of the pain inflicted in the past by interpretations that would be considered grossly unjust in our day and age.

Specifically as it relates to Bible study, how do we do this without tearing each other and our communal fabric apart? One path to ease our way into wider inclusivity and stronger connections is the democratizing, relevantizing, and concretizing of Bible study and the lessons it can teach. According to Brettler, "the Bible is a sourcebook that I—within my community—make into a textbook." Brettler considers the Bible a sourcebook because it conveys the interests of many different groups and one can find in it more than one opinion on almost any single issue of importance. But it is also a textbook that outlines the options available to us:

> I make the Bible into a textbook in several ways. The simplest is through "selection"—choosing one of the options that the Bible offers. How and why I make those choices is a complicated (and personal) issue. At any rate, in part I do this within my religious community—and in part I choose a community that has already made compatible choices.[14]

Picard echoes Brettler:

> I think that the right approach to dealing with the question of selection and boundaries in interpretation is bound to the ability to form an interpreting community....In the absence of an Archimedean point from which one may judge interpretation, this theoretical question becomes one of reality. Has a community been formed in which Jewish culture is a central characteristic of its existence? Such a community has the right to interpret tradition and to create out of it [interpretations] that are right and proper for

---

[14] Brettler, *How to Read the Bible*, 280–281.

> itself....A community that sees itself as part of the Jewish cultural continuum and manifests its values in the world of practice should create the hermeneutics through which it sustains and develops its own existence.[15]

Both Brettler and Picard in essence describe an already existing evolutionary trend which, in my opinion, bodes well for the survival of Judaism. And I, standing on the shoulders of such scholars, have seen time and again the wonder of (re)connection with roots and communities materializing and taking shape in the aftermath of a democratic approach that empowers readers—as part of their study process—to protest and reject interpretations that they find irrelevant, to recontextualize the texts, and to parse the reconfigured result for values that are meaningful to their reality and existence as Jews.

III. A Few Examples of Implementing the Both/And Approach when Teaching the Bible

The following examples demonstrate possible ways to navigate tensions raised by a multidimensional both/and approach. In my work with adult students over the past decade, the treatment of texts promoted here has engendered renewed interest in biblical texts and commentaries, and strengthened the goal of finding relevant insights in those resources.

I have used books in the K'tuvim (Writings) section of the Tanakh as a lens to shine a new light on concepts and theologies that originate in Torah and Nevi'im. Such concepts and theologies include retributive justice, intermarriage, and other post-exilic existential concerns that are still relevant today.

Wrestling with the issues raised by such an approach to Bible study goes far beyond acknowledging multiple variations of the same narrative, and how they might be harmonized through creative *midrash* or explained by source and literary criticism. What is called for here is reading the Tanakh "horizontally" or inter-textually, both within the Masoretic Text of the Bible and in conversation with older manuscripts such as the Septuagint and the Peshitta. Also, while considering each text's *Sitz im Leben* ("setting in life") and asking when, by whom, for whom, and why it was written, I strive to

---

[15] Picard, *Seeing the Voices*, 290. Further down on that page, Picard states that in his opinion, "the most appropriate space for such hermeneutic dynamics in order to change and rejuvenate Jewish culture is the State of Israel, where there is a national democratic sovereignty and where the public space is shaped by the Jewish majority culture." Having said that, he does not negate the idea of pursuing a similar task within voluntary and autonomous communities of Jews outside Israel.

keep our contemporary practical and existential concerns in mind. We study *midrash* through the ages and ask ourselves and each other whether, within these depositories of tradition, we can find links and correlations between the biblical text (or the commentary thereon) and our own reality.

For example, we studied Jeremiah not only in conversation with Ezekiel, but also in conversation with Daniel. Specifically, students reviewed the re-reading in Daniel 9 of Jeremiah 29:10–14 and considered the implications of Daniel's extreme measure throughout the ages to our day. Jeremiah, in a letter to the exiled community in Babylon, makes clear to them that return to the land and restoration will come, though not very soon. In seventy years, God will remember his people in exile and bring about their redemption. Daniel, who attempts to explain, after the seventy years have passed, why return and redemption had not yet come, reinterprets Jeremiah's prophecy to read "seventy periods-of-seven-years," thereby pointing to a period of roughly 490 years after the Babylonian conquest. The Book of Daniel is set in a period starting with the Babylonian empire and Nebuchadnezzar's ascendance to the throne in 605 BCE, and contains prophecies that appear accurate up to the time of the Hasmoneans, roughly 490 years later (115 BCE was the height of Yohanan Hyrcanus I's rule). Thus, scholars concluded that the text was actually written around the time of the Hasmonean revolt (c. 165 BCE), and that the author of the Book of Daniel points to the days of the Hasmonean rule and sovereignty as the fulfillment of Jeremiah's prophecy.

What does Daniel's *biblical* commentary on Jeremiah's *biblical* prophecy tell us about the efficacy and fulfillment of such prophecy? Did prophecy indeed stop, as rabbinic sages claimed, with the destruction of the Temple and the limited sovereignty that ensued during the fifth century BCE, or is Daniel too a type of prophet? Is there a place and a role for prophecy today? How so or why not? Is Daniel's creative maneuver in reinterpreting Jeremiah an example to be followed and used to justify reinterpretations of other texts: *aggadic*, *halakhic*, doctrinal, and theological?

Additionally, we tapped into scholarship on the political, social, and theological aspects of various Jewish communities at the time, from Susa and Babylon through the Judean province to Elephantine in Egypt, in order to create a more comprehensive context for the prophecies of biblical prophets during and after the destruction. As a result, students asked why those communities were marginalized by biblical and rabbinic texts and what that marginalization might mean for them as American Jews. In light of the yearning expressed by Jeremiah and Ezekiel for the ingathering and return of *all* Israel, including the (not only) lost (but also forgotten) ten tribes,

students concluded that it is possible to improve on past experiences of disenfranchisement, alienation, and marginalization within our nation by calling for the mutual acceptance and understanding of movements within modern-day Judaism(s). While fragmentation may be one aspect of the evolution of human communities with which we must come to terms, we can at least listen to hear different voices and modify our (sometimes excessive) particularity for the purpose of keeping more Jews in the tent.

Another modern concern was addressed when we studied Jeremiah 27:21–22, where the prophet states in God's name, "concerning the vessels remaining in the House of *Adonai*…they shall be brought to Babylon and there they shall remain until I take note of them." These verses are used in a Talmudic dispute to justify the position that Jews should remain in the diaspora until called to return to the land of Israel by God or God's messenger.[16] American Jewish students raised the question of whether this argument was motivated by the reality of a prosperous Babylonian diaspora reluctant to uproot itself and return to the land of Israel. They can easily relate to this reluctance as they themselves are exiles-by-choice and do not expect to immigrate to Israel anytime in the near future (or ever). Such an assessment highlighted new aspects of the relationship between Jews in the diaspora and those in the state of Israel. It also opened students' minds to thinking about the Book of Esther not only as a horror story for diaspora Jews but possibly as a blueprint for a continued, meaningful, and impactful Jewish existence outside Israel.

While vying to find commonalities with Jews everywhere, we are nevertheless forced to come to terms with the fact that each of us is a locus where various (and at times seemingly incompatible) aspects of being converge. This reality creates many options for how we choose to understand ourselves and others. It also impacts how we choose to interpret and learn from our history. For example, a close examination of each of the characters in the Book of Esther, both those traditionally cast as heroes as well as those cast as villains, reveals thought-provoking parallels between various characters.[17]

Mordecai and Vashti, despite never meeting in the book, have much in common. They can be understood as markers for "the other"; the former in a Jewishly particular context, the latter in a universal one. Both experienced a fall from grace because they publicly humiliated powerful men, and in

---

[16] This Talmudic dispute (also dubbed "The Three Oaths," *shalosh shevu'ot*) appears in b. *Ketubot* 111a. Incidentally, it may be viewed as the rabbinic way of using K'tuvim to shine a new light on Torah and Nevi'im, because it uses verses from Song of Songs to interpret Jeremiah 27:21–22.

[17] The discussion here relies heavily on issues of identity as analyzed in Timothy K. Beal, *Book of Hiding: Gender, Ethnicity, Annihilation, and Esther* (New York: Routledge, 1997).

both cases, the repercussions went far beyond punishment of the "offending" individuals. What light does this reading shed on rabbinic *midrashim* that vilify Vashti[18] and the ways in which we should be reading and teaching such *midrashim*? And while the collective punishment for women involved a ridiculous, almost humorous, edict to prop up a threatened patriarchy, the collective punishment for Jews was genocide. Students discussed, in this connection, how actions of certain individuals, at any time or place but particularly in a contemporary reality that is beleaguered with exclusionary social and political alliances that cast out "others," might be used to characterize and even vilify a whole group. They asked whether the Book of Esther tells us that we should take this human tendency into account when we are deciding whether and how to (re)act and what to say. The students were intrigued and delighted to find that some rabbinic sages made a similar point and that, intertwined with hagiographic *midrashim* on Mordecai, they also produced a minor crop of *midrashim* that criticized him.[19]

Another example: The description of Haman as he is called and rushed, almost violently, to Esther's first and second banquets (Est. 5:5 and 6:14) brings to mind the king's earlier command to bring Vashti (Est. 1:11). Thus—while previously, there was a similarity between Vashti and Mordecai (as "the other") and between the King and Haman (as their persecutors)—here, the text can be read as suggesting different parallels, by which Haman mirrors Vashti in the precariousness of their positions and ultimate demise, and the king in his role as oppressor might be aligned with Esther. This reading was deepened when we considered Esther's actions against Haman, his sons, and other Persians (who may or may not have actually attacked the Jews) (Est. 7:7; 9:7–13; and 9:16). Such observations led to a discussion regarding "proportional" retaliations against enemies and to students' realization that on this topic, too, one must be cautious when judging such actions—whether here in America or half a world away in the Middle East.

Lastly, a few observations on connecting students with the Book of Lamentations. Reading this text as more than an anthology of dirges expressing mourning and supplications mixed with hope allowed students to wrestle with several theological issues that are existentially relevant today. The book includes powerful language of protest that calls for a reassessment of traditional understandings of divine-human relationships and communication. Such reassessment led students to redefine the role and power of prayer and of other forms of communication with God in their lives. It also empowered students to reject a simplistic view that diminishes that which humans call "God" to an unflattering description of one who metes out retributive

---

[18] For example, b. *Megillah* 12b.
[19] For example, *Yalkut Shimoni* on Nach 1054:4.

punishments to excess and with whom any connection is always, in some major or minor way, transactional.

When speaking of protest, I have in mind texts such as Lamentations 2:5, where the poet claims that "Adonai has acted like a foe…," and 5:22, where the poet describes the state of the Judahites' relationship with Adonai in the starkest terms: "For truly, You have rejected us, bitterly raged against us." What makes this protest even stronger is the fact that this is the final verse in Lamentations; this is how the book ends.[20]

When speaking of transactionality and excessive retribution, I am referring to texts such as Deuteronomy 28, which is structured as a contract or transaction: If you keep the commandments, all will be well; but if you do not, it will be the end of the nation. Particularly disturbing are verses such as 28:63, "And just as Adonai once delighted in making you prosperous and many, so will Adonai now delight in causing you to perish and in wiping you out…"

"Really?!" asked the incredulous students, "Adonai will not only punish the wayward nation, but will delight in wiping them out?!" In addressing such incredulity, I remind the students of the human element in our tradition that not only mediates between us and the divine, but at times—in an honest but desperate attempt to clarify Torah and make it "speak in the language of humans"[21]—those who compiled and edited the biblical text may have distorted the divine message and done violence to its integrity. To quote Louis Jacobs, the late theologian and Orthodox rabbi, "The Bible may still be seen as an inspired work, but the inspiration has been channeled through the human psyche and colored by temperament, social background, and human reactions to events."[22] Thus, it is clear that voices calling for intellectual honesty have already created an arc spanning various types of Jews and Judaisms; from the secular (Ahad Ha'am), through the Reform and Conservative (Marx, Brettler, Wolpe, Neusner, and Frymer-Kensky), to the Orthodox (Picard and Jacobs). (Unfortunately, Jacobs paid a preposterous price for his brave honesty.[23])

---

[20] Traditionally, we repeat verse 5:21 at the end of the recitation to soften and change the tone of this ending. However, for many who study the text, this is not a satisfactory "solution." The fact that there is no response from Adonai only exacerbates the sense of abandonment and annihilation of the relationship (i.e., the covenant).
[21] b. *Berakhot* 31b.
[22] Louis Jacobs, *God, Torah, Israel: Traditionalism Without Fundamentalism* (Cincinnati: Hebrew Union College Press, 1990), 33–34. I am grateful to Rabbi Tal Sessler for bringing Jacobs and his work to my attention.
[23] For "The Jacobs Affair," see for example Michael Freedland and Jonathan Romain, "Rabbi Dr. Louis Jacobs Obituary" in *The Guardian*, July 4, 2006.

Incidentally, those who turn to Rashi for a deeper understanding of Deuteronomy 28:63 will find him quoting b. *Megillah* 10b. There, R. Elazar explains that based on the Hebrew grammar, the verb *yasis* should be translated as "God will cause [your enemies] to delight" instead of "God will delight in your destruction." This explanation does not resolve the theological quandary of God as a source of joy in connection with the obliteration of the Jewish people. Rather, this revised translation serves as another example of the desperate attempt to make Torah speak in the language of humans.[24] Quoting Jacobs again, "The sophisticated theist can address God as *Thou* and can pray to Him and yet, in that very prayer, admit, as he must, that God is unknowable."[25] In other words, our sages' attempts to make God more "knowable" resulted in untenable arguments.

Allowing adult students to express doubt and to challenge traditionally established interpretations of the Deuteronomistic "if you do this, then God will do that" proposition helped many of them to negotiate the reality of "bad things happening to good people," following Rabbi Harold Kushner's book by that title.[26] They thus move beyond past indoctrination, if any, or revulsion and disenchantment with that proposition. Included in this expansive and compassionate approach, partly explained in Kushner's book, is the reminder that God, too, has free will and should not be viewed as reducible to a formula that does not seem to be proven by reality. In the face of a silent (if not absent) God, several students made the case for continued faith in and commitment to selected (liberal) Jewish values—a socially just community, fruitful connections with others across intra-faith and interfaith lines, and healthy relationship with nature—regardless of the belief in or knowability of God. This makes possible and invites recontextualizing God as a life-force, energy patterns, relationships, peace-affirming processes, and the potential for healing and growth, in addition to thinking of the divine as an entity.

IV. Conclusions

Frymer-Kensky, having explored the nature of goddesses in the Ancient Near East, arrived at several revelatory and relevant conclusions that played a transformative and necessary role in exposing the damage caused by "millennia of misogyny and marginalization in the monotheist religions."[27] Thanks to pioneers like Frymer-Kensky, Wolpe, and others, we are in a better po-

---

[24] *Sifre Numbers* 12.
[25] Jacobs, *God, Torah, Israel*, 18, italics in the original.
[26] Harold Kushner, *When Bad Things Happen to Good People* (New York: Schocken, 1981).
[27] Frymer-Kensky, *In the Wake of the Goddesses*, viii.

sition, decades later, to give students and congregants tools to negotiate paradigm shifts in Bible studies. We are far from being the first Jews to decide that certain received traditions and understandings are no longer applicable to our way of life, its sensibilities, and its sensitivities.

Most Jewish adults I have encountered in the past decade appreciate going beyond pre-modern readings, searching for meaningful and relevant insights that expose weaknesses in certain received traditions. This search emphasizes the distinction, made by Wolpe and others, between historical and spiritual truths. It is encouraging to read in Gereboff's review of curricula of both denominational and nondenominational rabbinic schools that programs claim to "stress the academic nature of their study, while also noting that they want students to think about the wisdom and spiritual value of these texts and how they might transmit these insights to Jews *to develop meaningful connection to these sources.*"[28] Even some Orthodox scholars "have spoken of the emergence among Orthodox thinkers of a more systematic engagement with historical critical approaches."[29]

Furthermore, going back to the example of the Exodus, learning that a growing number of archaeologists now claim that the ancient Israelites did not conquer the land militarily, but rather emerged very gradually as a monotheistic movement from within Canaanite culture, sheds a new light on our self-understanding as the "Chosen People." That the ancient Israelite civilization emerged around the twelfth century BCE and only much later (probably around the seventh century BCE) established its founding narrative through stories such as the Exodus—and eventually distinguished itself by abolishing idols and child sacrifice and espousing (to a certain degree) humanistic and universalistic values such as the sanctity of life, care for the weak, and free will—moves the concept of chosenness away from a simplistic superiority and closer to the view of ancient Israelite civilization as an innovative movement that attempted to create a just and equitable society: a society that refused to accord rights based solely on might or ignore the plight and voices of disadvantaged minorities in its midst.

Such self-understanding balances the haughtier flavor of chosenness, distances it from unnecessary zealotry and fundamentalism, and endows it with more humanistic and universalistic tendencies. In an age of conspiracy theories and demagoguery, it is imperative that we deploy all of the tools at our disposal to instill habits of honesty, courage, accountability, sense, and sensitivity. If we are to take seriously the seventy modes of expounding

---

[28] Gereboff, "Denominational, Nondenominational, Transdenominational, Post-denominational or Pluralistic," 125; emphasis added.
[29] Ibid., 122, n. 4.

the Torah,[30] or the *midrash* that not just our ancestors but all of us and our descendants were present at Sinai,[31] we must make room at the table for as many voices and interpretations as possible. In the area of biblical studies, I have seen time and again how honest re-reading and wrestling with received traditions and interpretations can create or renew a sense of Jewish identity, belonging, and commitment to build stronger bonds to and within communities.

---

[30] *Numbers Rabbah, Naso*, 13:16.
[31] *Midrash Tanhumah, Nitzavim* 3:1.

Rochelle Robins responds

Revital Somekh-Goldreich's passion, as demonstrated in her writing, is to (re)connect and (re)commit adult Jewish educators and learners to a multidisciplinary, current, and interactive approach to biblical studies. A phenomenon of disenchantment is known to occur within seminarians from diverse traditions when they engage biblical and other sacred literature through the lens of historical and literary criticism for the first time. The notion of critiquing the Bible from a perspective of history, archaeology, comparative literature, and linguistic accuracy throws students off their spiritually innocent paths. A Christian student of chaplaincy, while feeling disoriented at his seminary as the result of this phenomenon, asked me, "Is this what I signed up for—to listen to my teachers deplete our Bible and tradition of spirituality and demand that I do the same?" I wondered if this were specifically a Christian seminarian's crisis, until a few weeks later, a Jewish student stepped into my office expressing seemingly identical anguish and spiritual distress over a biblical studies course.

When a student enters an academy of religion and first encounters the documentary hypothesis, for instance, a theory that states that the Torah (first five books of the Tanakh) was not written entirely—or at all—by God or Moses, it might startle, distress, anger, or disappoint them. Many professors and advisors have supported students through their initial astonishment over the perceived profanation of their devotional view of the texts. And, of course, there are also times when students have not received critical support over their shaken world. The good news is that, in my own observations, over time and more often than not, student astonishment and dismay is integrated into an increased set of scholarly skills that excavate expanded, multi-vocal, linguistically sound, and spiritually broadening readings of texts.

Somekh-Goldreich, in her chapter, "Intellectual Honesty: An Ethical Approach to Adult Jewish Education," proposes that an ongoing "process of evolution, revolution, and revelation" should be at the forefront of Torah teaching and Jewish studies in adult education, both at academic and lay levels. Her thought is centered in a deep concern that "Teaching the Bible either as literally true or as if its views (and those expressed by traditional interpreters) have aged well—when many are obsolete, one-dimensional, homophobic, xenophobic, androcentric, constricting, or otherwise offensive to modern sensibilities and identities—causes too many Jews to give up on any attempt to (re)connect with their Jewish roots and communities." Reading the Torah for accuracies and inclusivity is where Jewish life and literature are continually restored.

Somekh-Goldreich's answer to the concern about texts not aging well is to propose that Jewish education and biblical studies for adults, both within and outside the academy, should be centered in intellectual honesty, the confronting of myths, and "differentiating education from indoctrination." While her focus is on adult education, Somekh-Goldreich asserts that this differentiation is important to cultivate within children to prepare them to be steadfastly ready for intellectual rigor, honesty, and courage throughout their lives. And, while the focus of her chapter is on congregations and communities, she is also pioneering intellectual honesty on the graduate level at the Academy for Jewish Religion California. Though not stated explicitly, Somekh-Goldreich implies that the ethic of creating significant and applicable interpretations of a text within an authentic communal process has the potential to eliminate fundamentalism, extremism, and fanaticism, thereby establishing healthier human psyches and relationships.

Interpretation and reinterpretation of ideas occur not only in later rabbinic commentaries, but also within and between the biblical texts themselves. Intertextuality—the methodical and artful practice of reading, reshaping, and re-envisioning writings through establishing connections with other writings—is central to Somekh-Goldreich's teaching methodology. For instance, she provides a cross-reading of Ezekiel, Jeremiah, and Daniel to clearly demonstrate that biblical literature can interpret and reinterpret itself from one book to another, thereby showing that intertextuality is not a modern or contemporary phenomenon; it is as old as (or perhaps even older than) biblical literature itself. The sustained dialogical experience and continued revelation within Jewish study and culture possesses ancient and biblical roots. It is not new. Its foundations were set from the beginning and continue to grow.

In light of suggestions for further inquiry for Somekh-Goldreich and all of us, it is important to recognize those educators who are not at all hiding "reality thought" and intellectual honesty in their work. Somekh-Goldreich's assertion that textual studies are primarily literal or nil in the mainstream Jewish world is true and problematic. Yet, there are also many innovations and a growing group of scholars and practitioners who are influencing a holistic and honest approach to biblical and rabbinic intertextuality and interconnection, thus establishing a less bereft picture of opportunities for rich engagement. One example is artist Helen Burke (1916–1997),[1] who dedicated two decades of her life within the auspices of the Union of Amer-

---
[1] Leslie Katz, "Camp Swig Artist Dies at 81," *J. The Jewish News of Northern California*, May 2, 1997, https://www.jweekly.com/1997/05/02/camp-swig-artist-dies-at-81-created-holocaust-memorial/.

ican Hebrew Congregations Camp Swig for Living Judaism. There, among the redwoods on Big Basin Way in Saratoga, California, living fulltime, year-round at camp, Helen, an artist who happened not to be Jewish, breathed new life into ancient texts for thousands of Jewish adults and children in a collaborative process. There are innumerable lesser-known, semi-invisible teachers and leaders like Burke who have made immense contributions to mainstream Jewish explorations of intertextuality.

Another area of curiosity would be to magnify where ancient and medieval rabbinic study methods set a template for debunking myths and challenging status quos in thinking. One might suspect that, given the complexities in biblical and rabbinic textual readings, including the polysemantic quality of the Hebrew language and the multi-vocal nature of rabbinic discourse, there is room to explore the intertextual nature of what Somekh-Goldreich is proposing as both old and new. She clearly espouses this notion as she uncovers the biblical foundations of it. Perhaps what can be broadened is the rabbinic interplay with intertextuality and cross-readings of text throughout the rabbinic era. There is room to emphasize that Somekh-Goldreich's vision, educational model, and perspective on biblical literature is in many ways a modern version of what the rabbis attempted to create among themselves. Some of the views expressed by traditional interpreters throughout the ages might seem revolutionary and enlightened even in our own time. Such interpretive creativity is not a new endeavor, yet Somekh-Goldreich and others make it accessible to individuals of all educational levels.

Somekh-Goldreich begins her chapter by mentioning twentieth- and twenty-first-century "giants" in Jewish intellectual honesty in the realm of Torah study—Frymer-Kensky, Neusner, and Marx, to name a few. I would venture to say that Somekh-Goldreich herself is setting a higher standard for students of all ages and levels of engagement; she is transforming learning through (re)claiming and integrating the foundations of biblical discourse into a communal, artful, and life-changing opportunity. Her rigorous commitment to placing contemporary concerns at the forefront of study brings balance, continuity of thought, communal cohesion, and personal discovery to those who learn from and with her. Disenchantment and spiritual distress are not typical outcomes in her classroom. Somekh-Goldreich implements a style of biblical literary criticism that, combined with a relational and artistic multidisciplinary approach, has the potential to make everyone's Torah study shoulders as broad as giants.

Revital Somekh-Goldreich responds

In her essay, Rabbi Rochelle Robins charts an arc from biblical texts to contemporary reality, identifying and examining microcosmic injuries and their resolution. Acknowledging traditional interpretations and noting their bias, Robins points to instances where those interpretations read Miriam's definite and monovalent culpability as a forgone conclusion based on verses that should, in reality, be read as merely oblique and indirect allusions. She thus convincingly makes the case against such biased readings and creatively mines revelatory diagnostic and remedial insights from her more cautious and nuanced treatment of the text.

This approach is consistent with my own views on Bible teaching in the twenty-first century, which explains why it inspired in me a rapid chain reaction of association and epiphanies in connection with some of the issues with which I have been contending in recent months. Therefore, the following reflections are offered in three sections: "Assonance"—finding echoes of Robins' observations in the issues currently engaging me; "Dissonance"—pondering double-standard as a source of, and an opportunity to, reframe memories and history; and "Resonance"—raising questions and material for thought.

Assonance: Reread and Reframe

Despite the potentially cutting-edge nature of rereading texts, as suggested by Rabbi Robins, this approach is well-rooted in traditional Jewish exegesis. The rabbinic call, *Hafokh ba va-hafokh ba de'khola ba*[1]—typically translated as "Turn it over, and [again] turn it over, for all is in it"—is an appeal, permission, and instruction all rolled into one. It is the key to ongoing revelation and the prooftext for the idea that rereading, reframing, and re-contextualizing sacred texts and traditions is the most ethical approach to study and life. This ancient mandate could possibly be rendered even more powerful when translated as "Turn it and *overturn* it, for all is in it," thereby empowering scholars and leaders to explore and even dance in the liminal space between tradition and innovation, between order and chaos, for the sake of sustainable and life-affirming spiritual evolution.

Brave new understandings of human nature and the human condition in the twenty-first century are catapulting individuals and communities into realizing that expanded relationality is imperative. By "expanded relationality," I am referring to a shift away from binary, exclusionary, supersessionist (or supremacist) self-understandings, toward a compassionate acceptance of one

---
[1] *Pirkei Avot* 5:22.

another's right to be and to thrive. Expanded relationality is imperative if we are to survive as a species and avoid devolution away from the potential for peaceful coexistence, both as individual members within a community, and as local/particular communities that comprise the global/universal fabric of humanity. All voices must be heard and acknowledged, in all registers and frequencies. New concepts and terms, such as microaggression, non-binary identity, and intersectionality, as well as the microcosmic dynamic suggested by Rabbi Robins, are driving the search for ways and means to authentically address existential questions of ontology, morality, and justice.

The Academy for Jewish Religion California (AJRCA) in general, and Robins in particular, are at the forefront of efforts, continually turning and *overturning* dogmas and other traditional approaches to sacred texts and interpretations. Her suggestions in connection with the power dynamics featured in Numbers 12—that we "reconsider God, Moses, and Aaron's pact and privilege over/against Miriam"; that "just because God apparently disapproves does not mean there is not truth being spoken [by Miriam]"; and that "[Aaron] instigates his own suffering as he plays a role in originating the anguish of another"—point to rarely considered interpretations such as that Miriam's skin affliction was not a divine punishment, but rather a physiological reaction to unbearable injustice and tension inflicted on this exceptional person's soul. Robins' analysis invites exploration and reassessment of other power dynamics within biblical leadership teams, such as God/Devorah/Barak. Possible re-readings that foreground heretofore unheard voices are exciting and pregnant with the promise of growth and spiritual evolution.

Dissonance: Double Standard and Reframing Disappointment

"Is it possible to be a victim of our own privilege?" asks Rabbi Robins before proceeding to unpack the profound emotional pain, and even trauma, caused by the clash between the experience of one community or individual on the one hand, and the collective memories on the other, selectively honed to support the foundational narratives that continue to shape how an opposing community or individual defines and understands themselves. For many of us, the moral dissonance that results from the realization that we have been applying one moral standard in connection with "us" while denying the same to "them" is existentially alarming. The celebration of Thanksgiving in the U.S., as unpacked by Robins, is a powerful example. It reminded me of the inconvenient and often marginalized connection between Israel's statehood and the Nakba.[2] The choice to utilize this "Disappointment of Education" as

---

[2] Nakba means "devastation" in Arabic, and is the term Palestinians use for Israel's War of Independence in 1948–1949, when many Palestinians were displaced—some through

a tool for spiritual development, growth, and possible reconciliation between communities and individuals may be no less painful.

One of the keys to easing the pain is approaching the experience not as a zero-sum game but, consistent with Robins, as an opportunity to embrace and develop "the practice, skill, and a willingness to invite the age-old reality of diversity to reshape memory." Robins grounds such practice, skill, and willingness in "[a]n ethic of disappointment" that "urges us to accept new knowledge in all of its loss, navigate it, and *hold the tension respectfully*" (emphasis added). This requires tremendous maturity and the ability to admit being less than morally perfect while all the time aspiring to become better. It also requires creating space for complexity, as well as trusting and expecting interlocutors to do the same; namely, just as we are expected to understand the worldview and admit the legitimacy of at least some of our interlocutors' grievances, we are entitled to expect them to reciprocate the accommodation.

Accordingly, acknowledging that authority and hierarchy may lead to injuries should not be construed to support the claim that because hierarchy/authority imply privilege, they always come at someone else's expense, that they are therefore injurious by definition, and that they should be invariably abolished. Such abolition will effectively collapse the tender-yet-life-affirming tension between order and chaos, causing all involved to slip toward a mutually exclusive, and therefore diminished, reality of either/or. As emphasized by Robins, "strong leadership is not the same as undue power and authority." Rather, hierarchy is necessary to establish order and enable effective leadership. Balancing the tension between effective hierarchy and injurious privilege is a good example of "*holding the tension respectfully.*"

Resonance: Bridges and Other Infrastructure

Noting that "AJRCA bridges unnecessary divides," Robins also cautions that the process "can be as messy, frightening, and chaotic as it is exhilarating." I agree and would like to add that building bridges and reassessing age-old prejudices does not necessarily eliminate divides or completely dissipate tensions. Rather, bridges are part of the crucial infrastructure that helps us to navigate inhospitable terrain nonviolently, and to sustain a delicate balance alongside, around, or above such tensions and divides.

Beyond generous spirits and the ethics of mutual recognition and acknowledgement, what else is required in order to build strong bridges and strengthen weak ones? At times, attempts to remedy systemic injustice cross the line and breach the civil rights of those perceived as privileged.

---

expulsions and others fleeing—and became refugees.

Righteous indignation could deteriorate into bullying, with the previously injured becoming injurious. Who is to referee when the roles are reversed? Who is to adjudicate which aspects and rights of "privileged" identities are marginalized or jeopardized? What systems or ethics should we have in place to guard against such slips?

An incident at Evergreen State College, in Olympia, Washington, is a case in point.[3] For many years, minority students and faculty members would observe a Day of Absence. The idea, sparked by the plot of a 1965 play, was to demonstrate that such minorities were in fact essential to the proper functioning of the campus. In 2017, organizers decided that on the Day of Absence, they wanted white people to stay off campus. One professor posted a message on a campus email list in which he objected to the proposal: "There is a huge difference between a group or coalition deciding to voluntarily absent themselves from a shared space in order to highlight their vital and underappreciated roles, and a group encouraging another group to go away.... The first is a forceful call to consciousness, which is, of course, crippling to the logic of oppression. The second is a show of force, and an act of oppression in and of itself."

Material for thought.

---

[3] For more details, see Scott Jaschik, "Evergreen Calls Off Day of Absence," *Inside Higher Ed*, February 22, 2018, https://www.insidehighered.com/news/2018/02/22/evergreen-state-cancels-day-absence-set-series-protests-and-controversies.

Set Two

Spirituality and Ethics in Transdenominational Jewish Pedagogy

Stephen Robbins

Interpersonal Ethics: Our Partner in Digital Citizenship

Corinne Copnick

Spirituality and Ethics in Transdenominational Jewish Pedagogy

Stephen Robbins

In 2000, I became a co-founder of the transdenominational Academy for Jewish Religion California, along with Rabbis Stan Levy and Mordecai Finley. Our transdenominational philosophy and its application in educating Jewish clergy, chaplains, and community leaders requires that we teach the full spectrum of expressions of denominational and non-denominational Judaism and the complete variety of ceremonial, intellectual, spiritual, and professional approaches to the totality of living as Jews in America. I believe that nothing is more important than the establishment of a transdenominational approach to spirituality and ethics, as all spirituality demands to be actualized in ethical and moral behavior. This means that there must be a search for the fundamental spiritual, ethical, and moral themes in Judaism as a whole, transcending denominational distinctions of definition and application. In doing so, we provide our students, graduates, and ordainees with a language of unified theory and methodology to infuse their own students, congregants, and communities with a deep personal connection to the ethical actions required by all of Judaism, regardless of definition or denomination.

Spirituality and Ethics

The Jewish religion has its roots in mystical revelations of God to humans, which, in turn, were enacted by humans in relation to other human beings. From the beginning of the Book of Genesis, where the fulfillment of Creation is the goodness that humanity brings into the world over and against their capacity to destroy it, to the stories of Abraham, Sarah, Isaac, Rebecca, Jacob, Leah, and Rachel, we learn that spiritual experiences of the Holy One require an action on our part that is both ethical (communal) and moral (individual) in relation to the people we live with—whether in our own families or in the nations we come to dwell with.

The narrative arcs of these patriarchs and matriarchs are too complex to be given justice here. None is more startling than the narrative of Jacob when, after stealing the birthright from Esau, he flees to a place called Luz, where he believes God cannot find him because it was a place of Canaanite sacrifice (Gen. 27–28). In this narrative, Jacob has the famous dream of the ladder ascending from Earth to Heaven with the *malachim* (angels) ascending and descending, and God standing next to Jacob, promising that He will be with Jacob in his travels if he is faithful to Him. Jacob awakens and says, "God was in this place and I did not know it" (Gen. 28:16), thus establishing for all time that God is present in every place and every person at every time. God travels with us through all of our individual journeys, not just Jacob's.

This spiritual principle is then turned into action by Jacob, who is both faithful and unfaithful to God in his dwelling with his uncle Laban and the profound manipulations that transpire between them in his marriages to both Rachel, the one he desires, and Leah, the one he does not (Gen. 29). Jacob finds that he must return to Canaan to make peace with his brother Esau, which leads to the great second spiritual realization of Jacob: wrestling with the *"ish,"* man, who is undefined in the text (Gen. 32:22–32). At the end of his wrestling, Jacob will not let his mysterious opponent go until he receives a blessing. *Ish* obliges by changing Jacob's name from Yaakov, the "grasper," to Yisrael, the "one who has struggled with God and man and was victorious" (Gen. 32:28). With this, Jacob changes his behavior from *stealing* a blessing to *asking for* a blessing. In doing so, he changes his ethical and moral behavior, thereby transforming his identity from the negative to the positive—the unholy to the holy. We are called B'nai Yisrael, the children of Jacob/Israel, in his transformation and ours. This appellation teaches all Jews that the Holy One is present for all of us, in all of our journeys and all of our struggles, at all times.

This principle applies completely through the Book of Genesis. The transformation of Joseph from arrogant child (Gen. 37) to the grand vizier of Egypt (Gen. 41), who seeks to make *t'shuvah*, reconciliation, with his brothers and reunification with his father in order to save them from the famine in Canaan (Gen. 41–43), and brings them into Egypt where, after Joseph's death, there arrives a "Pharaoh who knew not Joseph" (Exod. 1:8). This imparts the lesson, on a larger scale, that our personal failures and successes in uniting the spiritual, the ethical, and the moral can also have a much greater impact on populations as a whole.

Following the Exodus from Egypt, the giving of the Ten Commandments at Sinai again connects the spiritual with the ethical and the moral (Exod. 20). Each of the ten has all three elements, especially the second five, which are transgressions committed in stealth. These sins—murder, adultery, stealing, lying, and envy—are often done in silence or hidden, such that the perpetrators believes they can get away with it, even though it is clear that nothing remains unknown.

From leaving Sinai through the Book of Numbers, we find the interplay of the spiritual, ethical, and moral exemplified many times in individual and group failures, along with individual and collective successes. These events show us the evolution of a people as a whole, as well as the individuals among them. The constant presence of God helps the people to uplift themselves, for example, at Mount Ebal and Mount Gerizim (Deut. 27), where they are divided and chant blessings and curses as they begin to pass into the land. This sets up the narrative of enormous conflicts between the Children of Israel and the Canaanite and Philistine residents, which leads to one disaster after another, including the anointing of Saul as king against the protest of Samuel, who speaks in God's name (1 Sam. 8–10).

Through the rest of Tanakh, we see the roles of priests, prophets, and kings being played out against the backdrop of the people, who must bear the burden of the shortcomings of one or the other. None of these stories is more profound than the narrative of David and Bathsheba (2 Sam. 11), which culminates in two results: (1) David makes *t'shuvah* before the Holy Ark, placing his hand on it, and is not destroyed, showing that he is forgiven; and (2) Solomon, the son of David and Bathsheba, becomes king and builds the Jerusalem Temple. Solomon's son, Jeroboam, and Rehoboam, son of Nebat, cannot find unity in ruling the Twelve Tribes. Thus, the Northern Kingdom is born and ultimately destroyed by the Assyrians in 721 BCE. This is a foreshadowing of the destruction and exile/dispersion of the people of Judah, the Southern Kingdom, first in Babylonia and then throughout the world at the hands of the Romans (70 CE).

It is left to the third section of Tanakh, *Ketuvim*, to be a compendium of narrative and wisdom tracts about spirituality, ethics, and moral behavior, such as in the theologically challenging books of Iov (Job) and Kohelet (Ecclesiastes). In Ruth and Esther, we find conflicting human behaviors. On the one hand, we have Ruth, the Moabite priestess who becomes an Israelite, the first "convert," and the great-grandmother of King David and the line of the Messiah (Ruth 1:16–17). Ruth, who shows compassion and *chesed* (lovingkindness) in caring for her mother-in-law, Naomi, goes to the field to collect food and is rewarded with the love of Boaz, the field's owner. Here, we see the spiritual and the ethical intertwined. On the other hand, in the Book of Esther, we find the saving of the Jews of Persia compromised by the vengeful massacre of 35,000 Persians—even though many of them wanted to convert and become Jews (Est. 8:17).

In my exploration of universal ethical principles, there are two texts that stand out for me. One is the Holiness Code, Leviticus 19:1-18, which culminates in that most profound statement, "You shall love your neighbor as yourself." The other is in the Book of Exodus: "You shall not wrong a stranger or oppress him, for you were strangers in the land of Egypt. You shall not ill-treat any widow or orphan" (Exod. 22:20-21). These passages establish that the principles of ethics and morality in Judaism are built on the spiritual principles of love and empathy, because they both flow from God.

The next great compendium on Jewish Ethics is, of course, *Pirkei Avot*, a collection of rabbinic ethical maxims and teachings commonly known as *Ethics of the Fathers*. Among its many gems are: "On three things the world stands: on Torah, on service, and on deeds of lovingkindness" (Shimon ha-Tzadik);[1] "Make for yourself a mentor, acquire for yourself a friend, and judge every person as meritorious" (Yehoshua ben Perachia);[2] and "If I am not for myself, who will be for me? And when I am only for myself, what am I? And if not now, then when?" (R. Hillel).[3] Before reading any *perek* (chapter or statement) in this compendium, we recite a meditation that articulates a profound affirmation of both communal and individual responsibility for ethical behavior in the world: "*Kol Yisrael yeish lahem cheilek l'Olam HaBah.*" This is usually translated as, "All Israel has a stake in the World to Come."[4] There are several alternate translations, which I combine and interpret into this: Each Jew has for each one of them a portion (*cheilek*) in this world in order that there be a World to Come. This translation moves the emphasis from the communal to the individual, from the distant, or transcendent, World to Come, to the moral obligation of each person in *this* world, so that there can be a World to Come. What this establishes is that reading any of the individual sayings in *Pirkei Avot* must be done with the intention of communal and individual responsibility.

This ideal is further epitomized in the statement of R. Akiva that Leviticus 19:18, the so-called "Golden Rule," is the most important principle of Torah.[5] One way of understanding this is that you can only love your neighbor as much as you are capable of loving yourself. This is a universal principle, not limited to any one denomination or philosophy; it is for every Jew and every human being. Even mysticism and Kabbalah, which focus on receiving and joining with God's presence, ultimately lead to one's behaving toward others in this world according to one's experience with the presence of God in your life.

The *siddur* (prayer book) is replete with examples of how *tefillot*, both communal and individual prayers, bridge the spiritual, the ethical, and the

---

[1] *Pirkei Avot* 1:2.
[2] Ibid 1:6.
[3] Ibid 1:14.
[4] m. *Sanhedrin* 10:1.
[5] *Sifra, Kedoshim* 2:4.

moral. Perhaps the best example is the *Sh'ma* (Hear, O Israel) and *V'ahavtah* (And you shall love), which focus on teaching and behaving according to the love of God. The *Sh'ma* teaches us, in so many ways, how God loves us—a gift that is freely given to us. This prayer is meant to open and enlighten us, as illustrated in the custom of enlarging the *ayin* at the end of the word *sh'ma* and enlarging the *dalet* at the end of the last word, *echad*, spelling the word *eid*, meaning "witness." A standard commentary is that we witness the receiving of God's love and then we, in turn, witness it to the world through our behavior—our ethics and morality—as taught to us by the *V'ahavtah*, the prayer that immediately follows. *V'ahavtah* obliges us to love "with all your heart, with all your soul, and with all your might." In this prayer, the word for heart, *lev*, usually spelled with one *vet* (v), is written with two, *levav*—an observation being that one *vet* is the *yetzer ha-tov*, the inclination to do good, and the other is the *yetzer ha-ra*, the inclination to do evil.[6] This symbolizes the challenge to love God even with a conflicted heart, which most of us possess. The prayer pushes us to eventually unify our heart by enacting and resolving the conflict in the way we behave.

V'ahavtah further implores us to do this *b'chol nafsh'chah*—"with all your soul"—which, in Jewish terms, really means the entire body; that is, the life force that sustains the body and soul's presence in it. This further reiterates the connection between the spiritual quality of our soul and the way in which we care for our bodies and use them in this world, whether in service of ourselves or in service to God and others. The last phrase, *b'chol m'odecha*, is generally translated as "with all your might," although some translate it as "resources," meaning all of our capacity to care for the world around us through our love and commitment to life. In other words, to help those in need, which is the highest ethical and moral standard in Judaism.

The rest of the paragraph is about studying and living as a role model for younger generations. This reminds us that all of the principles we have been taught need to be expressed and role modeled. Two concrete expressions of this are the customs of *tefillin* (phylacteries) and *mezzuzot* (ritual object on doorpost and gates). The wearing of *tefillin* is the joining of the dedication of the spirit, exemplified by the box on the forehead, and our action in the world, exemplified by the box on the forearm. *Tefillin* unifies mind, body, and spirit to ethical and moral behavior. The *mezuzah* affixed to our doorpost is tilted inward so that blessings flow into the home, influencing how we treat others. Both symbols possess two key features: one is the container itself, which is akin to the body, and the other is the scroll housed inside, which contains both the *Sh'ma* and the *V'ahavtah*. Together, they unify the

---

[6] b. *Berakhot* 54a.

spiritual and the physical.

Another profound ethical statement in the *siddur* occurs at the beginning of the *Amidah* (Standing Prayer). The first benediction, the *Avot* (Forefathers), which now also includes the *Immahot* (Foremothers), reminds us that we are descendants of the founders of our people and part of the ongoing history that they began. This ties us to their complex lives and all of their descendants, through the history of Judaism until the present, and imbues us with the complexity of their ethical and moral values and struggles.

For example, their names—especially when the *Immahot* are added—recall the complicated marriages of our ancestors, starting with Abraham and Sarah, who could not conceive. Abraham is unable or unwilling to wait on God's promise that he will be the father of a multitude, so in his impatience and distrust, he takes another woman. With Sarah's handmaiden Hagar (*midrashically* portrayed as a gift from Pharaoh[7]), Abraham fathers a son whose name is Ishmael, meaning "God listens" (Gen. 16). Later, Sarah, as a result of God's intervention, conceives a son whose name Isaac (Yitzchak) means "the one who laughs," referring to her laughter upon hearing that she will conceive (Gen. 21). It is noteworthy here that Sarah only becomes pregnant after Abraham circumcises himself (Gen. 17). With this act, Abraham faces and corrects his own lack of complete commitment, both to God and Sarah. Once he is circumcised, he demonstrates his absolute faith and trust in God and belief that the promise will be fulfilled. This demonstrates to each of us that we should, likewise, enter complete commitments with our spouses and with the divine.

Three days after the circumcision, Abraham, still recovering, is visited by God. From this, we learn how important it is to visit the sick (*bikkur cholim*). This is a general ethical and moral value that, again, crosses every philosophical and denominational line and is obligated to every Jew. Another universal lesson is Abraham's willingness, despite his pain, to get up and tend to the three visitors—in the text seen as "strangers"—men who are later revealed as messengers of God (Gen. 18). The principle here, again without any denominational emphasis, is that we invite and care for the stranger in our midst. This central concern is highlighted on Passover, in our Haggadah, which reiterates the biblical lesson cited earlier that we were strangers in the land of Egypt and therefore must behave in a compassionate and inviting way to strangers.

Of course, the relationships between our other forefathers and foremothers have their own unique challenges and insights. What is important for our discussion is that their stories, recalled when we mention their names

---

[7] *Genesis Rabbah* 45:1.

in *Avot*, give us a template to resolve our own familial conflicts and convey the necessity of resolving them through spiritual, ethical, and moral actions.

Contemporary Challenges

Beyond the classical literature, there are several volumes of ethical systems with particular importance for our contemporary world. Alexandre Safran's book, *Explorations in Jewish Religious Ethics*, provides a synthesis of the distinctions between the various dimensions of spirituality, ethics, and morals, and their expression in Judaism from biblical through contemporary times.[8] The introduction to this sweeping collection of teachings on the correlation between spirituality, ethical principles, and moral behavior offers profound examples, including: the simultaneous physical and spiritual creation of the world with the purpose of enabling "goodness to spread"; the commandment of Leviticus 19:18—"You shall love your neighbor as yourself"—encompassing all of the other commandments of the Torah (following Rabbi Akiva) because God's image is reflected in one's neighbor, thus loving the neighbor is also loving God; humanity is in search of God and God is in search of humanity—the "desire from below" meets up with the "desire from on high"—bringing the Heavens to the Earth and raising the Earth to the Heavens; the spiritualization of matter and the materialization of the spirit, allowing a "reparation" of the historical rupture between spirit and matter and "restoration" of the original unity of matter and spirit; the principle of *lifnim mi-shurat ha-din* ("beyond the line of the law") forbids a Jew from exploiting a possible interpretation based on the letter of the law so as to favor himself and disadvantage the other—especially when the latter is in difficulties (it is forbidden to act against the "spirit," or the "heart," of the letter of the law). Safran concludes his introduction with the quote of the prophet Micah (6:7), in which spirituality, ethics, morals, and the physical world are all joined in a simple statement: "He has shown you, O man, what is good; what does Lord require of you but to do justly and to love mercy and to walk humbly with your God?"

One of the most fundamental transgressions in our tradition is *lashon ha-ra*, the evil tongue. Our society, especially the media, is built on gossip. Understanding how *lashon ha-ra* impacts not only our society, but all levels of human behavior—including in our own family life—is fundamental to managing our ethical and moral behavior in the world. *Guard Your Tongue*, adapted from the Chofetz Chayim by Rabbi Zelek Pliskin, is a prime source

---

[8] Alexandre Safran, *Explorations in Jewish Religious Ethics*, trans. M. Pater and E. M. Sandle (Jerusalem: Feldheim, 1999).

for the myriad applications of this principle.⁹ This comprehensive work identifies thirty-one ways in which *lashon ha-ra* is enacted in everyday life and relates them to the weekly Torah portions (*parshiot*). Among these is the teaching that *lashon ha-ra* is the greatest of all transgressions for which there is no forgiveness in this world, only in the next. The gossiper transgresses three of the most fundamental principles of spirituality, ethics, and morality, in that he is akin to a murderer, an idolater, and an adulterer. As a murderer, he "kills" three people: himself, the one he gossips about, and the one who hears it. As an idolater, he worships his own power to decide who lives or dies in this world. As an adulterer he destroys the intimate relationships between people in order to possess them.¹⁰

The Ethics of Business, Finance, and Charity, by Rabbi Ezra Basri, provides a comprehensive overview in these areas of intense ethical challenges.¹¹ Examples of business ethics which stand out for me are: Do not withhold information in the making of a business negotiation and contract; When one gains, the other does not lose; One must not give *tzedakah* at a level that lowers their standard of living, so that the can continue to provide *tzedakah*.

Jewish medical ethics is yet another complex contemporary field, as demonstrated in Dr. Avraham Steinberg's *Encyclopedia of Jewish Medical Ethics*.¹² There are several obvious issues that face Jewish clergy and community leaders, and especially chaplains—for example, participation in the decision making of when to remove life support. Another is the issue of abortion and, in particular, considering when independent life begins and when abortion is permissible. Positions on these and other medical matters very greatly across denominations. Depending on the theology—i.e., the perceived relationship between humanity and God—Jews of different backgrounds have differing approaches to these important life issues and the balancing of practical and spiritual concerns.

These areas of ethical exploration—gossip, business, finance, charity, and medicine—and the general overview of Jewish ethics should be a required part of Jewish seminary education. To date, the Academy for Jewish Religion California (AJRCA) has no comprehensive, transdenominational survey course on applied Jewish ethics, nor sufficient guidelines for each course that specifically delineates the spiritual, ethical, and moral content of the

---

⁹ Zelig Pliskin, *Guard Your Tongue: A Practical Guide to the Laws of Loshon Hora Based on Chofetz Chayim* (Jerusalem: Pliskin, 1975).

¹⁰ b. *Arakhin* 15b.

¹¹ Ezra Basri, *Ethics of Business, Finance, and Charity*, trans. Eliyahu Touger (Jerusalem: KTAV, 1987).

¹² Avraham Steinberg, *Encyclopedia of Jewish Medical Ethics*, trans. Fred Rosner (Jerusalem: Feldheim, 2003).

subject matter. I propose that there be a faculty colloquy around this issue in order to clarify the pedagogy of spiritual, ethical, and moral teaching at AJRCA. In this colloquy, members of the faculty would study and report on one of these areas in order to discuss in toto how to approach these subjects.

While this proposal addresses our internal curricular development, it will also impact all who are served by our students. There are many Jews who yearn for depth of learning and meaning that integrates their spiritual, intellectual, and behavioral life. Unifying all of these in educating Jews will assist such Jews in understanding and applying Judaism in a way that is at the same time spiritual and practical. It is to these Jews, especially, that we must reach out to deepen their appreciation of their Jewish identities—and Jewish roles—in the world.

Interpersonal Ethics: Our Partner in Digital Citizenship

Corinne Copnick

Part One

Morality and Ethics as Co-Dependents

The Torah has endured in large part because it is believed to provide human beings with a divinely inspired blueprint for how to lead a moral life, an ethical life. History has taken humanity, and the Jewish people in particular, down diverse roads to far-flung places over the millennia. Customs have changed, ideas have been dissected, and new ones introduced time and again, yet the ethical map of permissible actions, while continually rethought in the light of new knowledge, remains basically the same. How do we explain, then, abstract words like "ethics" and "morality" in the complex present that is the twenty-first century? And do ethics and morality mean the same thing? Or are they co-dependents in the process of leading a just Jewish life? At a time when our society struggles with or has forgotten these concepts, how do we translate them today in interpersonal terms? How do we take our place in society as good—and well-informed—digital citizens?

First, we would do well to look back to our Torah, specifically to the Five Books of Moses. Unethical interpersonal behavior is the cornerstone of many biblical stories in the Chumash. Near the beginning of Genesis, we find the disturbing interaction between the formerly upright Serpent and Eve, who, by listening to this evil tongue, disobeys God by eating the fruit forbidden and persuading her husband to do so as well. As a consequence, she, Eve, at the time of expulsion, and Adam are sent out of the Garden of Eden to gain experience in life by toiling for food and to labor in giving birth to populate it. Thus, they bring shame into the world, and, by their own interpersonal actions, their children, Cain and Abel, bring knowledge of death as well.

As the five books of the Torah continue, we learn from the *Akeida* episode of Abraham and Isaac that, unlike other groups, we must not offer our children as sacrifices to God. Later, the interpersonal actions of Jacob (aided by his mother, Rebecca) with both his brother, Esau, and his father, Isaac, in stealing Esau's birthright, bring deceitful interactions into society—as well as directly addressing taking advantage of the vulnerable (i.e., "before the blind, do not put a stumbling block," Lev. 19:14). As stories in the Torah continue, we encounter the duplicity of Rachel, Jacob's wife, who steals idols from her father's house and lies to him.

In short, the first chapters of the Torah are about the development of families who must abide by a moral code and behave ethically with one another. This culminates in the giving of the Ten Commandments at Mount Sinai. Now there is a code of behavior carved into stone. The Children of Israel are connected to God and to each other by a covenant. In Exodus, as families learn to grow into tribes and eventually a nation, a code of ethics is established in regard to the prospective property division in the Promised land.

However, there is still a long way to go. The Golden Calf episode illustrates a rejection of ethical behavior as individuals and as a group. The people cannot function ethically without a leader, an authority, to tell them what to do. Their leader, Moses, is away on the mountain; his brother, Aaron, turns out to be spineless as a leader. It will take time to develop a nation with the national values to which they have already been exposed. The challenge is to live in accordance with them.

A big leap is taken in the Book of Leviticus. Here personal ethics are brought to a holy dimension. The Hebrew people, the *Ivri*, begin to understand that, with acceptance of the covenant, they are committed to living the moral life the covenant defines, not only in spiritual terms, but in the quality of the way they practice these tenets in everyday life. Furthermore, in accepting an abstract, eternal God as One, they must eschew all other gods—symbolized by the multiple idols the desert people surrounding the Hebrew tribes worship. In so doing, they create a sacred space, the Tent of Meeting, to worship their *Elohim*. This sacred space separates them both in time and space from the surrounding tribes. Their eventual goal will be to make the Promised Land they are determined to reach a sacred space in which they might live and prosper. And when the census is finally taken in Numbers, and a prospective property division in the Promised Land is defined, the tribes begin to stand together as a nation. Thus, we see the growth of the interpersonal into the social and the beginnings of economic integrity. By the end of the Torah, we have a moral blueprint for ethical behavior at many levels.

Intentionally, biblical heroes are not perfect. Human beings have flaws. So, we learn from our heroes how to be better people. The first Jew, Abraham, even argues with God to alter an angry divine action against disobedient humans, and God changes his mind! The Bible's stories encourage us to believe that, despite our failings, we can grow to overcome them. We can improve upon our morality and ethics, both in conception and action.

What is Morality?

Some commentators assume that ethics and morality are interchangeable concepts; others believe that these two words have subtle differences that need to be understood. In this latter view—in its simplest, most optimistic interpretation—morality is benign; it reflects the human desire to do good. That is why *Aseret HaDevarim*, the ten divine utterances (commonly called the Ten Commandments), intended to guide moral living, were enunciated at Sinai.

A covenant easily counted on ten ancient fingers, these commandments were intended to guide the Hebrews who had fled from oppression in Egypt to living as free people—with moral precepts to be both "heard" and "done" (*na'aseh ve-nishma*), even in the wilderness.[1] It is a covenant between the Jewish people and God that continues to bind them together everywhere and forever; but, at the same time, it is conditional to the Jewish people's adherence to its tenets. This covenant that has survived through the millennia until today embodies an enduring concept of morality, one later adopted by Christianity. "A covenant creates a moral community," writes the late Rabbi Lord Jonathan Sacks, former Chief Rabbi of the British Commonwealth and the author of an erudite book appropriately titled *Morality: Restoring the Common Good*; "it binds people together in a bond of mutual responsibility and care. It can be vast...it can also be small and personal."[2] If you follow these concepts, the Hebrew Bible instructs us, you will lead a just and moral life. They have survived through the millennia until today, embodying an enduring concept of morality. So, this covenant, this sacred moral code, is the WHAT.

It is further incumbent on the Jewish people—in following this moral code through actions and then internalizing the WHY of it through study—to serve as exemplars to the nations of the known world. In other words, although initially particularistic, most of this Jewish concept of morality has universal implications as well.[3]

---

[1] Exodus 24:3–7. "Hearing" may also be understood as "perception" in Hebrew, suggesting cognitive understanding, in addition to an aural faculty.

[2] Jonathan Sacks, *Morality: Restoring the Common Good in Society* (New York: Basic, 2020), 313.

[3] At the same time, as Cantor Dr. Jonathan Friedmann teaches, it should be recognized that the first four utterances are theological in nature (one god, no idols, do not take God's name in vain) and have ritualistic dimensions (the Sabbath), and thus do not apply universally. Thus, these first four are particularistic, "ritual *mitzvot*"—concerned with not offending God—as opposed to "ethical *mitzvot*."

What About Ethics?

Although there is some overlap, the concept of ethics is subtly different. Ethics represents the HOW.[4] Based on the moral code of the covenant expressed at Sinai, it embodies an intricate system of laws to ensure that people know how to carry out the WHAT, the moral code, the right way, a just way. That is why we have the Book of Leviticus. It teaches the HOW minutely. Centuries later, the Talmud endeavored to do so even more minutely, and with plenty of debate because not everyone sees the "how to" of leading a righteous life, a moral life, the same way.

So, a code of ethics, as I see it, incorporates more than an outline of what the right thing to do is or a philosophy of doing the right thing. It outlines the tools to accomplish these goals, to actually lead a moral life. In this way, ideally, morality and ethics combine to create just living, not only for individuals but also for societies. Of course, societies evolve with changing circumstances, and with them, moral codes alter, sometimes for the good, sometimes not; sometimes the long-term effects of these changes are not seen beforehand. But the moral code expressed by the Ten Utterances still stands.

As Americans, we strive to remain true to both the intent and substance of the Constitution; yet our system of government provides for occasional amendments to take into account changes in society over the centuries. In Judaism, after the fall of the Second Temple, our rabbis provided that function with vigorously diverse interpretations of the Holy Scriptures, yet with understanding that it falls to human beings to enact these understandings in their daily lives in situations that may be demanding. Taking the position in this chapter that morality and ethics are co-dependents, let us ask ourselves these questions: 1) How do these twin underpinnings of our Jewish life affect our ethical behavior as Jews today, in this current climate in America? 2) How does our ethical behavior stemming from our moral code affect our interpersonal relationships?

The more I consider this subject, the more convinced I become that interpersonal relationships between human beings are integral to *all* the ethical categories included in this volume: interpersonal, family, societal, medical, economic, and global. In this century, digital relationships have entered the fray at all levels as well, and present another ethical category. At the present time, we are confronted every day by the many ways our continually

---

[4] Just as there have been many discussions about definitions of morality in philosophical and religious literature, many scholarly discussions of ethics and various proposed models exist. What I am suggesting in this essay are practical definitions that are easier for most people to understand and hopefully to follow.

multiplying digital devices, powered by human input, can undermine—or advance—an ethical society. So, let us ask a third question: 3) How do the digital technologies of this twenty-first century affect our interpersonal behavior, such as friendships, and, consequently, our ethics?

I am a rabbi. I believe in the Judaic purpose "to do" in accordance with a moral code intended to be both particular and universal. Our laws are supposed to be particular to Jews, who in turn, by their behavior will be a light unto the nations; that is, set an example of moral behavior accompanied by fruitful actions that will encourage other peoples to do the same. "Believe in God because God is good." God is *tov* (good). Think *tov*, do *tov* (to yourself and others). Study why we do *tov*. Study how to do more *tov*. That is our moral code. The difficulty is interpreting what is "good," something we have debated in our Talmud, in our houses of study, in our congregations, in our hearts and souls, for thousands of years. And now, in our open society, we are asking, "Is everything relative, a moral equivalent?" So, my fourth question is this: 4) What's good?[5]

> He has told you, O Man, what is good.
> And what the Lord requires of you:
> Only to do justice,
> And to love goodness,
> And to walk modestly with your God (Micah 6:8).

Part Two

The Evil Tongue and How it Affects Society

The Torah, Talmud, and the vast collection of Jewish texts explore the area of interpersonal interchange at length. For example, our tradition teaches that *lashon hara* (the evil tongue) can undermine interpersonal relationships, with serious consequences. In fact, according to some interpreters, Moses' sister, Miriam, is punished for ridiculing Moses' wife for being a Cushite, that is, a black woman. As a result, God punishes her by inflicting her with a white, scaly skin disease.[6] While the punishment is temporary, she is banished outside the Israelite camp for seven days. We learn that the world God created has many colors.

---

[5] Our Hebrew liturgy includes the biblical refrain "*Mah tovu*" (how good it is!) taken from *Parshat Balak* (Num. 24:5). The pagan prophet, Balaam, has been hired by the Moabite king, Balak, to curse the people of Israel. However, when Balaam views the beauty and peacefulness of the orderly Israeli camp from a mountaintop, he changes the curse to a blessing.
[6] *Sifre Devarim* 275:1 and b. *Arakhin* 15b.

The evil tongue can lead to hurtful actions. So, the Talmud, compiled over several centuries by the great rabbis that continued to lead Judaism after the destruction of the Second Temple, further explores the evil tongue as a conveyor of ideas influencing actions harmful to both society and interpersonal relationships. In a rabbinic folktale often retold, the way hurtful words can inflict pain and ruin someone's reputation is effectively symbolized by comparing the spreading of nasty rumors to letting the feathers of a pillowcase fly away. As they scatter in all directions, it is impossible to retrieve them. The damage is done. We no longer have to imagine how this damage can be multiplied in the digital age.

In a chilling admonition, the Talmud also teaches us that destroying a person's reputation is akin to murder (the person pales from the pain inflicted by these words as the blood drains from his face). It is the murder of a reputation, something nearly impossible to regain.[7]

In fact, there is a special Hebrew name for pain inflicted by words, by the evil tongue: *ona'at devarim* (based on Lev. 25:14, 17). Just as there is *ona'ah* in monetary matters (i.e., willful deceit, fraudulent business dealings), there is *ona'ah* in words, when the intention or effect is to inflict pain.[8] We should not add pain with our words to people whom tragedy has befallen, who are suffering illness, or by implying that God does not allow innocent people to come to harm, and, in general, behaving like Job's so-called "friends." This concept is explored in the second century CE narrative of Akhnai's Oven (b. *Bava Metzia* 59a-b), told in a round-about Talmudic manner that inquires whether a person (symbolized by a broken oven that needs repair) who has been broken by hurtful words can ever be made whole again.[9]

As the Talmudic story develops in Akhnai's Oven, a jealous group of rabbis behaves unethically toward an individual, Rabbi Eliezer, the former leader of their group. Their words encircle him like snakes. Their behavior, in fact, resembles cyberbullying, the current digital maligning and shaming of an individual, even the destruction of that person, for reasons of jealousy—or because that person's views are different from one's own.

The Talmudic story then brings magical events into play to prove the point. Finally, a *bat kol*, a divine echo from heaven, enters the fray to support Rabbi Eliezer, but the rabbis are unconvinced. "It [the Torah] is not

---

[7] b. *Bava Metzia* 58b–59a.

[8] One may not cause pain to a repentant sinner by asking about his former misdeeds, nor to a convert about the deeds of his ancestors. "You shall not wrong a stranger, or oppress him, for you were strangers in the land of Egypt" (Exod. 22:20).

[9] This description of "Akhnai's Oven" is excerpted from Corinne Copnick, "The Staying Power of Hope in the Aggadic Narratives of the Talmud," M.R.S. thesis, Academy for Jewish Religion California, 2015. Other sections of that text are also brought into this discussion.

in heaven!" they declare. The divine voice, the *bat kol*, should not interfere in earthly matters. Rather, through free will and the social processes of decision-making, human beings have the ability to make their own decisions to effect change—for good or bad.

Even though Rabbi Eliezer is right in his opinion, the jealous rabbis, who are the majority, do not agree. After he leaves the meeting in disgust, they insist that the majority opinion will hold. Even if the decision is wrong, the process is right. Thus, they invoke the principle of majority rule. This is something to think about in contemporary times. What happens if the majority is wrong? Nevertheless, in the Talmudic story, the jealous rabbis go even further. In spite, they decide to excommunicate Rabbi Eliezer.

The Talmud does not pull any punches as it tackles the anguish that a group can inflict to magnify the pain. Their action is called a *herem*, and it means that no one in the community will talk to him; they will not have anything to do with him; he is excommunicated. Rabbi Eliezer, who has already been defamed by malicious words, is now hurt by the *withdrawal* of words. In other words, Rabbi Eliezer is dead to the community.

In the Talmudic story, nature takes its revenge as God punishes both the upstart rabbis and the community. Fortunately, Rabbi Eliezer's tears reach the gates of Heaven, which open wide for him because he has been painfully wounded by *ona'at devarim*.

Please note that, at least in theory, every opinion cited in the Talmud should be respected (even though rabbis did sometimes hurl their beliefs at one another).[10] In the current climate of contentious opinion in America, this might be considered a naïve position. However, the rabbis of the Talmud listened to all sides of a matter and were inclined to make their joint decision (which became law, *halakhah*) based on majority opinion.[11] At the same time, just as in the decisions of the U.S. Supreme Court, the minority opinion was still respected and became a valid point of view. Actually, when we examine how Jewish rabbis/judges exercised the law so many centuries ago, we find that American law has many resemblances to rabbinic law.

The rabbis of old argued vigorously and persuasively, enjoying the different points of view, and indeed the argumentation itself, but the situations they tackled were serious ones, and the decisions they made had conse-

---

[10] The Talmudic premise was that the rabbis made good faith arguments and were well meaning, even when they did not agree, whereas today's discourse is often intentionally misleading, purposely hateful, and gleefully harmful. We need not tolerate the intolerant—or hateful intentions.

[11] In fact, in b. *Eruv* 13a the rabbis explain that the position of the House of Shammai, even if deemed not the accepted view, comes first because they treated each other with civility.

quences of which they were keenly aware.[12] Usually acrimony was avoided because the rabbis recognized that there could be multiple truths, depending on one's perspective and knowledge of a situation.[13]

In our contemporary society, however, *there is a danger of multiple truths unless the whole truth is told.* This is where the practice of disseminating "sound bites," whether on television or on our other various electronic gadgets, can be downright dangerous. Through the plethora of commentators, the talking heads, celebrity personalities, online trolls, and politicians with their own agendas, the worldwide public becomes instantly acquainted not just with one version of the truth, but with a fraction of one version—and it can be recorded for future listening and/or for posterity also. We live in a world of recorded (and televised) fractals.

Sadly, decades after the Internet first made itself available to public and private usage with the best of personal, societal, and business intentions, *lashon hara* continues to invade social media, inflicting coarsened modes of expression and blatant disregard for both truth and the feelings of those individuals or groups, whether unwitting or complicit, who encounter its manipulative platforms. A growing disregard for integrity in interpersonal relationships disturbs family relations as well, evidenced by those who reveal too personal, sexual, or often damaging information, visuals included, on a widely distributed forum. In my view, the development of close friendships has also taken a hit.

The Transformation of Friendship Through Social Media Channels

Unfortunately for the world, including the U.S., perhaps the most insidious digital weapon today is social media. It has become that way over time. When I first began to use the Internet with the birth of the World Wide Web in 1991, the idea was to share information—free of charge. It involved a *giving*; we could not only communicate with other people, both in our own milieu and around the world, but we could also help one another. We could educate. It was such a beautiful idea. Relationships could be maintained from afar and friendships blossomed because distance was no longer an issue.

At a personal level, I had lived most of my life in Montreal, Canada, with a sojourn of fifteen years in Toronto when separatist issues became a prob-

---

[12] Sometimes there was not enough evidence to make a decision, and the discussion was deemed "undecided" and tabled. Sometimes rabbis who had greater scholarship or prestige carried the day.

[13] What I am stressing is that every point of view, sometimes expressed with hyperbole to make the point, was given consideration. That is why only one point of view out of many cannot be cited as the conclusive rabbinic position.

lem in Quebec. When I was sixty-five years of age, I moved to California to help my daughter, a single mother, raise her newborn child, my grandchild. Through the Internet I was able to keep long-held relationships with my Canadian friends and relatives current for many years. As the Internet developed, we could exchange photos and videos. No, it was not the same as person-to-person exchanges, with warm human contact and hugs, but it kept us close. The new friends I made in California at first were mostly colleagues or activity friends, and so the dear, online friends remained very special for me. They were my "pen pals," much like the ones I had on the cusp of my teen years, until the polio epidemic (years before Salk's vaccine largely eliminated the threat of that virus) made people worry about opening handwritten letters from abroad.

Writing to a pen pal of yesteryear and sending an email message today is different, though, in terms of expectation. Emails are like instant coffee. The sender expects a speedy answer; otherwise, the computer's system will send you an urgent nudge: "Two days have passed since you got this message!" Answering a pen pal's letter was a more thoughtful process. You savored the letter, perhaps discussed some of the contents about distant places with other people, had photos you wanted to send developed, and in a few days posted a considered response to your pen pal, with maybe a quote or two from your favorite authors. At least that was my experience. The post office worked promptly then. So, the development of real friendship with strangers—enduring friendship perhaps—is not a new concept. Technically it is different, of course, and the time for friendship to grow has telescoped.

While it is true that online friendships have tended to take on a somewhat glossy, superficial quality—with lots of "selfies" shared as recompense for our actual selves—our cell phones, our iPads, our computers have served as a means to meet people, to share our opinions. To develop and continue friendships that have the potential to become "real." It is also true, as my colleagues assure me, that many fruitful, life-affirming, and genuine relationships have been forged online. Many of us have a variety of online friends with whom we share ideas and offer life support, and whom we will likely never meet in person. This is particularly true of the younger generations.

In her online *Psychology Today* pre-pandemic article, "Are Online Friends Better Than No Friends At All?," Professor Suzanne Degges-White extols the benefits (and outlines some of the pitfalls) of online friendships.[14] Just

---

[14] Suzanne Degges-White, "Are Online Friends Better Than No Friends at All? Online Relationships offer support in ways face-to-face friendships may not," *Psychology Today*, Oct. 5, 2018, https:// psychologytoday.com/us/blog/lifetime-connections/20810/are-online-friends-better-no-friends-at-all. Dr. White is a Professor at Northern Illinois University.

as in "face-to-face" friendships, she explains, "there's a broad spectrum of relationship quality among online buddies." In some online friendships, there is a tendency to project our "best selves" in a virtual projection of who we really are. This is something difficult to maintain with real life friends. On the other hand, among the many online choices, we may find other friends with whom we feel safe in exposing our vulnerabilities, bringing "candid honesty and genuineness to the relationships." In fact, as Professor Degges-White writes, "Research shows that it is 'safer' to be open and honest about our struggles, deficits, and anxieties with 'online buddies' than with people we see on a regular basis. When we share intimate information and reveal information that is less than flattering...[w]e feel less exposed when we hide behind the keyboard."[15]

In the early, idealistic days of the World Wide Web, as I experienced it a generation or more earlier than Professor Degges-White, the catch was that soon business interests began to think of the Internet less in terms of friendship than as a hot merchandising tool. In fact, I, too, quickly established my own writing and editing business on the web in 1991, and when I moved from Canada to the U.S. in 2000, I could take my clients with me. By then, big business had discovered the web for its marketing purposes, and ads began to appear on everyone's webpage, trumpeting their messages in ever more appealing forms, even when we did not want them there. We soon learned to buy products on the Internet we were not even sure we wanted and pay for them on that same screen.

And then came a multiplicity of social media channels emphasizing brief messaging. Lengthy blogs and messages were out, and Twitter was in. Why not get our instantaneous thoughts online for the world to digest in seconds? What a great way to keep up connections—and circulate our comments widely! Our eyes and noses were soon buried in our screens.[16]

Sadly, the tenor of these brief posts with "connections" at home and around the world gradually changed, affecting concepts of friendship. Emphasis began to be placed on the superficial, on how you were viewed by others. How many people would "like" what you posted? Did they "see" what you posted? Friendships became calculated in terms of "followers" of these posts. And then some young people discovered the power of the web in a more malign direction. Cyberbullying became a new thing. Cyber-hacking was yet to come. Eventually, when political discourse took over the Internet with manipulative and divisive opinions expressed in attack modes on or by

---

[15] Ibid.
[16] I have complained to my grandchildren that I rarely see their faces. Even my dog lifts my fingers off the computer keys when I have been on too long!

"the other side," many people of all ages began to copy the politicians. They began to use the now familiar digital devices as vehicles, indeed weapons, to express hostility, hatred even—to whip up anger on ever-changing platforms in the service of questionable causes, even to incite violent action against those who did not share their views.

When it comes to friendship, however, Professor Degges-White has a kinder view. While she acknowledges that users should be aware of digital dangers, such as social networks supporting extremist views, she also points out positives, such as "the availability of support groups," and that "stigmas lose their power in virtual environments."[17] On the other hand, at a therapeutic level, she warns that some of the seemingly neediest people may turn out to be "emotional vampires," and that online platforms may feed narcissism. For these reasons, she advises always having an exit strategy if the contact is not going well.[18]

Let me be clear that I am an enthusiastic user of maintaining and developing contact—whether personal, business-related, in support of societal justice, or therapeutic—through email and various other electronic platforms. I love communicating with friends and relatives, or as a rabbi. In particular, in this time of the COVID-19 pandemic, I have been a devotee of Zoom technology. In fact, my calendar is full of Zoom meetings.[19] For me, technologies like Zoom, Skype, and FaceTime, as well as Gmail, Facebook, and my own website,[20] have enabled my way of life, and that of my family, to continue in this time of a virulent pandemic.

There are, however, still many worrying technological flaws and security issues to overcome. "Zoombombing" has become a problem, and pre-registration, waiting rooms, and passwords to enter a meeting are essential. My personal email has been hacked twice, as well as my rabbinic blog, and technological change is so rapid and has affected so many areas that it is hard for people (especially elderly people) to keep up. The biggest problem, as I see it, though, is the misuse of the medium. How do we keep the bad guys out, and who decides who the bad guys are?

---

[17] Degges-White, "Are Online Friends Better Than No Friends at All?"
[18] Ibid.
[19] As a rabbi, during this past year I have conducted in-person, very small funerals, and weddings on Zoom, and with accompanying services Zoom-relayed to relatives across the country. I have served as a *dayan* (judge in a rabbinic court) at a number of virtual conversions (with natural immersions) for a flourishing Los Angeles *bet din*, of which I am a governor. I am able to attend worthwhile meetings with colleagues and attend the lectures of distinguished speakers virtually. I have given weekly lectures of my own to the study group I founded, Beit Kulam, as well as readings of my 2020 book, *A Rabbi at Sea: A Uniquely Spiritual Journey*, across the U.S.
[20] http://www.rabbicorinne.com

It is truly distressing that both public pronouncements and interpersonal relationships on the Internet have taken a darker turn in the last few years. Over time, this twenty-first century mode of societal communication—instead of uniting people across the miles—has developed a harsh stream of invective, sparing neither enemies nor those formerly called friends, who can now be coldly "unfriended" with the click of a computer key. Teenagers, in particular, are cruelly affected emotionally as their self-esteem is decimated in public. There is, in general, an utter disregard for the feelings of those who are victimized. Has the rapid growth of the Internet actually been destructive to developing in-depth, positive interpersonal relationships?

Although private and public streams of communication have seemingly merged, it is not always in a benign way, especially now that competing political views have taken over available platforms or have established their own platforms to influence opinion. Too often this confluence of conflicting communication stirs up anger and prevents the public presentation of divergent views. At the same time, it should be remembered that respecting divergent views is not the same as tolerating hateful and harmful viewpoints.

As we have seen, what begins as interpersonal misbehavior can grow into a problem—a moral injury—that may eventually plague society with violence: When a group of people with fanatical views, for example, link together on the Internet and attack the Capitol of the United States and even plan further insurrections, we may indeed ask another question:[21] What may happen to our own society when ethical behavior becomes tinged with fanaticism—and when the time-honored Judaic principle of *lashon hara* (evil speech) is maliciously invoked on social media? Sadly, the answer may be moral injury, especially to younger generations.

Moral Injury

I first learned about the term "moral injury" from Rabbi Jonathan Sacks.[22] The combination of these two words was popularized by Pulitzer Prize-winning war reporter David Wood in his book, *What Have We Done? The Moral Injuries of Our Longest Wars*.[23] Wood was concerned that many battle-hardened soldiers returning from Iran and Afghanistan were affected by moral injury. Author Francisco Cantu, reflecting on his own experience as a border agent, further explained that people do not have to be on battlefields to be

---

[21] The incited vigilante attack on the Capitol in Washington, D.C. took place on January 6, 2021. The seat of government was threatened, and many people were injured or killed.
[22] Sacks, *Morality*.
[23] David Wood, *What Have We Done: The Moral Injury of Our Longest Wars* (New York: Little, Brown & Co., 2016).

exposed to moral injury.[24] It is something pervasive that can happen from immoral societal exposure, and it seeps deeply into individual consciousness. According to Rabbi Sacks, it is a gradual process.[25] The wounds develop slowly, as people are urged to accept things they know are wrong. Over time, they experience moral injury.

In turn, I too am deeply concerned about the moral injury, the psychic wounds our political atmosphere continues to inflict on a new American generation. Two of my grandchildren are currently seniors in university, and a third is a freshman this year, and I worry about their future and those of their classmates. Shaming and shunning—a modern-day *herem*—are seen as the just desserts of those who do not conform, with resultant psychological harm to teenagers in particular.

My own teenage granddaughter was injured by *lashon hara* (in the form of vile tweets and threats) for the honest opinions she expressed on Twitter, to the extent she needed supportive help from a therapist to recover her societal and personal equilibrium. It took considerable time until her anxiety and depression lifted and she felt like a normal teenager again. Fortunately, she had a strong Judaic code of morality and ethical conduct to help her back to mental health and enjoyment of life.

Although there was a good outcome for my granddaughter, it is tragic that, on a daily basis, intentions that are morally wrong are being deliberately transformed by misguided leaders into what is promoted as morally good. In an oft-quoted "Orwellian" kind of transformation, what is plainly evil to most thinking people is deceptively cited as the "right" path to follow for the ultimate good. Misused biblical quotations bolster grandiose speeches. Facts are simply overlooked in a society driven by instilled fear, divisions, and repeated lies. By wounds.

In America, as I write these words, we are watching these wounds begin to fester on a daily basis, through the mouths and actions—or inactions—of our leaders. The wounds first show themselves through acts of incivility, even hatred, through acceptance of lying as a new normal, through crazed individuals who vent their rage by shooting innocent people. And who flout their hatred on the Internet, creating new moral injuries.

After more than a year of a global pandemic that took vast numbers, while some Americans raced to have celebrations, vacations, or reunions with families, others have been slower to rejoin the in-person social sphere. Longtime friends and dearly-loved relatives may have succumbed to the pandemic. Grieving continues to play a role in our national character. Peo-

---

[24] Francisco Cantu, *The Line Becomes a River: Dispatches from the Border* (New York: Riverhead, 2018).
[25] Sacks, *Morality*.

ple turn off the news. Yes, there has been moral injury. But as Generation Z turns off its anxiety and returns to school with a new awareness, a deep sadness built into their collective consciousness, there is also a determination to make a better world, to correct what is "wrong." They are the new wave, and they are right. They circulate these views on the web too. They have lots of followers. Now it is time to heal by seeking out and deepening our meaningful friendships once again, hopefully face-to-face, in person.

Thankfully, growing segments of our society are beginning to raise their voices in outrage: Children—no matter where they come from—should not be forcibly separated from their parents and certainly not, to add insult to injury, without a coherent plan for reuniting them. School children should not have to worry about being shot when they go to school. We must move into the future as a nation: diverse, inclusive, unified. We have to heal our climate. If we can defeat this pandemic, we can do anything. And Generation Z wants to do something about it.

Once again, the words of Rabbi Sacks capture this moment: the resilience of a new generation, the power to recuperate from disaster emphasized in Judaism.

> There exists, within nature and humanity, an astonishing range of powers to heal what has been harmed and mend what has been broken. These powers are embedded within life itself, with its creativity and capacity for self-renewal. That is the empirical basis of hope. Nature favors species able to recover, and history favors cultures that can do so.[26]

In America, we have survived a physical crisis, at least for the time being. It is our task now to reinstate the moral compass, give ourselves a big collective hug, and rebuild an ethical way of life, one that puts aside hateful discourse and remembers that supportive friendships are more than comments exchanged on a screen.

As Jews, as members of *Am Israel*, we are fortunate to have our biblical blueprint, our tested guide to the what, why, and how of moral and ethical behavior. These "co-dependents" have served us well for thousands of years in many situations and locales around the world; they have helped us survive natural disasters, adverse historical events, even slavery, racial hatred, and multiple holocausts. Our blueprint has helped us to believe that a green shoot will always rise from the decimated trunk, that we will continue to improve not only our own condition, but also that of humankind.

---

[26] Sacks, *Morality*, 19.

Stephen Robbins responds

One of the enduring qualities of Judaism has been its adaptability to the historical, social, economic, and political realities in which it is practiced. There is an underlying ethical principle of Judaism to constantly interpret and respond to the challenges of whatever contemporary period, using the spiritual, ethical, and moral foundations that were given at Mount Sinai. The essay by Rabbi Corinne Copnick both expresses and expands on this principle. She herself emulates adaptability within an ethical framework of Jewish values. At the tender age of seventy-nine, she was ordained by AJRCA as rabbi in 2015 (along with my wife, Rabbi/Cantor Eva Robbins).

Rabbi Copnick embodies in her work the ideals on which the Academy was founded, and exemplifies why we seek out second-career students who bring profound knowledge and experience to their studies and, ultimately, to their work as clergy. This is precisely what she has accomplished in her years of service to our God, our people, and the individuals she serves in nontraditional settings, such as her work on cruise ships.

In her essay, Rabbi Copnick teaches us about the wisdom of the "aged ones," or *zakeinim*, who are also referred to as "wise ones." Her breadth of experience has given her a unique vantage point on the digital age in which we live, and its challenges to Jewish moral and ethical teachings. Among the most important lessons gleaned from her essay is the unfortunate atomization of society in the digital age, so that we no longer relate to the whole person, but only to images and texts of what people wish us to know about them, and them about us. At the core of Judaism is that life is with people. Yet, our interactions have been disrupted, fragmented, and ripped apart by digital platforms and the COVID-19 pandemic. As such, she points out, we tend to formulate false images of ourselves as well as false images of others.

At their worst, digital platforms become a means of shaming, shunning, and bullying of those with whom we differ or compete. They can be—and in many cases have become—a modern-day *herem*, or excommunication, leading to unspeakable damage and even suicide. Furthermore, as Rabbi Copnick cautions, the digital age has taken away our privacy, a vital possession in Jewish ethics. As we discussed together, this is a realization of Orwell's dystopian *1984*, only in this case we do not know who is watching. It can be anyone anywhere who wants to intrude on our lives.

Jewish ethics, in all its iterations, centers on individual life and the autonomy of individual thought. In contrast, digital platforms thrive on followers, not independent thinkers. The purpose of the original ethical framework given at Sinai—*Aseret ha-Dibrot* or "Ten Commandments"—is to be a paradigm for self-responsibility in moral and ethical behavior and thought. Rabbi Copnick rightly asserts that, as Jews, we must be careful to use digital platforms, perilous though they are, to *re-engage*, so that we do not lose our connection to each other, to Torah, and to God.

I would like to see Rabbi Copnick develop her discussion of moral inquiry further, and specifically how she would apply it as a teaching tool for Jews living on the Internet. There is much potential here, and her wisdom, passion, and insight in this area are vital. Her work as a rabbi and as the author of this essay is a shining example of what Jewish responses to contemporary challenges are all about.

Corinne Copnick responds

I am truly honored to respond to this comprehensive essay on spiritual, ethical, and moral themes in Judaism by Rabbi Stephen Robbins, one of the three esteemed founders of the transdenominational Academy of Jewish Religion California. What we learn from Rabbi Robbins' fine essay, above all, is that spirituality is an integral part of reflections on ethics and morality. As he suggests, an extended focus on these themes would greatly enhance religious studies for prospective clergy, especially in a time of multiple contemporary challenges to our way(s) of life. With this goal in mind, Rabbi Robbins' essay first takes us on a thought-provoking exposition of how these themes are both deeply embedded and intertwined in the biblical stories about our patriarchs and their wives.

Not only does the mystical revelation of God to humans in the Torah's early chapters require human moral action in the physical world, but when Jacob dreams about a ladder stretching to heaven, his dream evolves into an understanding that God is present for all of us—and each of us—in all places and times, as each of us sets out on our individual journey. This is a teaching sorely needed in a time when our own dreams are being eroded by a pandemic that seemingly will not quit.

The Torah, however, perseveres. By the time of Joseph's large administrative role in Egypt, the twelve estranged brothers are encountering issues of reconciliation and reunification (themes we urgently need to resolve in the twenty-first century, as Rabbi Robbins later articulates in more detail), and we learn from Robbins that "ethics and morality in Judaism are built on spiritual principles of love and empathy, because they both flow from God." The Jewish people have already been gifted with a Holiness Code so that they can put these concepts into practice as they evolve as a people.

Rabbi Robbins' essay also takes us into the world of the Nevi'im (Prophets), to the transgressions of King David and Bathsheba, as well as the kingship of Solomon, in whose reign the Temple was built, only to culminate in destruction and exile. We learn in Ketuvim (Writings) that both Ruth, who adopted the Israelite people as her own, followed her widowed mother-in-law, Naomi, to a strange land, and offered herself at Naomi's behest to Boaz so they could survive, and Esther, who hid her Jewish identity in order to marry a Persian king for the survival of the Jewish people, both compromised their values to achieve a necessary goal. Yet we learn from Rabbi Robbins that both women also brought an emphasis on compassion and *chesed* (lovingkindness) into their respective worlds.

Two questions trouble me in regard to these dilemmas: How much can we, as individuals and as a community, even as a country, allow ourselves to erode our values in order to achieve goals we perceive as necessary for survival in the world and time in which we live? What strengths must we find in ourselves in life-or-death situations?

Perhaps Rabbi Robbins has an answer, as he takes us beyond the wisdom of the Bible to another kind of wisdom gained from experience—to *Pirkei Avot*, the *Ethics of the Fathers*. It is a lay text that has endured the test of time, and, as Robbins writes, affirms "the moral obligation of each person in this world, so that there can be a World to Come."

Of specific interest to me, because my own essay in this volume places emphasis on *lashon hara* (the evil tongue) as encountered in Jewish texts, including the Talmud, is Rabbi Robbins' brief commentary on this issue. I plan to order the book he recommends, *Guard Your Tongue* (adapted from the Chofetz Chaim by Rabbi Zelek Pliskin). Sadly, *lashon hara*—compared in scope to the cardinal sins of murder, idolatry, and adultery—is very much a part of our everyday life in today's global, technologically interconnected world.

In sum, with such a vast cornucopia of knowledge literally at our fingertips today, surely clergy and laypeople alike can learn from the many biblical and post-biblical Judaic examples of instances requiring spiritual/moral/ethical behavior, and the ways in which humans can find the qualities within themselves to step up to the plate. What we learn from Rabbi Robbins is that in our age-old, expounded Jewish views cast a strong light on these issues in the here and now.

Set Three

The Human Covenant: Toward an Ethic of Jewish Political Engagement

Shaiya Rothberg

Fear of Sin and of One's Teacher in Early Rabbinic Judaism

Joel Gereboff

The Human Covenant: Toward an Ethic of Jewish Political Engagement

Shaiya Rothberg

Politics is a notoriously difficult subject for Jewish communities. The common denominators that bring people together in shared communities often do not include explicit political agendas. It is generally easier to avoid political issues than to address them. But politics is the realm of social justice and injustice, and one that as Jews we cannot abandon. In this essay, I propose that cultivating a commitment to what I will call "the human covenant," consisting of international human rights norms, is incumbent upon us today as part of our historical mission as the People of Israel and should stand at the center of our religious identity.

Mending the Body and Soul of Humanity

Of the many gates to Judaism's teaching on social justice, I find the work of the Rambam (Moses ben Maimon; Maimonides, 1138–1204) particularly evocative. One compelling way to read the Rambam's complex literary legacy is that he believes that the Torah has a twofold purpose: *tikkun ha-guf* and *tikkun ha-nefesh*, to mend the body and soul of humanity.[1] By "mending the soul," Rambam means realizing each human being's full spiritual potential, which he understands as the process through which we realize our potential to reflect God's image.[2] His idea of "mending the body" involves the "body politic," human collective political power. Mending the body includes shaping politics so that all people have the material and social necessities they need, like housing, education and protection from violence, so they can "mend their souls."

A graphic image of "the body politic" appears on the frontispiece of Hobbes' seventeenth-century book, *The Leviathan*, which analyzes "the form and power of the commonwealth."[3] The engraving shows a colossal man,

---

[1] The Rambam is a famously esoteric and multivocal writer and no single interpretation can claim to fully represent him. My interpretation of *tikkun ha-guf* and *tikkun ha-nefesh* is grounded in reading *The Guide of the Perplexed* 2:40 and 3:27 in light of the *Laws of Kings*, Ch. 12, quoted below.

[2] See *Mishneh Torah*, Foundations of the Torah, 4:8.

[3] Thomas Hobbes, *Leviathan or The Matter, Forme and Power of a Commonwealth Ecclesiasticall and Civil* (London: Andrew Crooke, 1651).

composed of countless tiny images of individual people, wielding the king's sword in one hand and the bishop's staff in the other. He is the Leviathan, and symbolizes the power of the collective, the political dimension of human existence. While Hobbes' conception of political authority is problematic, this image of the collective-human Leviathan remains a potent symbol for the realm of the political and will be a useful image in this essay.

Imagine the Leviathan as a dynamic creature who can appear not only as human but in different shapes. When political power acts destructively rather than benevolently, the Leviathan takes the shape of a wild beast, perhaps as a dragon in the spirit of the biblical origins of this word (e.g., Isa. 27:1; Job 3:8, 40:25). However, if the power of the political is directed towards "mending" people rather than devouring them, then we can imagine the Leviathan in the shape of a benevolent human being. This is how I propose we understand the Rambam's "mending the body," that is, as an attempt to shape and humanize the Leviathan, to transform human political power from the form of a devouring beast into a shape that nurtures and protects us.

In the closing section of his monumental *Mishneh Torah*, literally "Repetition of the Torah/Law," the Rambam offers a vision of what we as a species will look like after all the Leviathans are humanized and global resources are directed to mending the body and soul of humanity:

> In that era, there will be neither hunger nor war, neither jealousy nor competition. Blessings will be abundant, comforts within the reach of all. The sole vocation of the entire world will be to know God. Thus they will become greatly wise, and will know hidden and deep matters; grasping the knowledge of their Creator to the utmost capacity of the human mind, as it is written (Isa. 11:9), "[They will not hurt nor destroy in all My holy mountain] for the earth shall be full of the consciousness of God as the waters fill the sea."[4]

This vision of redeemed humanity embodies Rambam's ideal of mending

---

[4] Rambam, *Mishneh Torah*, *Hilchot Melachim* 12:5; *Machon Mamrei* version, my translation. In the printed editions of the *Mishneh Torah*, this paragraph accrued the word "Israel" so that it states that "Israel will be greatly wise…" But another version is preserved in manuscripts without the word "Israel," so that it is humanity that will become greatly wise. This is almost certainly the correct version of the text. See Menachem Kellner, "Farteitcht un Farbessert (On 'Correcting' Maimonides)" in *Bedarkei Shalom*, ed. B. Ish Shalom (Jerusalem: Beit Morasha, 2007), 255–263 [Hebrew] and translated into English by Joel Linsider in *Mekorot* (Yeshivat Chovevei Torah Rabbinical School) 6:2 (2007): 1–11.

THE HUMAN COVENANT 81

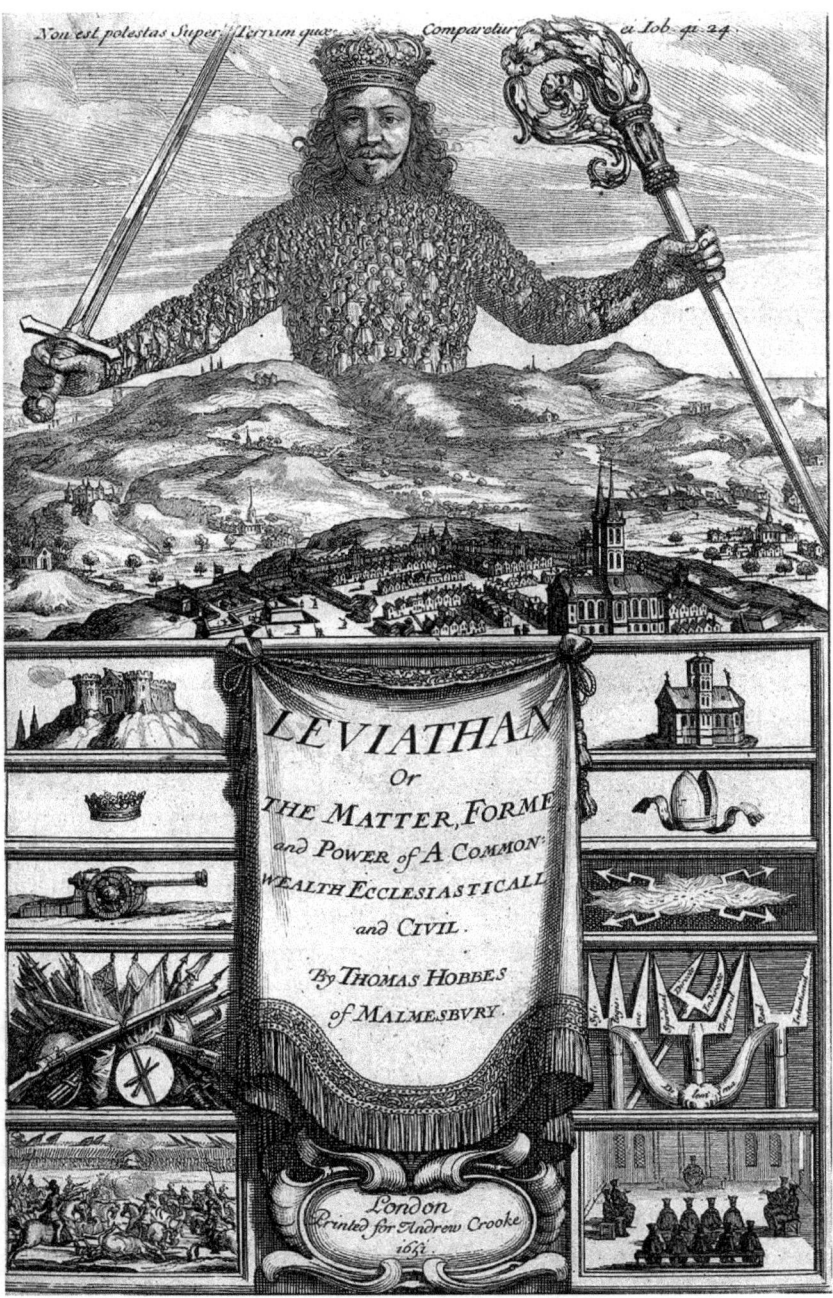

Thomas Hobbes, Leviathan, frontispiece;
engraving by Abraham Bosse (1651) (Library of Congress).

the body and soul of humanity. Because the body politic of humanity has been mended, there is no hunger, war, jealousy, or competition, and blessings and comforts are abundant for all. With its body mended, the sole vocation of humanity is to mend its soul through knowledge of God.

Mending the body, then, provides the necessary conditions for mending the soul. But the relation cuts both ways. In his interpretation of Gan Eden, the Rambam imagines that before the sin, the first humans knew God to their utmost capacity, and thus had already achieved the end goal depicted above: They were deeply wise, caused no hurt or destruction, and existed in a kind of spiritual bliss.[5] After eating from the Tree of Knowledge of Good and Evil, however, their consciousness constricted, and they became obsessed with judging things according to what they wanted or did not want. For the Rambam, *etz ha-da'at tov vera* would be better translated as "the tree of obsessive thoughts about fears and desires." It offers no real "knowledge": "good" is what you want and "evil" is what you do not want. The sin and punishment are one: Entrapping yourself in endless thoughts about what you want is the sin; being entrapped in those thoughts is the punishment. According to the Rambam, this entrapment is the exile from Eden.

The spiritual predicament of exile carries political implications. Entrapped in their narrow desires, humans compete for material riches and political domination, and so doom themselves to a world of hunger, war, jealousy, and competition.[6] The tragedy is that true value—knowledge of God—is free, and its attainment requires no competition. The opposite is also true: the more knowledge of God that you have, the more opportunity there is for me to acquire it too. And, since for the Rambam knowledge of God is closely associated with the virtues of wisdom, justice, and compassion, the more it abounds, the greater my chances of living in a just and well-ordered society. Our political and spiritual brokenness are intertwined, and so too is the work of our mending.

The Rambam's vision is a synthesis of biblical religious inspiration and medieval philosophical rationalism. His doctrine of structuring the state so that it provides the material and social conditions necessary for human flourishing combines the moral and spiritual grandeur of the Bible with Greek wisdom about human nature and the polis. I find his synthesis beautiful and compelling. Because we live in a culture permeated by Graeco-Western thinking about politics, the Rambam's interpretation draws the Bible closer to our world. He gives the vision of the prophets a political form that makes

---

[5] See Rambam, *The Guide of the Perplexed*, Part I, Chapter 2. The Rambam only explicitly speaks about the first man in this context.
[6] The Rambam explores this dynamic in *The Guide to the Perplexed*, Part III, Chapter 12.

sense in light of the political thought in his day, thereby mediating between tradition and reality, in keeping with his rabbinic vocation.

One element of his vision that I find particularly compelling is its way of entwining spirit and justice. There is a widespread sense that liberalism and liberal democracy cultivate a spiritually vapid, hedonistic consumerism that ultimately undermine themselves. Think of the Rambam's version of exile from Gan Eden: forever thinking (and posting) about our fears and desires. This spiritual exile from Eden seems to fragment society, cause alienation, and facilitate the rise of dangerous, dysfunctional political leaders. Judaism contains deep wisdom about cultivating loving communities grounded in spiritual practices. The Rambam's teaching emphasizes that this wisdom is important for engaging politics.

Another aspect of combining spiritual vision with political ideals involves the Rambam's expansive utopian-prophetic envisioning of a redeemed humanity. In contemporary politics, we rarely fantasize about what we, as a species, might look like if we could pull ourselves together. When is the last time you wondered how wise, compassionate, and just the human species could realistically become? Let us imagine that, by some miracle, for the next two hundred years we followed the Rambam's advice and invested everything we have—all of our vast collective wealth and knowledge—in protecting all humans from harm and raising them in spiritually grounded, loving communities. What would humans look like then? Would we still recognize "politics" after two hundred years in the life of a humanized Leviathan? How might the responses and capabilities of our species to global crises like the COVID-19 pandemic and climate change be different than they are now?

When I imagine the Rambam's redeemed world, filled with wise people loving God and each other, and the total absence of war, injustice, and poverty, it ignites in me an optimism and a love for the human species that I do not feel when I read the news. In fact, following the news and engaging in social justice work often seem like an engine that burns optimism and love of humanity for fuel. Since we need that engine, we need a source for its fuel. When we connect in the right way to sacred texts from our tradition that invite us to engage in utopian-prophetic envisioning, and chant them out loud together on Shabbat and holidays, we uncover a source for the spiritual energy that social justice work requires.

The clause "in the right way" in the previous sentence requires emphasis. Since particularistic identities, including ours, are often weaponized to dehumanize others, the Rambam's ideal, according to which Judaism serves God's plan for the human species and not just the Jewish people, is a crucial first step for any Jewish ethic of political engagement. The Rambam's human-centric approach undoubtedly reflects his Aristotelian philosophical commitments, but it also follows the simple meaning of the biblical story. Abraham is chosen by God to be a leader of nations immediately after the disasters of the Flood and the Tower of Babel. The larger context is that God is clearly attempting to get humans established on earth. The simplest explanation of God's choice of Abraham is that this is a new divine strategy to accomplish that same goal. "Mending the body and soul" is the Rambam's medieval conceptualization of the biblical story.[7]

Ultimately, the Rambam understands Jewish tradition as a blueprint for accomplishing the divine plan for humanity: to mend our bodies and souls so that we become, in the Rambam's terminology, *adam*—that is, fully human. For the Rambam, "humanity" is not a description of who we are but the name for our highest moral and spiritual ideal. It is when we have mended our bodies and souls through wisdom, justice, and compassion that we realize our human potential to reflect God's image.[8] We need to be careful with this idea, because treating "humanity" as an ideal rather than a description has in the past been used to dehumanize those who deviate from the ideal, as the history of colonialism clearly shows. But having acknowledged that danger, Rambam's use of the term "human" as our highest ideal emphasizes the universal scope of Judaism's aspirations, our commitment to protecting and nurturing every single human being. That holistic spiritual-political commitment to directing our species' wealth and knowledge to cultivate *adam*—humanity—strikes me as the very core of authentic Jewish political engagement as it emerges from the Rambam.

While the Rambam's vision draws elements of the biblical vision closer to contemporary reality, it still leaves us deep in the Middle Ages. The Rambam imagines that a kind of theocratic monarchy will serve as the best engine for mending humanity.[9] That probably made sense in twelfth-century politics. But to integrate the compelling elements of his spiritual-political envisioning into contemporary reality, we need later figures who have continued the process of mediating between Jewish teaching and reality in light of more modern developments.

---

[7] For a succinct interpretation of Abraham's election along these lines, see Sforno's introduction to Genesis and commentary on Exodus 19:6.
[8] On the use of "human" in this way, see the fifth of Rambam's *Eight Chapters* (Commentary to the *Mishnah*, Introduction to *Pirkei Avot*). On wisdom, justice, and compassion, see *The Guide to the Perplexed*, Part III, Chapter 54.
[9] See Rambam, *Mishneh Torah*, The Laws of Kings.

To Dwell in Zion

I find two modern Jewish thinkers, Rabbis Shimshon Rafael Hirsch (1808–1888) and Chaim Hirschensohn (1857–1935), particularly compelling in this context. Both imagined how Judaism could contribute to humanizing the global Leviathan through a Jewish engagement with politics. And, like the biblical prophets of old, both of them did so by envisioning the role of Zion in global affairs. This is also true of the Rambam, who imagined that human redemption would begin in Zion and then, like flowing waters, spread out to the rest of the planet.[10] In light of the significance of Zion for the Jewish spiritual-political envisioning that we are exploring, let us first briefly consider the symbolism of Zion in Jewish tradition more broadly.

We first encounter what will later be known as Zion as the unnamed "land that I will show you" to which God commands Abraham in *Lekh Lekha*. Our first encounter with Zion is thus as a *destination*. It is a physical destination, but only secondarily, because Abraham is commanded there as the space in which to realize his divine *mission*. In Buber's words, "The story of Abraham, which connects the gift of Canaan with the command to be a blessing, is a most concise resume of the fact that the association of this people with this land signifies a mission."[11]

But just a few verses after entering the land, Abraham is promptly driven from it by famine (Gen. 12:10). From this moment, and throughout Jewish history, Zion is not only mission and destination, but also our mythical lost origin, for which the people yearn, and to which, according to the biblical prophets, they are destined to return. Zion destroyed is the meaning of *exile*. Zion rebuilt is the meaning of *redemption*. In Kabbalah, Zion is the conduit through which God's abundance flows into the world.[12] When Jewish figures like Isaiah, the Rambam, and Rabbis Hirsch and Hirschensohn envision Zion, they do not merely touch on a location, but offer us an opportunity to see the origin, mission, destiny and ideals of Israel through their eyes.

The first vision we will explore is that of Rabbi Shimshon Rafael Hirsch. Rashar Hirsch was a founder of modern Orthodoxy, one of the first Jewish civil rights activists, and was perhaps the first Torah scholar to center his Torah worldview on the idea of human rights. Like the Rambam, Hirsch conceived of the Torah as a blueprint for the realization of humanity's higher potential, to cultivate what he called "Mensch-Jissroel," the human-Israel-

---

[10] For the stirring of redemption first in *Eretz Yisrael*, see Rambam's *Commentary to the Mishnah, Sanhedrin* 1:3. On the final redemption, see the closing passage of the *Mishneh Torah*, quoted above.

[11] Martin Buber, *On Zion* (New York: Schocken, 1973), xix.

[12] See Rabbi Joseph Gikatilla, *The Gates of Light*, trans. Avi Weinstein (Lanham, MD: AltaMira, 1994), 100.

ite, who embodies a universal human ideal: "The Jewish task must not be conceived as something alien to and divorced from the human task....So it is that we begin the windings of our *tzitzit* with a white-colored thread, representing pure humanity, continue with a blue thread representing Judaism, and finish off by returning to the white thread. Pure Judaism always returns to pure humanism."[13]

We can explore Rashar Hirsch's thinking about human rights by comparing his boldly anachronistic commentary on the Torah to the ideals he evoked in his own civil rights activism. Pharaoh enslaved the Jews by denying "that it is not race, not descent, not birth, or country or property, altogether nothing external or due to chance, but simply and purely the inner spiritual and moral worth of a human being, which gives him all the rights of a man and of a citizen."[14] Following the same logic, Hirsch argued that Germany's refusal to grant Jews "full emancipation, complete unrestricted equality of rights" also amounted to enslavement. In a letter to the Reichstag, which had extended civil rights to some hitherto disenfranchised populations but not to Jews, Hirsch wrote, "The Jewish members of the state...had been the most enslaved people in the land...no one was robbed of the holiest inalienable rights as they were. If atonement is to be performed, here is where it should be carried out."[15]

What did Rashar Hirsch mean by "human rights"? When he decries Pharaoh's denial of "the rights of man and of the citizen" he clearly means to remind us of the French "Declaration of the Rights of Man and of the Citizen" of 1789. But we need not assume that he believed that ancient Egyptians could have understood modern civil rights.

In a passage quoted below, Hirsch suggests that the Noahide laws may be understood as a standard of human rights. He uses the term "human rights" to designate the legal and political justice appropriate to a given context. In his time, he believed that meant human rights in the modern sense of the French Declaration. This does not mean he would have accepted contemporary human rights.

The French Declaration, for example, did not extend rights to women and, as far as I know, Hirsch was no suffragette. He was also no friend

---

[13] Samson Raphael Hirsch, *The Collected Writings, Volume III: Jewish Symbolism* (New York: Feldheim, 1984), 329.
[14] Hirsch, Commentary on Exodus 22:20. Quotations from the commentary are drawn from Isaac Levy's translation in *The Pentateuch Translated and Explained by Samson Raphael Hirsch* (London: L. Honig & Sons, 1956). I have made slight changes based on other translations.
[15] Michael Miller, *Rabbis and Revolution: The Jews of Moravia in the Age of Emancipation* (Stanford, CA: Stanford University Press, 2011), 200–201 and 215–216.

of Jewish religious pluralism. In seeking to identify elements of tradition relevant for a contemporary ethics of Jewish political engagement, we are reading Hirsch selectively, as we did with the Rambam.

Hirsch's activism embodied a political ideal, a human shape for the Leviathan, the cultivation of which he believed is part of the mission of Israel. He envisioned what might be called a Jewish politics of human rights, in which the spiritual grounding of Judaism would moralize politics: "Deception and murder which in individuals lead to prison and gallows, if exercised on a grand scale in the 'interests of the state' are crowned with laurel and medals. The Abrahamic nation is to know nothing of these national institutions… [but rather] to dedicate themselves with all devotion to the Divine purpose… to re-establish man to its original pure calling of אדם [*adam*–humanity]."[16]

In Hirsch's imagination, the mythical past and future meld into one ideal vision of Zion. The Jewish state of yore was faithful to the Torah which (the text is italicized in the original for emphasis), "…*knows no distinction between the rights of man and the rights of citizen. Everyone who acknowledged the moral laws of humanity—the seven Noahide laws—could claim the right of domicile in Judea.*" For the Torah, "it is *not nationality which bestows human rights, but human rights that bestow nationality!*"[17] Human rights in Zion were not "conditional on anything other than on that simple humanity which every human being as such bears within him."[18] So it was, and will be again, when God "sees fit…to unite again His scattered servants in one land, and the Torah shall be the guiding principle of a state, an exemplar of the meaning of Divine Revelation and the mission of humanity."[19]

Hirsch's vision of Zion goes beyond the civil rights for which he struggled. He did not demand that Germany collapse the division between human and citizen rights by granting all people the right of domicile. Nor did he claim that European national identities were constituted by human rights. It is because Israel (unlike other nations for Hirsch) exists to serve God's vision for humanity, that a truly Jewish state is *transnational*: its very national identity constituted by universal human rights, and its borders open to all. Hirsch promulgated his vision of Zion not as a practical program for a Jewish state (he opposed modern Zionism), but as an ideal for Jews living in diaspora where God sent them to educate the nations.[20] The mission of Israel as Hirsch lived it was to embody practical, realistic human rights

---

[16] Hirsch, Commentary on Genesis 12:2 (use of the word "אדם," in Hebrew, in the original).
[17] Hirsch, Commentary on Exodus 1:14 (emphasis and exclamation point in original).
[18] Hirsch, Commentary on Exodus 22:20.
[19] Hirsch, *The Nineteen Letters*, trans. Joseph Elias (New York: Feldheim, 1994), Letter 16.
[20] See for instance, Ibid., Letter 8.

activism in the country in which he lived, with his eyes fixed on a mythical Zion, where human rights would reach their ideal fulfilment.

The second vision of Zion, that of Rabbi Chaim Hirschensohn, was also seen from diaspora, in the United States in 1919, two years after the Balfour Declaration, and was offered as a proposal for the use of the Temple Mount under the auspices of a modern Jewish state. Rabbi Hirschensohn was born and raised in Palestine, but settled around 1903 in Hoboken, New Jersey, after being excommunicated by Orthodox authorities in Jerusalem for advocating the study of modern Hebrew and secular subjects.[21] In exile, he fell deeply in love with American democracy, and envisioned a modern Israel which embodied the ideals of democracy and international law:

> Among the issues that stand as a serious obstacle for any religious [Jew] and which mars his happiness in regard to the salvation which God has done for us through the English Declaration [is]...the question what will we do with the place of our Temple which is the height and primacy of the glory of His praise even now...
>
> [I]t is not far off to think that this period is the one about which Isaiah prophesied "In the days to come, the Mount of the Lord's house shall stand firm above the mountains, and tower above the hills, and all the nations shall stream towards it"....And this is because in this House will be the Peace Palace—but not like the Peace Palace in the Hague, where the peace representatives bow down before the glory of those whose power casts its shadow over the world.... And it will be more than the League of Nations...which in any case has more good will than legal power, but rather it will be the "Court of the Nations" which will judge the peoples in justice and the nations with righteousness, and iniquity will no longer rule in the world, and the corrupted idea that nationalism justifies iniquity and evil will be banished, and justice for every nation will be like justice for every individual, for each one has the right to develop in his own unique way, but without damaging his fellow, and there will be no more tyranny: not by man on man, nor

---

[21] See David Zohar, *Jewish Commitment in a Modern World: Rabbi Hayyim Hirschenson and His Attitude to Modernity* (Jerusalem: Shalom Hartman Institute, 2003) [Hebrew]. On Hirschensohn's approach to democracy, see Shaiya Rothberg, "The Democratization of the Jewish Political Tradition," Ph.D. diss., Hebrew University of Jerusalem, 2008, https://archive.org/details/Democratization [Hebrew].

nation on nation, nor nation on man, nor man on nation, nation shall not take up sword against nation, neither will they learn war anymore.[22]

Like the Rambam and Rashar Hirsch, Rabbi Hirschensohn understood the mission of Israel as mending humanity. But unlike Rashar Hirsch, he was a religious Zionist who believed that Israel's mission required the physical return to Zion through the establishment of a modern Jewish state. He therefore imagines that the people of Israel will contribute to mending humanity not only as citizens in other countries, but also through an international court of justice that will sit on the Temple Mount in the Jewish state like the Peace Palace in the Hague. Given his emphasis on protection from tyranny, and the iniquity and evil of nationalism, it seems likely that had he lived in 2002, the year the International Criminal Court was established, he would have advocated erecting it on the Temple Mount in Jerusalem.

According to Rabbi Hirschensohn's *halakhic* analysis, the international law of his day was a branch of Torah law. He argued that in *halakhic* terms, the treaties upon which international law are based constitute "the covenants of the peoples," and that such covenants are absolutely binding in Torah tradition, like the covenant at Sinai. He cites the Talmudic ruling (b. *Gittin* 46a) that violating a covenant with a foreign nation is a desecration of God's name and forbidden, even if compliance with the covenant contradicts an explicit commandment.[23] The binding Torah authority of international law was already in effect according to his analysis, even without his imagined Court of Nations on Mount Zion. But if so, why did he imagine it?

Rabbi Hirschensohn watched the international community labor at the task of protecting humanity through the global rule of law. They sought to prohibit the cruelest war tactics, to protect non-combatants, to defend national minorities, to establish labor standards and to prevent war. These are the historical foundations of the same body of international law that exists today. He yearned to express the religious significance he saw in these efforts, and the role that the modern Jewish state should play in their success. He envisioned the Court of Nations on Mount Zion to express the sacred importance of this role in fulfilling Israel's mission in history.

Rabbi Hirschensohn based his vision of Zion on the instruments of international law and politics of his day, the Peace Palace in the Hague, rooted

---

[22] Chaim Hirschensohn, *Malki Ba-Kodesh*, Vol. 1, p. 13 in David Zohar's edition (Ramat Gan: Bar-Ilan University Press, 2006), 10–12.
[23] See Chaim Hirschensohn, *Eleh Divrei Habrit*, Vol. 1 (Jerusalem 1926), 71 [Hebrew] and Shaiya Rothberg, "Human Rights on the Mountain of God," *Tikkun* 32:3 (2017), 29–33.

in the early Hague and Geneva conventions, and the League of Nations. But his vision, like that of Rashar Hirsch, surpasses the ideals of his era. His idea of an international law that protects not only nations from each other, but every individual on earth, even from their own states ("...nor nation on man, nor man on nation...") exceeded the international law of his day and foreshadows the development of contemporary human rights.

For Rabbis Hirsch and Hirschensohn, something very close to contemporary human rights stands at the center of their take on the Jewish mission in history. For Rashar Hirsch, the emphasis is on human rights as the self-evident morality of his time. He saw the necessity of extending equal civil rights in the modern state to Jews as a moral fact, the denying of which was tantamount to the endorsement of slavery. For Rabbi Hirschensohn, on the other hand, the emphasis was on international law and "the covenants of the nations." He also believed that democracy and equal rights reflected the morality of his day,[24] but he believed that moral standards evolve over time, and vary from culture to culture, so that it is necessary for nations among themselves, and all the nations together, to enact covenants embodying explicit agreement about concrete norms at each stage of human development.[25]

A Politics of Human Rights

Both Hirsh and Hirschensohn captured something important about the contemporary idea of human rights. In fact, their two perspectives have been the dominant justifications for human rights offered by theorists over the decades since human rights became globally prominent in the second half of the twentieth century.[26] Earlier generations of theorists offered arguments for the universal validity of human rights as moral truths, reflecting Enlightenment philosophical traditions from earlier centuries. Contemporary thinkers, having internalized the post-modern and post-colonial critiques of such "Eurocentric" arguments, emphasize the need to build global consensus through covenants and treaties. For these later thinkers, the validity of human rights rests less on claims about human nature and more on the actual agreement of almost all the world's 200 states to the key international covenants on human rights.

Looking back to the Rambam, we might say that these two rabbis seek to update the Rambam's Jewish political agenda. Like the Rambam, they seek a

---

[24] See, for example, Hirschensohn, *Malki Bakodesh,* Vol. 1, in David Zohar's edition (Ramat Gan: Bar-Ilan University Press, 2006), 65–67.

[25] See Chaim Hirschensohn, *Eleh Divrei Habrit,* Vol. 1 (Jerusalem 1925).

[26] For a summation of these developments, and an exploration of models combining human rights and religious tradition pertinent to the thesis suggested here, see Linda Hogan, *Keeping Faith with Human Rights* (Washington, D.C.: Georgetown University Press, 2015).

practical rational way, through engagement with the political realities of their day, in which Judaism can help mend the body and soul of humanity. But rather than the Rambam's theocratic monarchy, Hirsch and Hirschensohn identify the modern project of human rights as the political engine needed to humanize the Leviathan. I think that they were right in important ways, and that this has concrete implications for contemporary Jewish life, as I will explain. But first I need to clarify what I mean by human rights.

Let us begin by dividing human rights into two parts: 1) the corpus of human rights norms; and 2) the movement to realize them. To get a handle on the corpus of norms, we will briefly explore the 1948 Universal Declaration of Human Rights (UDHR) as it emerges from research into its drafting.[27] It is a mistake to imagine, as is sometimes thought, that the framers offered human rights as timeless moral truths supposedly deriving from human nature. In fact, they understood themselves to be addressing the concrete political conditions after World War II. For authority, they appealed not only to moral truths, like Rashar Hirsch, but also to the agreement of real people, motivated by different religious, philosophical, and cultural convictions, like Rabbi Hirschensohn. They used the language of "rights," not because of an existential preference for "rights" over "obligations," but because rights language can provide effective protections for human security in the context of modern legal systems.

We might say that the framers of the UDHR visualized what a dignified human existence could look like given the resources available to states after World War II. They sought to translate that vision into a set of practical norms to which most humans alive in their day would agree and which could be readily integrated into existing systems of political power. In other words, the framers estimated what the Leviathans alive in their day were capable of, what kind of human lives they could cultivate, and what code of norms could ensure that they did so. To understand the Universal Declaration's thirty articles, we need to approach them not as abstractions, but three-dimensionally, by imagining the actual human lives they envisioned. We will do this by considering the lives of a mother and child in light of each of the thirty articles.[28]

First of all, mother and child enjoy an adequate standard of living, including food, clothing, housing, medical care, and social services (Articles 22 and 25). The parent works at a job she chose with good conditions, equal

---

[27] See Johannes Morsink, *The Universal Declaration of Human Rights: Origins, Drafting, and Intent* (Philadelphia: University of Pennsylvania Press, 1999).
[28] The Universal Declaration of Human Rights can be found at the UN website: https://www.un.org/en/about-us/universal-declaration-of-human-rights.

pay for equal work, and an adequate salary for herself and child (if not, her salary is supplemented). She may form a labor union and will receive social security in case of unemployment, sickness, etc. (23). She works limited hours with paid vacations (24).

Mother and child were educated in free public schools focused on the full development of their personalities (26). They participate freely in cultural life (27), may choose any religion or none (18), and once of age may marry or divorce (16). They are free to express their opinions (19), to organize political movements (20), to run for office or be appointed to public service, and live under a government based on the will of the people as expressed in periodic free elections (21).

The life, liberty, and security of mother and child are protected by the state (3). They may not be arbitrarily arrested, detained or exiled (9), or enslaved (4), or subjected to cruel punishment (5), or denied their nationality (15). Their privacy, honor, reputation (12), and property (17) are legally protected. They are free to move within the state, or to leave it and return (13), or to seek asylum in another state (14), while always being recognized as people before the law (6) who are entitled to equal protection (7). If their rights are violated, they receive effective remedy by a competent tribunal (8). If accused of a crime, they are presumed innocent (11) and entitled to a fair public hearing by an impartial tribunal (10).

Mother and child are entitled to all the above "without distinction of any kind, such as race, color, sex, language, religion, political or other opinion, national or social origin, property, birth or other status" (2). This is what it meant by being "born free and equal in dignity and rights" (1). Finally, they are entitled to a political order that protects their human rights (28–30), so that they may enjoy the four freedoms laid out in the preamble to the Universal Declaration: "Freedom of speech and belief and freedom from fear and want."

The corpus of human rights as it emerges from the Universal Declaration is not complete. Additional articles were needed regarding gender, children, the environment, and other issues. While some of these lacunae have been addressed in the seventy-five years since the UDHR was written, the corpus is still evolving. Nonetheless, imagining the human reality behind the thirty articles gives us a sense of the kind of human existence that the human rights project seeks to provide all human beings.

One might argue that while these goals are laudable, human rights are too embedded in the present nation-state system to mend the body and soul of humanity. The change we need is more radical, like a socialist transformation of how we manage global resources; or a paradigm shift to environmentally sustainable forms of life; or a fundamental reorientation about what gender means; or a spiritual awakening, following which we educate for mindfulness rather than consumerism. Indeed, I feel certain that we need all those things. The argument here is not that human rights are enough, but rather that they are necessary precisely because they are embedded in the state system.[29] Modern states are effectively omnipotent for people subject to their power. The Nazis exemplified that power for evil, but since World War II we have also witnessed how modern states can liberate people from extreme poverty, expand literacy, reduce child mortality, provide clean water, and protect free societies. For good and for evil, the Leviathan we face today takes the form of the modern state. Human rights are designed to establish shared norms for states to obey that overlap international law, national constitutions and legal systems, and global civil society discourse.

We will now shift our focus from the corpus of human rights norms to the movement for their realization. Clearly, in one important sense this movement has been a failure: the rights of billions of human beings are regularly violated. But since the human rights project entails the liberation of all people from poverty and injustice, it is a rather large task, and incremental partial successes are significant. I want to focus on one such incremental partial success: the establishment of a global nearly pan-human consensus around human rights norms.

In general outline, the Universal Declaration's envisioning of dignified life has been codified into law, ratified in international covenants, and adopted into the national constitutions and legal systems of almost all the world's 200 existing states. In parallel, global civil society discourse is often explicitly grounded in the language of human rights. NGOs and activists in (almost) all of the world's countries, cultures, languages, and religions communicate their agenda by reference to human rights.[30] This language enables them to make their claims in terms that enjoy a significant degree of globally shared meaning, and which overlap international law and the legal systems of most countries. Even systematic violators of human rights generally do not deny human rights standards, but rather deny that they are violating them. Never in the history of our species has a set of legal and

---

[29] For an illuminating discussion of the limitations of human rights, see Samuel Moyn, *Not Enough: Human Rights in an Unequal World* (Cambridge, MA: Harvard, 2018).

[30] For a fascinating history of human rights and their rise to prominence, see Samuel Moyn, *The Last Utopia: Human Rights in History* (Cambridge, MA: Harvard, 2010). For the proliferation of human rights across international bodies and national legal systems, see Zachery Elkins, Tom Ginsburg, and Beth A. Simmons, "Getting to Rights: Treaty Ratification, Constitutional Convergence, and Human Rights Practice," *Harvard International Law Journal* 54 (2013): 61–95.

moral norms been so widely accepted across cultures and languages and throughout existing systems of political power and social discourse.

It seems to me that the development of this nearly pan-human consensus about basic norms to protect humans everywhere is a significant milestone in the history of our species. Perhaps it belongs to that family of developments that ultimately reshaped our lives, like the agricultural revolution and the advent of writing. In the spirit of Rabbi Hirschensohn's idea of the "covenants of nations," we might identify this milestone as the emergence of the human covenant. If we inhabit the narrative spun by the Rambam about the Abrahamic mission and the Torah as a blueprint for a redeemed humanity, the emergence of the human covenant can only be recognized as a critical new chapter. I think that Rabbis Hirsch and Hirschensohn started writing that chapter when they framed the redemption of Israel in Zion, and humanity everywhere, in light of human rights.

If we find this new chapter about human rights by Rabbis Hirsch and Hirschensohn compelling, it should move us to articulate our religious commitment to this emerging human covenant in our Jewish lives. Rashar Hirsch, in addition to his civil rights activism, embedded his commitment to human rights in his Torah commentary, so that the members of his community understood that he identified Pharaoh's oppression with the denial of the "rights of man and of the citizen," and regarded modern civil rights as part of the justice and freedom intended by God. Rabbi Hirschensohn took it further by seeking to erect what amounts to an international court of human rights on the Temple Mount.

We, too, must find ways of empowering the movement for human rights through the strength of our tradition. Jewish education should highlight the profound religious significance of the emergence of the human covenant as a milestone in the divine mission to mend the body and soul of humanity. When we address current events in our synagogues, youth movements, schools, and institutions of higher learning, our commitment to the human rights of all people should be bedrock to our discourse. And when we embrace the pluralism of political outlooks in our communities, our mutual respect should be grounded in the knowledge that while we may disagree about the means, we share a commitment to the goal of achieving for all people the dignified human existence envisioned in the Universal Declaration of Human Rights.

Commitment to human rights does not preclude disagreement about particular norms or their application. Only ongoing critical engagement with diverse peoples can correct distortions in the evolving corpus of norms and keep the government and civil society actors that apply those norms honest. Such critical engagement is all the more necessary today, because as human rights language has increased in power, so too has its abuse become more common. However, it is generally not difficult to distinguish between authentic and bogus uses of human rights. When human rights rhetoric is employed to justify violence against civilians, for example, clearly the agenda involved is not human rights. So too, when claims of human rights violations are dismissed not due to an examination of the facts but through delegitimizing organizations and activists, clearly the result is not to uncover the truth but to conceal it.

We stand at a critical juncture in the history of our species. The ideals of democracy and human rights championed in the post–World War II global state order appear more fragile today than in recent memory. Climate change and other crises are already taxing the capacities of our political systems. As crises deepen, there will be increasing pressure to disregard human rights standards. By seeking to unite diverse Jewish communities, across denominations, behind a shared commitment to the human covenant, we lend spiritual strength to the ongoing effort to humanize the Leviathan. By speaking a shared human language about basic norms, we build bridges not only across Jewish denominations but also to other faiths, helping to enlarge the mosaic of faith-based communities lending their strength to mending humanity's body and soul. At the dawn of the human rights era, Rabbis Hirsch and Hirschensohn began writing a crucial new chapter in the story of Judaism's political engagement with the world. In light of the almost unimaginable success in building global consensus around the norms that they championed, it is now our task to continue the work they began.

Fear of Sin and of One's Teacher in Early Rabbinic Judaism

Joel Gereboff

Words and phrases associated with "fear" are ubiquitous in biblical sources and appear frequently in early rabbinic (*tannaitic*) literature. Three different types of terms express "fear." First, there are words that are generally translated as fear, such as *yirah*. Second, some words describe bodily manifestations of fear, such as trembling or shaking (*charad, ra'ad*). Third, phrases using metaphors generally focused on embodied experience portray fear. These include: "melting heart" (*nimas lev*), "weak heart" (*rakh lev*), or "weak, fallen hands" (*rafeh lev*).[1]

Many rabbinic descriptions of fear parallel those of the Bible. Thus, both biblical and rabbinic texts express the terror and fear of wild animals, aspects of nature such as thunder or earthquakes, or of violent military enemies. Both biblical and rabbinic sources also frequently invoke the "fear of God" (*yirat YHWH, yirat Elohim*) or the equivalent rabbinic term "fear of Heaven" (*yirat Shamayim*). In addition to new nuances for these expressions in early rabbinic texts, those sources also introduce a number of novel concepts and issues. For example, rabbinic texts sort out the relationship between the commandments to honor and fear parents, distinguish between fear and love of God, and describe toiling in the study of Torah as increasing one's "fear of God" and derivatively, one's "observance of commandments." This paper focuses on two novel uses of fear in early rabbinic literature: the fear of sin (*yirat chet*) and fear of one's teacher (*morat rabbo*). The analysis will seek to determine the meaning of these expressions, and in particular, draw upon recent scholarship on the study of emotions. This is relevant to the theme of this volume, as many religious and secular ethicists have discussed whether fear in general, and fear of God in particular, should play a role in a person's moral and religious life.

Contemporary Studies of Religion and the Emotions

The past two decades have seen a continuing interdisciplinary interest in the study of emotions. Many anthropological and historical works on the emotions adopt a social-constructivist approach, a view that analyzes how various cultures understand what emotions are and how they depict and

---
[1] I wish to thank my colleagues Francoise Mirguet and Jonathan Friedmann for their continuing support of my research and for their suggestions for improving this paper.

see particular emotions as appropriate or inappropriate. With regard to biblical and rabbinic texts, a number of recent studies have identified a set of challenges related to the study of emotions in these works. Francoise Mirguet, David Lambert, Phillip Lasater, and Ari Mermelstein have written a number of pieces on these matters as they relate to biblical and Second Temple Jewish writings, and I recently published an essay on hate in early rabbinic Judaism.[2] That essay of mine opens with a long discussion of the theoretical and methodological challenges related to studying emotions in rabbinic texts. Here I note that there is no specific concept of "emotions" in these works, no terms for a distinct human factor we label as emotions.

In general, and as we shall see, the understanding of human psychology, differentiating features that shape and are expressed through human behavior, is not fleshed out in terms of a clear inner and outer self. As Lambert, Mirguet and Lasater observe, we should not impose upon these works Cartesian and Victorian notions of the self that posit a distinct interior self. The understanding of the term "heart" (*lev*), for example, does not draw clear distinctions between the body, emotions, reason, desire, and other aspects of the human. As such, emotions, or perhaps better labeled as passions per Lasater, are often connected to the heart, and as such, are not irrational "emotions." Rather, they are a combination of cognition, appraisal, will, and affect. Love, fear, hate, and joy are observable and enacted, and in that way come into being in relationships and actions. Much of the most recent research argues that in many instances, these terms emphasize power rela-

---

[2] Francoise Mirguet, "The Study of Emotions in Early Jewish Texts," *Journal for the Study of Judaism in Persian, Hellenistic and Roman Period* 50 (2019): 557-603; Ari Mermelstein, "Beauty or Beast? The Pedagogical Function of Metaphor and Emotion in Midrashim on the Law of the Lovely Captive," *Journal of Ancient Judaism* 8 (2018): 388-409; David Lambert, "Refreshing Philology: James Barr, Supersessionism and the State of Biblical Words," *Biblical Interpretation* 24 (2016): 532-556; Phillip Lasater, *Faces of Fear: The Fear of God in Exilic and Post-Exilic Contexts* (Tubingen: Mohr Siebeck, 2019); Joel Gereboff, "Hate in Early Rabbinic Judaism," in *To Fix Torah in Their Heart: Essays on Biblical Interpretation and Jewish Studies in Honor of B. Barry Levy*, eds. Jacqueline S. du Toit et al. (Cincinnati: Hebrew Union College Press, 2018), 59-83. Additional studies of emotions in rabbinic texts include: Jonathan K. Crane, "Shameful Ambivalences: Dimension of Rabbinic Shame," *AJS Review* 25 (2011): 61-84; Joshua Levinson, "The Divided Subject: Representing Modes of Consciousness in Rabbinic Midrash," in *Self, Self-Fashioning and Individuality in Late Antiquity*, eds. Joshua Levinson et al. (Tubingen: De Gruyter, 2018), 169-185; Ronit Nikolsky, "Parables in the Service of Emotional Translation," in *Parables in Changing Contexts: Essays in the Study of Parables in Christianity, Judaism, Islam and Buddhism*, eds. Annette Merz et al. (Leiden: Brill, 2020), 37-56; Jeffrey Rubenstein, "The Role of Disgust in Rabbinic Ethics," in *Strength to Strength: Essays in Appreciation of Shaye J.D. Cohen*, ed. Michael L. Satlow (Providence: Brown Judaic Studies, 2018), 421-436; Shulamit Valler, *Sorrow and Distress in the Talmud: Judaism and Jewish Life* (Brookline, MA: Academic Studies, 2011).

tionships and positionality between beings and highlight embodied physical behaviors and responses. Rhetorical references to emotional terms also serve a sociological function when they call for members of a group either to or not to experience and express a particular emotion such as fear, hate, disgust, or love *vis à vis* certain individuals.[3] One can be taught or implored to have or avoid certain emotions. This paper argues that concepts such as fearing sin and one's teacher contribute to delineating the actions of the ideal Jew, one who belongs to the imagined community of sages (*chakhamim*).

Several recent studies have analyzed various terms associated with fear and related terms, such as love and hate.[4] Philip Lasater's 2019 book, *Faces*

---

[3] Studies of the political and sociological nature of the rhetorical usage of emotional terms, especially of fear, include: Sara Ahmed, "The Affective Politics of Fear," *The Cultural Politics of Emotions* (Edinburgh: Edinburgh University Press, 2014), 62-81, and Martha C. Nussbaum, *Monarchy of Fear: A Philosopher Looks at our Political Crisis* (New York: Simon and Schuster, 2018). For examples of similar uses in Second Temple and rabbinic sources, see: Ari Mermelstein, "Love and Hate at Qumran: The Social Construction of Sectarian Emotion," *Dead Sea Discoveries* 20 (2013): 237-263; and "Emotional Regimes, Ritual Practice, and the Shaping of Sectarian Identity: The Experience of Ablutions in the Dead Sea Scrolls," *Biblical Interpretation* 24 (2016): 492-513.

[4] Phillip Michael Lasater, *Faces of Fear*; Francoise Mirguet, "Love and Hate in Deuteronomy," in *The Oxford Handbook of Deuteronomy*, ed. Don Benjamin (New York: Oxford University Press, forthcoming); Phillip Michael Lasater, "'The Emotions' in Biblical Anthropology? A Genealogy and Case Study with *YR'*," *Harvard Theological Review* 110 (2017): 520-540; Angela Thomas, "Anatomical Idiom and Emotional Expression," *A Comparison of the Hebrew Bible and the Septuagint* (Sheffield: Sheffield Phoenix, 2014); Angela Thomas, "Fear and Trembling: Body Imagery in the Hebrew Bible and the Septuagint," in *The Reception of the Hebrew Bible in the Septuagint and the New Testament: Essays in Memory of Aileen Guilding*, eds. David J. A. Clines and Cheryl Exum (Sheffield: Sheffield Phoenix, 2013), 115-125; Jon D. Levenson, *The Love of God: Divine Gift, Human Gratitude, and Mutual Faithfulness in Judaism* (Princeton: Princeton University Press, 2016); Bill T. Arnold, "The Love-Fear Antinomy in Deuteronomy 5-11," *Vetus Testamentum* 61 (2011): 551-169; Sara Kipfer and Jacob L. Wright, "'Fear (Not)!'—Emotion and Ethics in Deuteronomy," *Journal of Ethics in Antiquity and Christianity* 2 (2020): 5062; David S. Vanderhooft, "'AHABAH: Philological Observations on '*ahab/'ahabah* in the Hebrew Bible," in *Ahavah: Die Liebe Gottes in Alten Testament*, ed. Manfred Oeming (Leipzig: Evangelische Verlagsanstalt, 2018), 41-56; Bernard J. Bamberger, "Fear and Love of God in the Old Testament," *Hebrew Union College Annual* 6 (1929): 39-53; James Alfred Loader, "'Trembling, the Best of Being Human': Aspects of Anxiety in Israel," *Old Testament Essays* 14 (2001): 260-280; Mayer I. Gruber, "Fear, Anxiety and Reverence in Akkadian, Biblical, Hebrew and Other North-West Semitic Languages," *Vetus Testamentum* 40 (1990): 411-422; Stephen M. Wilson, "Fear, Love, and Leadership: Posing a Machiavellian Question to the Hebrew Bible," *Journal of Biblical Literature* 139 (2020): 233-253; Matthew Richard Schlimm, "The Paradoxes of Fear in the Hebrew Bible," *Svensk Exegestisk Arsbok* 84 (2019): 25-50; and Ronit Nikolsky, "'To Love' in the Bible: A Cognitive Evolutionary Approach," in *Language, Cognition and Biblical Exegesis: Interpreting Mind*, eds. Ronit Nikolsky et al. (London: Bloomsbury, 2019), 70-87. There are also studies of the notion of fear in various Second Temple texts including Ben Sira, Philo, and

of Fear: The Fear of God in Exilic and Post-exilic Context, discusses previous scholarship on fear in biblical sources, with a particular focus on fear of God, and challenges the longstanding understanding that fear focuses primarily on emotions. He also claims there are two distinct senses of fear of God in biblical text: one that focuses on fear or terror of the divine due to threats of punishment; and a more advanced sense of the emotion of fear, often translated as "awe" or "reverence." Instead, fear of God signifies and demands the person's behavioral submission to the deity and has little to do with an inner experience, whether of dread or awe. This hierarchical relationship gives rise to embodied expressions, such as lowering of one's hands, bowing, and recoiling. In a similar vein, biblical texts calling for the "love of God" underscore the acceptance of the authority of God and demand an emotional experience or reaction. Although it would be overstated to claim that biblical sources lack a sense of an embodied reaction of terror and fear resulting from encounters with vicious animals, threatening enemies, or terrifying natural occurrences, one should not presume and impose our notions of emotions upon the meaning of biblical, Second Temple, and early rabbinic sources employing terms associated with fear. The following draws on these recent understandings of emotional terms and offers an analysis of the novel rabbinic concepts of fear of sin and fear of one's teacher.

Fear of Sin

Only one study has analyzed some of the *tannaitic* sources using the term *yirat chet*, fear of sin. In it, Marc Hirshman examines several of the traditions in Mishnah and Tosefta, arguing that the concept of fear of sin reflects one of two somewhat conflicting early rabbinic approaches to the religious life. Hirshman contends that fear of sin was associated with "the early pious ones" (*chasidim rishonim*) who viewed it as requiring an ascetic way of life that culminates in a person being able to experience the "holy spirit" (*ruach haqodesh*).[5] He contrasts this model of the religious life with the dominant

---

Qumran literature, and in New Testament sources. Space limitations do not permit me to list all those studies, or to note differences among these sources regarding their theorizing "emotions," and whether all references to "fear" describe an emotion in the contemporary understanding of the term.

[5] Marc Hirshman, "On the Concept of Fear of Sin," in *Studies in Jewish Thought in Honor of Sara A. Willensky*, ed. Moshe Idel (Jerusalem: Magnes, 1994) [Hebrew], 155-162. Additional studies discussing other dimensions of fear in rabbinic literature include: Adolf Buchler, "The Service of God for the Love or Fear of Him and the Right Attitude toward Suffering," *Studies in Sin and Atonement in the Literature of the First Century* (London: Oxford University Press, 1928), 119-211; Ephraim Urbach, "Acceptance of the Yoke of the Kingdom of Heaven: Love and Reverence," *The Sages: Their Concepts and Beliefs* (Jerusalem: Magnes, 1979), 400-419; Elias Bickerman, "The Maxim of Antigonus of Socho," *Harvard Theological*

rabbinic emphasis on study of Torah as the ideal way to serve God. He concludes that fear of sin requires extreme carefulness to avoid sin (*zehirut*) and recoiling or withdrawal from sin (*ritiyah*). Hirshman's study thus seeks to trace the history of the development of the notion and its societal correlates. Although he does not situate his analysis in conversation with scholarship on the emotions, his conclusions correctly emphasize the behavioral aspects of fear of sin. In the following analysis of all appearances of "fear of sin" in early rabbinic documents, inclusive of the *halakhic midrashim*, I will reinforce Hirshman's observations on the primacy of the behavioral elements of the notion. I will also modify his conclusion regarding the strong opposition between the behavioral aspect and "Torah study," as a number of traditions see it as a valuable component of the way of life and character of sages, judges, and students of Torah.

Fifteen units of traditions in early rabbinic documents include the term "fear of sin." Only one source (M. Sot. 9:15) directly connects fear of sin with piety (*chasidut*). Several other sources, however, make connections between the "first pious ones" and the call to avoid sin, or they contrast the fear of sin with the value of Torah study. M. Sot. 9:15 contains a saying ascribed to the odd early rabbinic figure, Pinchas b. Yair, a person generally described as a miracle worker and not as an individual particularly learned in Torah.

> Rabbi Pinchas ben Yair says, "Heedfulness leads to cleanliness, cleanliness leads to purity, purity leads to separation, separation leads to holiness, holiness leads to modesty, modesty leads to **fear of sin, fear of sin** leads to piety (*chasidut*), piety leads to The Holy Spirit, The Holy Spirit leads to the resurrection of the dead, and the resurrection of the dead comes from Elijah, blessed be his memory, Amen."

Hirshman notes the sequencing of certain character traits and their associated behavior that lead to receiving the Holy Spirit. Although the behaviors that exhibit fear of sin (as well as the other traits) are not delineated, this source sees it leading to piety. Praise for the avoidance of sin appears in two additional traditions about the "pious ones," Tos. Suk. 4:2 and Tos. Ned. 1:1, though neither uses the expression "fear of sin." In the former, pious ones

---

Review 44 (1951): 153-165; Joel Weinberg and Wim Beuken, "Job versus Abraham: The Quest for the Perfect God-Fearer in Rabbinic Tradition," in *The Bok of Job*, ed. Wim Beuken (Leuven: Leuven University Press, 1994), 281-196; and Deena Grant, "How to Love God: Deuteronomy, Early Rabbinic Literature and Gospel Texts," *Journal of Interreligious Studies* 26 (2019): 58-71.

and persons of deeds (*chasidim ve-anshei ma'aseh*) would dance with torches at the celebration of the water drawing ceremony (*simchat beit ha-shoevah*) and say, "Fortunate is a person who has not sinned (*chata*), and anyone who has sinned, shall be forgiven."

In the latter tradition, two rabbis, R. Judah and Simeon b. Gamaliel (though most likely R. Simeon), note the avoidance by "the early pious one" of taking on Nazirite vows, for doing so would indicate they have sinned as Nazirites must bring a sin-offering upon concluding their vows. Hirshman also cites M. Avot 2:8, which appears to contrast the value of Torah learning with fear of sin. This source enumerates the five disciples of R. Yochanan b. Zakkai as follows:

> R. Eliezer b. Hyrcanus, R. Joshua b. Chananiah, R. Yose the priest, R. Simeon b. Netanel and R. Elazar b. Arakh. He used to list their praises: R. Eliezer b. Hyrcanus [is like] a plastered cistern which does not lose a drop; R. Joshua b. Chananiah, happy is the woman who gave birth to him; R. Yose the priest, a pious person (*chasid*); R. Simeon b. Netanel, **sin-fearing**; And R. Elazar b. Arakh, an ever-flowing spring.

This tradition concludes with two statements prioritizing the value of Torah learning:

> He [Yochanan b. Zakkai] used to say, "If all the sages of Israel were on [one side] of the scale and R. Eliezer b. Hyrcanus on the second side, he would outweigh them all." Abba Shaul said in his name, "If all the sages of Israel were on [one side] of the scale and R. Eliezer b. Hyrcanus with them, and R. Elazar b. Arakh on the other side, he would outweigh them all."

For Hirshman, this source contrasts Torah study with piety and fear of sin, contributing to his understanding of the latter two in opposition to the former in early rabbinic texts.

Hirshman, however, overlooks sources that do not see the two values opposed. Since the purpose of this paper is not so much to trace the history of the notion of fear of sin, I would argue that even if Hirshman's reconstruction of the early association of the term "fear of sin" with "piety" is correct, other rabbinic texts see a harmony between fear of sin and Torah study or wisdom. A clear expression of the harmony of the two values is in a saying recorded in M. Avot 3:9, ascribed to Chaninah b. Dosa, a person also often seen more as a miracle worker than a Torah sage.

> Rabbi Chaninah ben Dosa said, "Anyone whose **fear of sin** precedes his wisdom, his wisdom is enduring, but anyone whose wisdom precedes his **fear of sin**, his wisdom is not enduring." He [also] used to say, "Anyone whose deeds exceed his wisdom, his wisdom is enduring, but anyone whose wisdom exceeds his deeds, his wisdom is not enduring."

According to this tradition, fear of sin—whatever it exactly entails—is essential for a person's wisdom, which I assume means Torah learning, to endure. Clearly here, the two are not seen in opposition. This view reiterates Proverbs 9:10, "The fear of the Lord is the beginning of wisdom." Another joining of the two values appears in the comments in M. Ed. 5:6 about the debated excommunication of R. Aqavia b. Mehalalel:

> Aqavia b. Mahalalel testified concerning four things. They said to him, "Aqavia, retract these four things that you say, and we will make you the head of the court in Israel." He said to them, "It is better for me to be called a fool all my days than…" Whereupon they excommunicated him; and he died while he was under excommunication, and the court stoned his coffin. R. Judah said, "God forbid [that one should say] that Aqavia was excommunicated; for the courtyard is never locked for any man in Israel who was equal to Aqavia b. Mahalalel in wisdom and the **fear of sin**. But whom did they excommunicate? Eliezer b. Chanoch."

In disputing the claim that Aqavia was excommunicated, R. Judah underscores the combination of wisdom (*chokhmah*) and fear of sin in this controversial early sage.

A good number of sources list fear of sin as a valuable trait and behavior, and do not set it in opposition to Torah learning. A tradition in M. Sot. 9:5 details the impact of the death of various sages and ends with the results of the death of R. Judah the Patriarch, the person who is taken to be the editor of Mishnah itself. Among those identified on that list are:

> When R. Meir died, the composers of fables ceased.
> When Ben Azzai died, the diligent students [of Torah] ceased.
> When Ben Zoma died, the expounders ceased.
> When R. Joshua died, goodness ceased from the world.
> When R. Akiva died, the glory of the Torah ceased.
> When R. Chaninah ben Dosa died,
> men of wondrous deeds ceased...
> When R. Yohanan ben Zakkai died,
> the splendor of wisdom ceased.
> When Rabban Gamaliel the elder died, the glory of the Torah ceased, and purity and separateness perished.
> When R. Ishmael ben Fabi died, the
> splendor of the priesthood ceased.
> When Rabbi [Judah the Patriarch] died,
> humility and **fear of sin** ceased.

Although the list connects the ending of Torah knowledge with a number of sages other than R. Judah the Patriarch, it is debatable whether one should see the various valued traits and behaviors as opposed to each other. Clearly, Mishnah considers R. Judah the Patriarch as a learned sage. A second saying in M. Sot 9:5, in noting what will occur "in the footsteps of the messiah," also lists Torah learning and the fear of sin separately. It would, however, be inappropriate to see them as opposed to each other:

> Rabbi Eliezer the Great says, "From the day the Temple was destroyed....In the footsteps of the messiah insolence will increase, and the cost of living will go up greatly; the vine will yield its fruit, but wine will be expensive...the wisdom of the learned will rot, **fearers of sin** will be despised, and the truth will be lacking; youths will put old men to shame, the old will stand up in the presence of the young."

While "the wisdom of learners" appears separately from the "the fearers of sin," it would be a stretch to see the two as entirely distinct and opposed types of people. All in all, this text again praises "fearing of sin." Similarly, in a saying in M. Avot 2:5, "fear of sin" is seen as a valued trait and behavior:

> He [R. Gamliel the son of R. Judah the Patriarch] used to say, "A brute (*boor*) is not **sin-fearing** (*yarei chet*), nor

is an ignorant person (*am ha'arets*) pious (*chasid*), nor can a shamefaced person learn, nor can an impatient person teach, nor will someone who engages too much in business become wise. In a place where there are no persons, strive to be a person."

One might see in this source a distinction, though not necessarily an opposition, between those who are sin-fearing, pious, or learned. Equally plausible is to see all these traits as valued for a student of Torah. By contrast, other texts endorse explicitly being sin-fearing along with other traits as necessary features of praised groups of people. Tos. Ta. 3:7 describes individuals who sought to circumvent restrictions imposed by external authorities on bringing offerings to Jerusalem as "fit (*kasher*) and sin fearing." According to T. Sanh. 2:9 (T. Sanh. 7:1), those appointed by the Sanhedrin as local judges were to be "humble, easy going, sin-fearing, and pleasing to everyone." Mekh de R. Ishmael Amaleq 1 (Mekh R. Simeon b. Yochai 17:9) contains alternative explanations of Exodus 17:9:

> "And Amaleq came and fought with Israel at Rephidim, Moses said to Joshua, 'Pick some men for us, and go out and do battle with Amaleq.'" R. Joshua says, "Choose for us warriors." R. Eliezer the Modiite says, "Chose for us **fearers of sin.**"

In this text, fear of sin is seen as a necessary trait for those going to battle. Below we will examine a tradition that excludes from going to battle those who are fearful because of their transgressions, which is understood to mean fearful of the impact of sins they have already committed.

Several additional *tannaitic* sources praise sin-fearing. Among the various commentaries offered in Sifre Deut. 323 (Mid. Tan. 32:33), an interpretation of Deuteronomy 32:33, "Their wine is the venom of asps, the pitiless poison of vipers" speaks of Israelites who "envenomed the leaders of Israel," the latter are described as "pious (*chasidim*), modest, fit (*kesherim*) and sin fearing." Finally, in commenting on Deuteronomy 32:8, "When the Most High set the inheritance for the nations, He set the divisions of man…in relation to Israel's numbers," a number of interpretations in Sifre Deut. 311 draw distinctions between the people of Israel and all the nations. However, one of the comments asserts that when giving inheritance to those among the nations, God distributed it to "those were fit (*kasher*), and fearing sin." In light of the sharp distinction in the commentary between Israelites and the other nations, and the generally negative view of the latter, traditional and contemporary analysts of this statement take this to be a reference to proselytes who join the people of Israel. This understanding treats the term "sin-fearers" as similar to the term "God-fearers," which in some cases means proselytes, or at least those who affirm the one God.

The above sources praise sin-fearing, generally not setting it in opposition to study of Torah. However, none of them makes clear exactly what it means to be "sin fearing." The meaning of the term appears to be self-evident. This is similar to the use of terms like "modest" or "fit," which are also left undefined. Hirshman cites M. Sheq. 5:6 as providing a sense of the meaning of fear of sin. That source states:

> There were two chambers in the Temple, one the chamber of secret gifts and the other the chamber of the vessels. The chamber of secret gifts: **sin-fearing persons** (*yirei chet*) used to put their gifts there in secret, and the poor who were descended of the virtuous (*benei tovim*) were secretly supported from them. The chamber of the vessels: whoever offered a vessel as a gift would throw it in, and once in thirty days the treasurers opened it; and any vessel they found in it that was of use for the repair of the temple they left there, but the others were sold and their price went to the chamber of the repair of the Temple.

In this source, sin-fearing people are described in behavioral terms. They give donations in such a way as not to embarrass those who receive those gifts of charity. Although this one text is a limited basis to determine the exact meaning of being "sin-fearing," I add to Hirshman's view that sin-fearing is described in behavioral terms. One source, however, does draw a connection between what may be understood as an emotion—shame—and being sin-fearing. Mekhilta de R. Ishmael Bachodesh 11 notes that connection in its comment on Exodus 20:17. In that verse, after experiencing the revelation at Sinai, which is described as including terror-inspiring fear due to thunder, lightning, and the voice of God, "Moses answered the people, 'Be not afraid; for God has come only in order to test you, and in order that the fear of Him (*yirato*) may be ever with you, so that you not sin.'" An anonymous comment in Mekhilta observes:

> "And so that His fear be upon your faces." "**Fear**" [here] is shame-facedness (*boshet*). Shame-facedness is a good sign

in a man. "So that you not sin." We are hereby apprised that shame-facedness leads to **fear of sin**, as it says, "Were they ashamed that they committed abominations?" (Jer. 6:15)

This tradition expresses the importance of a person understanding their relationship with God. One who grasps their need to submit to God would experience shame if they did not act appropriately. As a result, having that sense of shame leads to the fear of sin, the avoidance of sinful actions. The verse from Jeremiah makes evident the ultimate behavioral significance of fearing sin.

The above survey of all *tannaitic* sources using the term "fear of sin" makes evident that none employs a modern notion of the emotion, a feeling interior to an individual. Rather, fear of sin is a character trait one is implored to acquire, and having it is manifested in various behaviors, especially in the avoidance of sinful actions. It is interesting to compare this understanding of "fear of sin" with the far more analyzed concept "fear of God." Both terms appear in nominal construct forms—fear of God (*yirat Elohim/YHWH*) and fear of sin (*yirat chet*), as well as the construct form for those who fear God (*yare, yirei Elohim/YHWH*) and the fearer of sin (*yare, yirei chet*). With regard to God, verb forms are also used—one is commanded to "fear God," while no one is commanded to "fear sin."

An additional point of contrast pertains to the nature of the relationship in the two cases. According to recent analyses of "fearing God," one is commanded to submit to God (*l'yirah et YHWH*). In contrast, "fear of sin" is understood to avoid sin. Although the partitive *min*, "from," is not attested (*yirah min chet*), this is the apparent meaning of the term. In the case of God, one is to seek connection, but to submit, manifested in bodily prostration before the divine. By comparison, one is to distance oneself completely from sin, to recoil from it. In both cases, the behavioral element is primary with little attention given to an affective component. In addition, in both instances the appropriate action flows from a cognitive appraisal. In many biblical passages, one's submission to God is expressed through a person's observance of the commandments based on Israel having entered into a covenant (*brit*) with God. In the wisdom tradition, it appears the fear of God grows out of one's recognition of the predictable nature of how the world works. Similarly, it appears that "fear of sin" stems from one's recognition of the wrongness of violating divine commands. Thus, even if there is an affective component to both "fears," the required action or response to God or sin is grounded in a cognitive evaluation of one's relationships.

In addition to the above traditions that use the terms *yirah* and *chet* in either of two construct forms, *yirat chet* or *yirei chet*, two texts describe certain people as *mityariim min aveirot*, fearful because of transgressions. Another tradition uses the unique term, *charedim al hamitzvot*, trembling regarding the commandments. All three texts differ in some ways from passages using the notion of "fear of sin." The last of these items, Sifre Num. 68, comments upon the situation described in Num. 9:6-7, of individuals who were unable to observe Passover in the month of Nisan.

> But there were some men who were unclean by reason of a corpse and could not offer the Passover sacrifice on that day [the fourteenth of Nisan]. And they came before Moses and Aaron on that day. Those men (*anashim hahemah*) said to him, "Though we are unclean by reason of a corpse, why must we be debarred from presenting the Lord's offering at its set time with the rest of the Israelites."

The *midrash* comments on what may be taken as unnecessary words in the text, "those men," as the passage could simply have stated, "And they said." The *midrash* interprets these superfluous words:

> "To indicate that they were people [who were] fit, righteous and **trembling on account of the commandments** (*kesheim, vetzadiqim vecharedim al hamitzvot*)." R. Judah the Patriarch dissents from this interpretation and says, "One need not [interpret] thus the saying, 'Those men said to him.' What does, 'Those men said to him' come to teach? This indicates that only those affected by the matter should inquire."

Relevant to the discussion of fear of sin is an anonymous, unattributed description of these individuals. This interpretation combines fitness and righteousness with the single appearance in *tannaitic* literature of those "who tremble on account of the commandments."[6] In the context of the biblical text, it appears that these Israelites were concerned that they would not be able to fulfill the commandment of properly observing the commandments

---

[6] Simon J. De Vries, "The Fear of God in the Qumran Scrolls," *Revue de Qumran* 5 (1965): 233–237, highlights a passage from 1 QS 4:2, "These are the ways in the world of the enlightened of the heart of man so that the path of righteousness may be made straight before him and so that the fear of the laws of God (*pachad mispetai YHWH*) may be inscribed in the heart, a spirit of humility and patience..." The words here differ—*pachad* and not *charedim*, *mitzvot* and not *mishpat*—but the idea may be similar: relating to the laws of God with fear.

of Passover. They do not appear to be concerned about avoiding doing something that is sinful.

The two traditions, M. Sot. 8:1-5 and Sifra Shemini de Miluim 2:4, describe people being "fearful because of transgressions." Both passages focus on already committed sins, not on avoiding sinful behavior. They appear to presume the possibility of divine punishment due to these errors. M. Sot. 8:1-5 relates to the law of conscription for battle presented in Deuteronomy 20:18. The biblical text calls for all Israel to go forth to battle without fear, but does excuse four groups of people from this requirement: people who are newly married, have built a home but have not occupied it, have planted a vineyard but have not ever harvested it, and those who are "fearful." The Mishnah comments on the two portions of the biblical text, Deuteronomy 8:3 and 8:8, that speak of the "fearful and fainthearted":

> And he shall say to them: Hear Israel, you draw near today to battle against your enemies; let not **your heart faint; fear not, nor be alarmed, and do not be terrified of them**" (Deut .20:3)…."Let not your heart faint" due to the neighing of horses and the sharpening of the enemy's swords. "Fear not" due to the knocking of shields (*terisin*) and the noise of their boots (*calgassin*). "Nor be alarmed" by the sound of trumpets…."And the officers shall speak further to the people, and they shall say: What man is there that is fearful and fainthearted? Let him go and return unto his house" (Deut. 20:8). Rabbi Akiva says, "That is fearful and fainthearted" is to be understood as it indicates: that the man is unable to stand in the battle ranks and to see a drawn sword because it will terrify him. R. Yose the Galilean says, "'that is fearful and fainthearted'; this is one who is **afraid because of the transgressions** (*mityare min averot*) that he has. Therefore, the Torah ascribed to him all the other reasons [mentioned as valid excuses for not going forth to battle], and he may return due to them [so as not to embarrass him by his having to admit he returned due to his concern about his sins]."

Both the anonymous comment and the one attributed to R. Akiva interpret "fearful" in a contextual manner as a person who is fearful of battle, a person who would undermine the courage of his fellow soldiers.[7] By contrast,

---

[7] Lawrence Schiffman, "The Law of Conscription in the War Scroll," in *Qumran Cave*

R. Yose the Galilean offers the novel view that the person fears suffering a negative consequence in battle due to transgressions he has committed. The final statement of the passage appears to understand the fear of sin at least initially to be something interior to the person. It explains that the Torah lists the fearful person along with the others excused from battle to avoid publicly embarrassing the person. Not knowing why the priest excuses him, other soldiers can attribute this to one of the other legitimate reasons for avoiding conscription.

The tradition in Sifra Shemini de Miluim 2:4 also uses the expression "transgression that you are in fear of" (*averah sheatem miyarim mimenah*). The exegesis of Leviticus 9:1-4, in which the expression occurs, is complicated. For the purposes of this chapter, what is clear here is that this *tannaitic* source also invokes the notion of people being afraid of punishment due to sins. The *midrash* asserts, however, that according to the biblical text, those fears can be allayed as atonement has been attained via already offered sacrifices. Again, the term *aveirah*, and not *chet*, appears; therefore, it seems to attest to a notion of fearing punishment due to already committed transgressions. It does not deal with the type of "fear" noted in passages that speak of "fear of sin." As already observed, those passages foreground the cognitive desire and correlated behavior of avoiding committing sins.

Fear of One's Teacher

A second novel use of terms associated with fear found in *tannaitic* sources is the notion of "fear of one's teacher" (*morat rabbo*). Although a number of Second Temple sources describe the relationship between teachers or scribes and their students, none prescribes "fear" as the required attitude or behavior.[8] A statement in M. Avot 4:1 expresses this unique rabbinic concept:

---

1 Revisited: Texts from Cave 1 Sixty Years after their Discovery, eds. Sarianna Metson et al. (Leiden: Brill, 2010), 179-189, analyzes the treatment of this passage in various texts from the Dead Sea Scrolls and makes clear that all understand the biblical text in this straightforward manner.

[8] Studies of student-sage relationships include: Benjamin G. Wright III, "From Generation to Generation: The Sage as Father in Early Jewish Literature," in *Biblical Traditions in Transmission: Essays in Honor of Michael A. Knibb*, eds. Charlotte Hempel and Judith Lieu (Leiden: Brill, 2006), 309-332; J.W. McKay, "Man's Love for God in Deuteronomy and the Father/Teacher-Pupil Relationship," *Vetus Testamentum* 22 (1972) 426-435; Elisa Uusimäki, "Maskil Among the Hellenistic Jewish Sages," *Journal of Ancient Judaism* 8 (2017): 42-68; Elisa Uusimäki, "The Rise of the Sage in Greek and Jewish Antiquity," *Journal for the Study of Judaism* 49 (2018): 1-29; and John J. Collins, "The Sage in the Apocalyptic and Pseudepigraphic Literature," *Seers, Sibyls and Sages in Hellenistic-Roman Judaism* (Leiden: Brill, 1997), 339-350.

Rabbi Elazar ben Shammua said, "Let the honor of your student be as dear to you as your own, and the honor of your colleague as **the fear** [reverence] (*mora*) of your teacher, and the fear [reverence] for your teacher as the fear [reverence] of heaven."

The mandate to fear one's teacher also appears in Mekhilta de R. Ishmael Amaleq 1 (on Exod. 17:9) and in Sifre Zuta 11:28. The former asks, "From where is it derived that the honor due to one's friend is to be as beloved by a person as the fear of his teacher?" The text cites how Aaron addresses Moses in Numbers 12:11 as "my lord." He did so even though he was his younger brother. This supports the contention about fearing one's teacher. The passage in Mekhilta, which parallels the tradition in Sifre Zuta, goes on to provide a second example of how, in Numbers 11:28, Joshua addresses Moses as "my lord."

Two aspects of this demand "to fear one's teacher" require an explanation. First, what is the basis for treating a teacher in this manner? Second, exactly what does "fear" entail? The answer to both these issues is straightforward. Already in Proverbs and in Ben Sira, teachers address their students as "my son."[9] A *tannaitic* passage, Sifre Deut. 34 explicitly depicts the teacher-student relationship as equivalent to that between fathers and sons. It states:

> "And you shall teach them to your sons" (Deut. 6:7)—These are your disciples. And thus do you find in all places that disciples are called "sons." [Scripture states], "And the sons of the prophets came forth" (2 Kgs. 2:3). Now were they the sons of the prophets? Were they not disciples? This shows that disciples were called "sons"....And just as disciples are called "sons," so too is the teacher called "father." As it is stated, "And Elisha saw [Elijah being borne aloft] and he cried out 'My father, my father—the chariot of Israel and its riders'" (2 Kgs. 2:12). And he saw him no more, and he took hold of his own garments and rent them in two (2 Kgs. 2:12–13). And [similarly] it says..."And it is written, 'And Elisha fell ill with the illness of which he would die, and Yoash the king of Israel came down to him and wept before him and cried, 'My father, my father'" (2 Kgs. 13:14).[10]

---

[9] Both Wright, "From Generation to Generation," and McKay, "Man's Love," note this mode of address.

[10] For discussions of the master-disciple relationships in rabbinic sources see: Catherine

The equation of teachers with fathers also makes evident what "fear" actually means. A number of *tannaitic* traditions detail the nature of fear of parents, noting the connection with the fear of God, and spell out the difference between honor and fear with regard to parents.[11] The briefest expression of this notion is in Sifra Qedoshim Parasha 1:4:

> It says, "A person his mother and father shall you **fear**" (Lev. 19:3), and it says, "The Lord your God you shall **fear**" (Deut. 6:13). It [Scripture] equates the **fear** (*mora*) of the father and mother with the **fear** of the Lord.[12]

This passage uses the same language as M. Avot 4:1, which draws a parallel between the fear of one's teacher and the fear of God.

> Sifra Qedoshim Parasha 1:10 specifies in behavioral terms the respective requirements of "honor" and "fear" of parents:

> Which is **fear** (*mora*)? He shall not sit in his place, and he shall not speak in his place, and he shall not contradict his words. Which is honoring? Giving him to eat and to drink and clothing and covering and bringing him in and taking him out.[13]

The difference between the required actions for honor and fear is that the former are performative, behaviors one must do, while the latter, fear—or often here translated as "respect"—are actions to be avoided. In neither case, however, are honor and fear understood to be about interior feelings. Rather, they demonstrate to the hierarchical relationship of parents and children.

Similarly, two roughly parallel traditions, Tos. Meg. 3:2 and Sifra Qedoshim Pereq 7:12 delineate the meaning of the requirement in Leviticus 19:32 "to show deference to the elder (*zaqen*)":

Hezser, *The Social Structure of the Rabbinic Movement in Roman Palestine* (Tubingen: Mohr Siebeck, 1997); Jonathan Schofer, *The Making of a Sage: A Study in Rabbinic Ethics* (Madison: University of Wisconsin Press, 2015); and Steven Fraade, *From Tradition to Commentary: Torah and Its Interpretation in the Midrash Sifre to Deuteronomy* (Albany: SUNY Press, 1991).

[11] Several passages, such as in M. Ker. 3:9 and M. B.M. 2:11, privilege the teacher over the father in situations when they are in direct competition with each other.

[12] The same notion appears in a longer exegesis in Mekhilta de R. Ishmael Bachodesh 8 and Mekhilta R. Simeon b. Yochai 20:12.

[13] Tos. Qid. 1:11 has the same list but adds, "he washes his face, hands and feet."

"Rise before the aged and show deference (*hodarta*) to the elder"—I might think even for a wicked [elder]; it is, therefore, written "elder," an elder being one who has acquired wisdom, as it is written, "Gather for Me seventy of Israel's elders of whom you have experience as elders and officers of the people" (Num. 11:16). R. Yose the Galilean says, "An elder (*zaqen*) is one who has acquired (*zeh sheqanah*) wisdom, as it is stated, 'The Lord created (*qanani*) me [wisdom] at the beginning of his course'" (Prov. 8:22). What constitutes "showing deference"? Not sitting in his place, not speaking in his place, and not contradicting his words.[14]

This text equates behaving with deference as requiring the avoidance of the same behaviors that other texts define as the "fear" (*yirah*) of a parent and a teacher. This interpretation of the verse aligns with the frequent equation in rabbinic texts of elders, *zeqenim*, with wise people, sages, and teachers of Torah.[15] Again, it is action, not an interior feeling (emotion) that is demanded to demonstrate "fear" or "deference."

Conclusions

Fear is a core human experience pertaining to relationships with various people, as well as with other species and aspects of reality. Being fearful is also a character trait, not so much an emotion. Ethicists have written much about the nature and appropriateness of behavior and relationships based on fear, often depicting them as undesirable. Similarly, virtue ethicists have commented on whether developing the character trait of being fearful is ever warranted. Finally, many psychologists treat fear as a negative emotion. While they recognize its value as a deterrent in situations of imminent danger and trace it to the evolutionary development of the "fright-flight-fight syndrome" exhibited by humans and other species, they characterize the use of fear in interpersonal relationship as psychologically unhealthy and label a person with excessive fear as suffering from destructive anxiety.

Early rabbinic sources have much to say about "fear." For the most part, the rabbis viewed "fear" behaviorally more than as an interior emotional

---

[14] Tos. Meg. 3:24 specifies that the opening portion of Leviticus 19:32, "rise before the aged," requires positive actions that other traditions understand to be the requirements of "honor." It also lays out a slightly expanded list of actions to avoid doing out of reverence and fear (*mora veyirah*). Sifra Num. 92 also interprets God's directive to Moses "to gather for Me seventy of Israel's elders" as demanding they be treated with honor as well as with reverence (*eimah*) and fear (*yirah*).

[15] See Fraade, *From Tradition*, 75–83, for additional texts equating elders with sages.

experience. In terms of the two novel concepts of "fear" analyzed in this chapter, fear of sin and fear of one's teacher, these sources see behaviors and relationships characterized as "fear" in a positive light. Being cautious and avoiding sin and treating one's teacher with "fear" are approved types of behavior. As such, rather than describing an interior emotion, fear in these cases can be observed in the public behavior of people. Rhetorical uses of the term fear also serve to shape the broader rabbinic community by specifying behaviors to avoid and the required postures and actions to perform *vis à vis* others.

Later rabbinic traditions go on to develop a more complex view of the self and note interior dialogues within a person. As other studies have charted, by the medieval period, in all strands of Jewish thought—philosophical, Kabbalistic, moralist (Mussar), and homiletics—fear of God, fear of sin, fear of one's teacher, and the contrast between fear and love of God occupy a central focus of Jewish ethical and religious writings and life.[16]

---

[16] For such analyses see: Louis Jacobs, "The Fear of God," *A Jewish Theology* (New York: Behrman House, 1973), 174-182; Byron Sherwin, "Fear of God," in *20th Century Jewish Religious Thought: Original Essays on Critical Concepts, Movements and Beliefs*, eds. Arthur A. Cohen and Paul Mendes-Flohr (Philadelphia: Jewish Publication Society, 2009), 245-254; Warren Zev Harvey, "*Yirat Shamayim* in Jewish Thought," in *Yirat Shamayim: Awe, Reverence and Fear of God*, ed. Marc D. Stern (Jersey City, NJ: Yeshiva University Press, 2008), 1-26; and Jonathan Garb, "From Fear to Awe in Luzzatto's *Mesillat Yeshari*," *European Journal of Jewish Studies* 14 (2020): 285-299.

Shaiya Rothberg responds

I found reading Dr. Joel Gereboff's "Fear of Sin and of One's Teacher in Early Rabbinic Judaism" fascinating. It is an excellent example of how academic research can change the way we understand texts and, for those for whom these texts play a role in our lives, also our understanding of ourselves. The article is part of a larger project of research into the meaning of emotions and how these appear, or seem to appear, in rabbinic texts.

This essay focuses on the meaning of "fear" in early rabbinic (*tannaitic*) literature. In particular, the fear (*yirah*) of sin and of one's teacher. The idea of "fearing" sin or one's teacher raises interesting questions: Why would one "fear" these things? Is it because sinning or crossing my teacher might result in punishment that I fear? Or because I fear seeing myself, or others seeing me, as a bad person or student? And what kind of fear is involved here? Is it the kind we feel before speaking in front of a group? Or the sort of fear that we experience when a ferocious dog bounds our way? Or is it a more general anxiety, like when we feel that some important plan is going awry?

All these interpretations of fear involve imagining that the authors of these texts thought about and experienced themselves like we do. But it seems that they did not. Gereboff points out that in rabbinic texts there is no specific term for "emotions" in a modern sense. Furthermore, our conception of emotions involves the idea that we have what he calls "outer" and "inner" selves. We think of "fear" as something we experience "inside" that may or may not be visible to others. But, as Gereboff makes clear, rabbinic thinking "is not fleshed out in terms of a clear inner and outer self…we should not impose upon these works Cartesian and Victorian notions of the self that posit a distinct interior self."

But if these texts do not assume an "interior self" that experiences emotions like I do, what could they mean by fear? The answer in brief is that terms like fear and love in early rabbinic texts refer not to what we would call emotions (at least not primarily so) but rather to physical behaviors expressing hierarchy and power relations. Fear of sin, for example, may have little to do with what one "feels inside" but rather is embodied (literally, manifest in the actions of the body) by one who carefully avoids sin. Fear of one's teacher is embodied in not sitting in their place or contradicting their pronouncements. Gereboff's conclusion seems warranted: "Early rabbinic sources have much to say about 'fear.' For the most part, the rabbis viewed 'fear' behaviorally more than as an interior emotional experience…rather than describing an interior emotion, fear in these cases can be observed in the public behavior of people."

Internalizing this perspective on ancient texts transforms what they seem to mean. If the texts involving "love" and "fear" that we recite from the Bible and rabbis are understood this way, then our understandings of these texts, the way they inform our religious lives, seem to become more *midrash* than *peshat* or simple meaning: When I read in the blessings of the *Sh'ma* that I should "love" God, my religious imagination understands this love as part of my inner life, which scholarship reveals is probably not what the authors intended. Of course, our religious lives are not limited to the historical meaning of ancient texts, and rich conceptions of our inner and outer selves are an important part of subsequent Jewish tradition. But understanding the meaning of our more ancient texts in historical context challenges what they mean when we pray and perform rituals. We might say that these re-discovered meanings "have a vote but not a veto"; that is, we hear their voices but are not bound by them, and this hearing enriches our religious lives.

At this point, I would like to raise a layperson's question regarding the absence of "emotions" and "inner self" in ancient texts. One scholar mentioned in the article, Lasater, argues that it would be more accurate not to refer to emotions at all in the context of ancient texts, but rather "passions," which combine cognition, appraisal, will, and affect, and which would have made more sense for ancient people who had no concept of an "inner self" and "emotions." But this suggestion seems to me to highlight a problem with this kind of methodology (or, more likely, with my understanding of it).

Are we to limit our interpretation of ancient texts to the conceptual apparatus of those who produced them? I admit that if I interpret an early rabbinic text in light of my conception of an inner self and emotions, I am surely skewing its meaning, given that the authors seemed to have no such conceptions. Hence (if I understand correctly) the suggestion that we use terms like "passions" that would have made more sense in that historical context. But what happens if we turn the clock back further, to a time that humans did not use language at all? Are we to assume that nothing in our "inner lives" and "emotions" is relevant for the interpretation of the lives and artifacts of such people?

This line of reasoning conflicts with my heartfelt conviction (by which I mean an emotionally charged opinion held by my inner self, rather than a visible physical behavior expressing the power dynamic in our relationship) that my dog, Georgie, experiences a range of emotion not unlike my own. I have always been insulted (for him) when, upon wagging his tail and leaping upon us when we return home, my wife quips that he must be hungry. Why interpret his motivations so narrowly? I felt vindicated in this belief when

I read somewhere that when a dog meets their human pack (I doubt that "master" is the term Georgie would choose, given how he clearly believes that he is in charge), the part of the brain that becomes activated is roughly the same part as when a human child sees a parent, and not the part associated with hunger and food. In fact, my superficial reading into the emotions of dogs (or perhaps "passions," in deference to Lasater), suggests that they experience love, fear, loss, playfulness and a host of other inner states and emotions, regardless of their (relative) lack of vocabulary to describe them.

Similarly, I believe, without evidence, that the various Homo species, whether or not they could speak, and probably also many other species, experience much of what we think makes our human lives unique and valuable. If so, surely the biblical and rabbinic authors, who are surprisingly foreign to us in some ways but also our twins in comparison to humans without speech or other species, probably also experienced emotions and inner lives, even if they did not have terms for them. This gives me pause to think: Perhaps the texts about fear of sin and fear of one's teacher focus on behavioral aspects, and not on "inner emotion," because they had terms for the former but not for the latter, while in fact their "inner experience" was much like ours.

Gereboff is careful not to overstate his case. He does not argue that *yirah* involves no "inner emotion," but rather that the texts seem to signify physical behaviors and publicly observable expressions of power-relationships, rather than what we would call emotions. His conclusions seem both justified and important. But when I posed to him my questions about the methodology and its conclusions, he seemed to think that they had some merit. He also suggested that perhaps my dog might make an appearance in this response. For this, Georgie was deeply appreciative, but expressed his heartfelt emotion only through a wag of his tail and a shake of his head.

Joel Gereboff responds

Drawing upon his extensive knowledge of Jewish thought on connections between the political and the spiritual, Dr. Shaiya Rothberg makes a strong argument for the central role of contemporary Jewish engagement with efforts to foster human rights. Through examining in some detail the views of Maimonides, Rabbi Samson Raphael Hirsch, and the lesser-known Rabbi Chaim Hirschenson, Rothberg demonstrates that all three saw the role of Torah and the mission of the Jews as having a universal orientation. Torah serves to enable the attainment of higher spiritual value. But attention and engagement with political efforts by Jews and others are necessary to mend the body politic of humankind. While noting how each of these three Jewish thinkers reflected broader currents of his time and spoke to the particular situation of Jews in their era and location, Rothberg concludes that they all share the above call for Jewish involvement with the political—or, using Hobbes' image for the political, in the effort at humanizing the Leviathan. In the course of his essay, Rothberg moves from Maimonides' advocacy of a theocratic monarchy as the vehicle for ensuring the humanizing of the political, through the spiritual values of Torah, to what he somewhat anachronistically sees as Hirsch and Hirschenson's promotion of human rights. In Rothberg's words:

> If we inhabit the narrative spun by Rambam about the Abrahamic mission and the Torah as a blueprint for a redeemed humanity, the emergence of the human covenant can only be recognized as the critical next chapter. I think that Rabbis Hirsch and Hirschenson started writing that chapter when they framed the redemption of Israel in Zion, and humanity everywhere in light of human rights.

Based on this conclusion, Rothberg ends his piece by noting briefly its implications for present-day Jewish activities:

> If we find this new chapter about human rights by Rabbis Hirsch and Hirschenson compelling, it should move us to articulate our religious commitment to this emerging human covenant in our Jewish lives.... We, too, must find ways of empowering the movement from human rights through the strength of our tradition. Jewish education should highlight the profound religious significance of emergence of the human covenant as a milestone in the divine mission of mending the body and soul of humanity. When we address current events in our synagogue youth movements, schools and institutions of higher learning, our commitment to the human rights of all people should be the bedrock to our discourse.... By seeking to unite diverse Jewish communities, across denominations, behind a shared commitment to the human covenant we lend spiritual strength to the ongoing effort to humanize the Leviathan.

Rothberg's case is compelling and adds religious depth to the high degree of what is often a very secular or thinly religiously grounded Jewish involvement with promoting universal rights of all humans.[1] It also implicitly critiques those Jews who focus narrowly upon the spiritual, for example through excessive devotion to Torah study, and to those who tend to separate Jewish causes from those of other people. From our extended discussion of our papers, I also learned that Rothberg lives these values in his own activities promoting respect for the human rights of all those living in the state of Israel, and in activities seeking to enhance peace between Jews and Arabs.

The limitations of space assigned to Rothberg for his essay led to his having to discuss only in a cursory manner the depth of the political vision of each of the three thinkers he introduces. Each wrote voluminously about the nature of Jewish and human life. An issue which I would have hoped for Rothberg to explain in greater detail is the anthropological assumptions of each writer. What does each see as the nature or inherent dispositions of humans (if any)? By appealing to Hobbes, for example, one is struck by that thinker's somewhat negative view of human nature compared with what Maimonides takes to be the ability and task of all humans to strive for human (spiritual) flourishing. Noting this also speaks to another key difference among these thinkers and others who promote the centrality of "rights." Like other medieval thinkers, Maimonides thought in terms of the "good" and not in terms of "rights." Rothberg's essay could analyze in greater detail how Hirsch and Hirschenson, and other contemporary Jewish thinkers, have integrated notions of rights with the primary Jewish discourse of duties and visions of the good.

Space limitations also did not allow for Rothberg to situate the views of these thinkers in relation to broader contemporary religiously grounded Jewish views of the political and of human rights, for example those of David Novak, Milton Konitz, and Michael Broyde.[2] David Wermuth's

---

[1] On the leading role of Jews in the drafting and promotion of the United Declaration on Human Rights, see James Loeffler, *Rooted Cosmopolitans: Jews and Human Rights in the Twentieth Century* (New Haven: Yale University Press, 2018).

[2] See for example, Michael Broyde and John Witte, eds. *Human Rights in Judaism: Cultural, Religious and Political Perspectives* (Lanham, MD: Jason Aronson Publishers, 1998); Milton Konvitz, ed., *Judaism and Human Rights*, 2nd ed (New York: Routledge, 2017); David Novak, "A Jewish Theory of Human Rights," in *Religion and Human Rights: An Introduction*, ed. John Witte and M. Christian Green (New York, Oxford University Press, 2011), 27-41; Asher Maoz, "Can Judaism Serve as a Source of Human Rights," *Tel Aviv University Law Faculty Papers* 7 (2005): 665-721; and S. Daniel Breslauer, *Judaism and Human Rights in Contemporary Thoughts: A Bibliographical Survey* (Westport, CT: Greenwood, 1993). On Hirschenson in particular, with references to broader analysis of his work, see David Ellenson, "Rabbi Haim Hirschenson: An Orthodox Rabbi Responds to the Balfour Declaration," *American Jewish*

detailed analysis of contemporary *halakhic* writings and Israeli court decisions regarding human rights would also serve to provide richer and more recent comparative information for situating the much earlier views of figures such as Hirsch and Hirschenson, who spoke in terms of the rights of mankind and prior to the formulation of the United Nations Declaration of Human Rights.[3]

Finally, the broader issue of how to develop universal views of human rights while respecting the particular position of various communities, be they religious, indigenous, feminist, or otherwise, would need to be considered to determine the salience of the very claim that there are universal human rights. Yet, Rothberg's compelling argument that all Jews should engage with advancing the goal of the human body politic adds a critical element to the intellectual and practical tasks of Jews today.

History 101:3 (2017): 247-269.

[3] David Wermuth, "Human Rights in Jewish Law: Contemporary Juristic and Rabbinic Conceptions," *University of Pennsylvania Journal of International Law* 32:4 (2011): 1101-1132.

Set Four

Growing from Interfaith Environmental Conversations

Nina Perlmutter

A Difference of Degree: Toward a Post-Anthropocentric Judaism

Jonathan L. Friedmann

Growing from Interfaith Environmental Conversations

Nina Perlmutter

Introduction

The license plate on my Prius says "ECORABBI," expressing my two deepest passions. However, while growing up I was unaware that environmental protection was part of Jewish tradition. I embraced only the imperative for social justice activism. Decades later I became active in environmental issues, long before becoming an informed or "spiritual" Jew. Discovering Jewish teachings and *mitzvot* relevant to environmental issues became a major impetus for my "coming home" to Judaism. It also significantly changed how I think and speak about environmental issues with the many secular and religious, Jewish and non-Jewish, environmentally concerned folks with whom I have long interacted.

As head of philosophy and religious studies at the local community college, I spent decades teaching ethics and created the first college-level environmental ethics class in Arizona. Discovering Jewish environmental teachings seriously changed what I had taught earlier. I had come to understand that my earlier ignorance about Jewish texts and interpretations had contributed to my perpetuating a misleading but popular idea in both academic and activist circles: that the real "root of our ecological crisis" can be found in the Jewish creation story, implying that Judaism is largely responsible for inspiring environmental abuse.

Over time I found that I was not alone as a Jew with only minimal (or mistaken) understanding of Jewish environmental teachings, no less how to "think Jewishly" about important issues, including the environment. In what follows, I will first describe major points on my personal saga. Then I will share how non-Jewish audiences and colleagues often respond to learning about Jewish environmental thinking. Finally, I will share how engaging with non-Jewish environmentally concerned folks as a now-informed Jew has impacted me.

Part 1: Adding "Eco-" to my sense of Jewish identity

My parents were adamantly "cultural" or "secular" Jews, and well-known leaders in interfaith, liberal political activism. My dad, the late Nate Perlmutter, spent his life in the Anti-Defamation League and died as its national director. So, it was in my bones to believe that life was about acting on the Jewish impulse for social justice. Dad and his interfaith, liberal colleagues fought against bigotry and for the Civil Rights Act. Growing up in Florida, I vividly recall segregated buses, bathrooms, water fountains, and signs declaring "No Coloreds, No Jews, No dogs" at many hotels and exclusive residential communities. My parents' mission was clear and assertively Jewish.

Back then, interfaith activist agendas and encounters usually did not include talking about their respective faith traditions. Focus was on the work to be done. Some worried that exploring their respective religions might diminish the sense of unity they needed to promote their shared political goals. And some, like my parents, did not really know much. As first generation American-born Jews, my parents were more focused on becoming Americans and improving America. They were not interested in maintaining their immigrant parents' "old-fashioned" traditions.

Happily, Dad did impart his love for the ocean, birds, trees, and the Everglades. Being out in nature was part of his American dream, not part of his Jewishness. While many of my friends went to Jewish summer camps, my parents sent me to Girl Scout camp (where I had my first memorable antisemitic experience). While appreciating the outdoors, taking political action to protect the natural world was not on my folks' to-do-list. I felt similarly. To be sure, Girl Scout camp opened me to loving the outdoors, yet I was later disappointed, even angry, at those hitting the streets for Earth Day in 1970 but not doing the same to protest the invasion of Cambodia that same month.

Given my own generation's mostly positive American Jewish experience, I was more in touch with helping other communities than with focusing on antisemitism.[1] My priorities—and for years my professional job—was organizing against the Vietnam War and then against nuclear weapons. Hiroshima and Nagasaki survivors whom I knew (and who brought me to Japan) taught the importance of opposing the entire nuclear fuel cycle, as radiation and other side effects of uranium mining (for both weapons and power) and nuclear waste storage were taking serious tolls worldwide.

Being against nuclear implied supporting alternatives. So, when then-Governor Bruce Babbitt opened the Arizona Energy Office to promote solar energy, conservation, and recycling, I was hired to help promote those across the state. More personally, my husband and I joined other "back-to-the-landers," moving to more rural country and hand-building

---

[1] Even before I knew it, parts two and three of Hillel's famous quote were more my reflex than part one: "If I am not for myself, who will be? If I am only for myself, what am I? And if not now, when?" (*Pirkei Avot* 1:14).

our passive solar earth home. I taught about solar construction and solar oven cooking at the local community nature center, promoting energy as an environmental issue. But throughout those many years, I never saw my impulses coming from a Jewish space.

The Academic Thread in My Journey

For decades in both academic and environmental activist circles, it was common to cite the "Judeo-Christian" tradition in general, and Hebrew Bible in particular, as a major source—sometimes *the* major source—of attitudes inherently destructive to the environment.[2]

The allegation became crystallized and more respectable with a widely distributed article by medieval historian Lynn White in *Science Magazine*. His 1967 piece, "The Historical Roots of Our Ecological Crisis,"[3] came at the time of growing awareness and concern about global environmental problems. It quickly became a classic, a mainstay in college environmental ethics and philosophy textbooks, including those I used. It remains the standard prooftext for the view that the Hebrew Bible is the primary source for arrogant exploitation of nature.

White's piece initiated a tidal wave of reactions. It was instrumental in inspiring a whole new academic area of study called "eco-theology" and activism in faith communities now called "eco-justice theology." In both fields, people explore religious teachings about the appropriate relationship between humans and the non-human world, encouraging actions based on those teachings. "Religious environmental activism" was born.

Back then, I knew almost nothing about Jewish history or teachings. Nor did I know that what we call "Judaism" is rabbinic, coming after the biblical period. And when I discovered Jewish texts and commentaries pertaining to the environment, it was a shock, a wake-up call, and an invitation. The more I encountered the history, content, and process of Jewish thinking, the better I understood that some voices within Judaism have long promoted very responsible consideration of the non-human world, and provided obligations and guidelines (*mitzvot*), character values (*middot*), unique insights, and processes for embracing what is now called "environmental ethics." In short, I found Jewish perspectives leading us in virtually the opposite direction from some of White's and his followers' assumptions.

---

[2] Those espousing this position are not necessarily antisemitic. In fact, some are Jews themselves. Their critique often results from ignorance and misunderstandings about Judaism and its history, about the complicated history of the term "Judeo-Christian," and about *how* Jews have long engaged with their sacred texts.

[3] Lynn Townsend White, Jr., "The Historical Roots of our Ecological Crisis," *Science* 155 (Mar. 10, 1967): 1203-1207.

As mentioned, this discovery significantly contributed to my spiritual saga. What (in ignorance) I thought Judaism taught about nature had been a major impediment to embracing my heritage. Correcting and deepening my understanding helped me see how many of my reflexes had unknowingly been Jewish all along. That discovery motivated my becoming a late-blooming practicing Jew.

After graduate-level Jewish studies and rabbinical school, I committed to making Jewishly grounded environmental ethics and experiences a significant part of my rabbinate. In 2009 I became the designated Jewish contact at the South Rim of Grand Canyon National Park, where I had long taught environmental ethics before becoming Jewishly engaged. I do *shabbaton* events, *b'nei mitzvah* ceremonies, Jewish river trips, and weddings at Grand Canyon and in other nearby Arizona and Utah locations. Programs include sharing diverse Jewish teachings about nature, sharing ancient blessings to the Source for natural phenomena, introducing nature-related words for the divine, and more. My goal is to model and encourage respect for both of my commitments as an "eco rabbi" and to help open Jews to possibilities they never imagined.

How far I am from teaching Lynn White as gospel truth! Or from thinking like those Jews who assume caring for the non-human world requires us to leave Judaism behind and embrace instead secular ethics, or only "liberal" Jewish commitments, or else their highly romanticized, Americanized versions of Buddhism, Taoism, Wicca, or some simplified, generic versions of Native American traditions. Having had numerous Jewish students and colleagues report "feeling guilty" for being Jewish when it came to environmental thinking, I can now respond more competently.

Interestingly and importantly, Lynn White never promoted "going East." As a Christian, his real agenda was to inspire Westerners, especially Christians, to take a more Franciscan approach towards creation.[4] In some ways his historic article was actually more critical of Christianity than of Judaism. That said, his repeated emphasis on how the "Judeo-Christian" tradition is responsible for problems, his only citing "dominion" in Genesis 1:26–28 ("Be fertile and increase, fill the earth and master it; and rule…all the living things that creep on earth") without ever mentioning the contrasting stewardship imperative "to till and to tend (protect)" the Garden of Eden in Genesis 2:15—nor the more nuanced and respectful ways Jews are to engage with animals and the land—all supported widely accepted oversimplifications.

Also, White's portrayal of Judaism as if it promotes only a simplistic

---

[4] On Easter Sunday 1980, Pope John Paul II proclaimed Saint Francis of Assisi the Patron Saint of Ecology, following Lynn White's recommendation.

"anthropocentric" (human-centered) ethics totally ignored its more "theocentric" (God-centered) emphasis in ethical decision making. While it is true that Judaism places humans in an elevated position, our ethical choices are not to be based solely on what we crave for ourselves.[5] Rather, we are to think and act from a space remembering and considering the Divine.

We are to yield to the latter for they are even "higher" on the hierarchy of ethical consideration. Talmud specifically expands on the importance of not being misled by whims, sensory and other personal desires, based on Numbers 15:39.[6] For example, even when I feel inclined towards killing and eating meat for personal pleasure, I am not to stop there. *That* would be "anthropocentric." Rather Jews must consider the Divine will, which overrides personal impulses. This more "theocentric" view of ethics underlies rules of *kashrut* and dietary discipline even when they go against my personal preferences. Anthropocentrism always places human desires first, as "central" to ethics. Theocentrism places God in the "center" of ethical thinking, with humans required to yield to the divine's will.[7]

In addition, I found that White's followers too often mistakenly equate Jewish and Christian understandings of key terms and concepts in the Hebrew Bible. Also, a dangerous over-simplification emerges by not knowing that "Judaism" is rabbinic—meaning, post-biblical—with centuries of sages' interpretations, debates, and expansions of Torah presenting more nuanced and numerous understandings. I will never forget being asked where contemporary Jews are sacrificing all those animals now!

My goal now also includes showing problems resulting from White's overly equating the two sides of the so-called "Judeo-Christian" perspective. I acknowledge that the term is often meant to inspire a sense of interfaith

---

[5] The work of Ellen Bernstein from Shomrei Adamah and Ronald H. Isaacs helped open my mind early on, as did Rabbi David Seidenberg, who has long challenged any extreme anthropocentric reading of Torah as deeply misleading. Seidenberg's recent book is recommended: *Kabbalah and Ecology: God's Image in the More-than-Human-World* (New York: Cambridge University Press, 2015).

[6] In Numbers 15:39, we are told that the fringes of our tallit are to help us "recall all the commandments of the Lord and observe them, so that you do not follow your heart and eyes in your lustful urge."

[7] Concentric circles have long been central to college ethics classes when discussing ethical priorities. Most important is what appears in the middle as "central." Additional circles show how far out we have ethical responsibility. The modern "animal rights" movement began when the British Humane Society added a layer for horses and domestic animals. Later, non-domestic animals were added. The classic exploration of this appears in the text I long used, Roderick Frazier Nash's *Rights of Nature: A History of Environmental Ethics* (Madison: University of Wisconsin Press, 1989).

commonality. Still, my sense is that in this context, the phrase can distort more than help. I agree with my colleague Jonathan L. Friedmann that "Judeo-Christian" is itself a Christian term that has nothing to do with Judaism. He notes how it was first used to describe Jewish converts to Christianity in the nineteenth century, was revived during the Cold War as a political term in the U.S., and has since sometimes been used by white Evangelical Christians to erase both the distinctiveness of Judaism and the existence of Islam in America's history.[8] Again, differences in how our traditions approach biblical texts in general, and environmental thinking in particular, are sometimes significant.

It is also important to share that Jews are mandated to lovingly "wrestle" with God (one meaning of our name, *Yisrael*), with our texts, and with each other about important issues, and the imperative to consider insights from multiple perspectives. We are to remember that the subtlety of the Hebrew language impacts our understanding of the text, and that while we can find some meaning by interpreting texts literally, we are also to acknowledge other layers and insights from other levels of interpretations (psychological, intellectual, spiritual, etc.).

In my interfaith encounters, history is not my focus. But I often mention how another turning point for me was learning ways that Judaism was less influenced by the Greeks' "absolutist" and "either/or" logic than were Christianity or Islam. My mentor, Rabbi Dr. Byron Sherwin, z"l, at Spertus College of Jewish Studies, always emphasized how Jewish thinking has long been a "both/and" approach more than "either/or." He described it as a "large buffet table," while cautioning that not everything was allowed on it.[9]

My point is that the famous quip "two Jews, three opinions" is more than a joke. Indeed, it is canonized. The theology of Deuteronomy versus Job is but one example: Job's friends insist he "deserves" suffering as punishment for misdeeds, as per Deuteronomy; but God sides with Job against the friends' analysis, affirming how much is beyond human understanding. We are taught that all Jews—past, present, and future—were at Sinai, and we are to ask each other what we heard there. Talmud is packed with respectful differences of opinion, with the Houses of Hillel and Shammai being the most famous and respected models. In my rabbinical thesis on approaching environmental issues Jewishly, I suggested that the Jewish approach to environmental issues and living an ecologically sensitive life actually seems more "alive" and "natural" precisely because it is not totally fixed or absolute.

As a result, no simple, monolithic, final or fixed Jewish "environmental

---

[8] Jonathan L. Friedmann, email to author, August 23, 2021.
[9] See Byron L. Sherwin and Seymour J. Cohen, *How to be a Jew: Ethical Teachings of Judaism* (Northvale, NJ: Jason Aronson, 1992).

ethic" can be found. Instead, key Jewish values, priorities, approaches, and discussions, disagreements, and open-ended conversations are at least acknowledged. While not all strands of Jewish thinking about the non-human world are positive in my view, I do believe we can learn something from all, and hopefully remember to disagree "for the sake of Heaven."

My overall message: the Jewish mandate to "wrestle" with texts and with life has yielded many ethical, positive results for the natural world and how we relate to it. Overly simplistic, or absolutist anthropocentric or ecocentric positions are not the only options. The theocentric, organic, dialectical processes that characterize Jewish thought are underappreciated contributions to responsible environmental decision-making and action.

Learning about Jewish environmental thinking expanded what I teach in my Jewish studies, environmental ethics, and Southwest ecology classes. My audiences have been college students, affiliated and unaffiliated Jews, Christians, interfaith communities, senior community education students, Hopi environmental activists, and others.

With increased awareness of climate change and other serious environmental crises, there is an increase in religious environmental conversations and interfaith activism. More awareness and activist groups exist across the Jewish spectrum as well. From Orthodox to Reform to secular, there are increasing Jewish resources and organizations for those seeking to act both as Jews and as colleagues in interfaith environmentalism.[10]

While happy these now exist, I still mourn the loss of Jews who left Judaism before such awareness arose, and those who remain uninformed and unable to consider or articulate environmental matters from a Jewish perspective. They mirror who I once was. When I encounter such Jews, I strive to approach them "where they're at," share my history, and speak in a voice both personal and academic. And I try to model caring for the non-human world Jewishly as integral to what being consciously Jewish can mean.

Part 2:
Responses to Jewish Environmental Thinking by Non-Jews

Overall, when I share Jewish approaches to environmental issues in interfaith settings, many report gaining more respect for, and curiosity about, "eco-Judaism" in particular and Judaism in general. Most often, their first response is surprise.

Before our more open dialogue time, I give a heads-up to always expect

---

[10] Canfei Nesharim was an early organization of this kind and still a favorite of mine (www.CanfeiNeshirim.org). For a general list of Jewish groups, see American-Based Jewish Environmental Organizations, "Aytzim: Ecological Judaism," https://aytzim.org/resources/educational-materials/155abjeo.

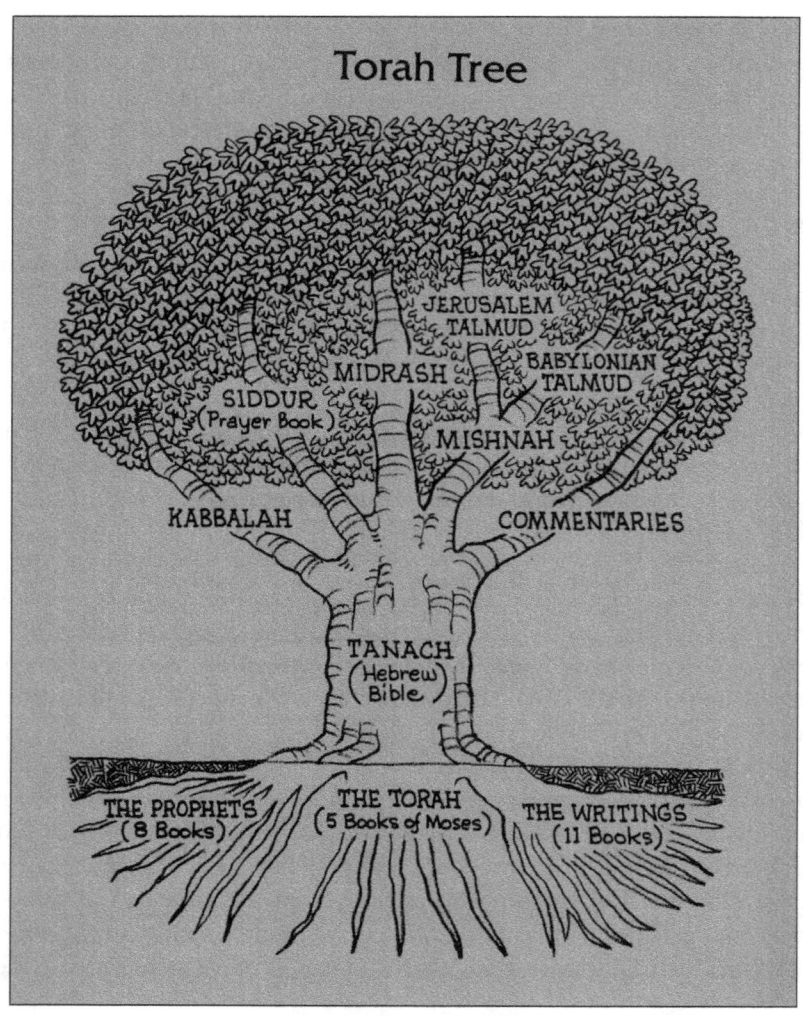

different Jewish views. We chat some about the word "Torah" being understood in both a narrow sense (as the Five Books), or in a larger sense as all of Jewish learning, and how on all levels it is "living": the *Eitz Chayyim* (Tree of Life), with leaves still being added. I present the pictured handout showing how a tree model illustrates "how Jews do Judaism."[11] Only then do we discuss more environment-related specifics.

The following topics seem to touch my non-Jewish audiences most quickly and deeply:

—*The diversity of views across the broad spectrum of Jewish life and practice.*

---

[11] From Molly Cone, *Listen to the Trees: Jews and the Earth* (New York: UAHC Press, 1995).

The fact that there is not even the expectation of a single, absolute, or "final" position often leads me to remind folks that "Judaism has no Vatican." They laugh. They also are intrigued upon hearing that "two Jews, three opinions" is demonstrated throughout commentaries and key texts.

—*That Jews are not required to "love" the Earth before carrying out obligations towards the natural world often leads to larger conversations about "love" in our respective traditions, about mitzvot, and about the "inner" and "outer" dimensions of religious Jewish life.*

"Love" is assertively central to Christian consciousness and (ideally) motivates compassionate action. My pastor friend Jan Flaaten sums up Christian environmental responsibility by quoting John 3:16: "God so loved the world that He gave his one and only Son…" Therefore, Christians must love the world—which implies caring for and protecting it. This inner attitude, love, becomes the vital, necessary first step for all Christian ethics, including environmental ethics. As such, Christians are often surprised that Jews do not necessarily have to love recipients of our good actions. Jews are to perform *mitzvot* even if our inner motivation is not so inclined (yet). We must treat humans and non-humans ethically even if we never come to love them. It is taught that doing *mitzvot* helps transform our inner world. But we must not wait for the ideal inner state to be cultivated.

Of course, loving God and neighbor are both valued in Judaism. But not all Christians know that Jesus' imperatives to "love your neighbor" and "love God with all your heart and soul" (Matt. 22:35–40 and Mark 12:31) originated in Torah (Lev. 19:18 and Deut. 6:5).

This conversation sometimes spurs some larger exploration of *mitzvot*. Non-Jews with whom I have engaged are intrigued that *mitzvah* can be understood as more than "commandment," but also as "good deed" (in the case of ethical commandments) and even as "bridge" between us and the divine (in the case of both ethical and ritual commandments).

—*Sharing my "Jewish response" to Lynn White often leads to conversations about the phrase "Judeo-Christian."* I express appreciation for how, in contemporary times, the phrase is often intended as a positive, pointing to what our traditions share. But I assert hope that we can respect each other even when we are *not* "the same." I often share some history about the term, including the negative undercurrent in its original use, even if unintended now. And I recommend *The Dignity of Difference* by Jonathan Sacks, the late Chief Rabbi of the United Hebrew Congregations of the Commonwealth (Britain).[12] Audiences smile when I show my wedding ring, sharing the

---

[12] Jonathan Sacks, *The Dignity of Difference: How to Avoid the Clash of Civilizations* (New York: Continuum, 2003).

inscription inside: "we're one, not two; two, not one." And I mention the Jewish goal is *not* to have us always totally agree or be the same, as per the Tower of Babel story.

—*Folks are usually surprised to hear how Jews can see, identify with, and learn from both Genesis 1 and 2 as separate and complementary.* These texts include imperatives to be applied appropriately in different proportions under different circumstances.

—*Many appreciate how Jewish prayer services include many psalms describing creation as alive—not just inanimate.* We discuss how this slows any impulse to see the non-human world as just material things or resources.

—*When talking about Genesis, I invite going back to its opening where the first five days are declared "good," then on day six, when humans appear, it is "very good."* I suggest an alternative to only focusing on us. Rather, I suggest the divine be seen as the "First Ecologist" who especially appreciates that the *whole system* has now come into being. Creation would be less good without us, but also without all that came before us. That's when I share my tremendous respect for Christian writer and agrarian spokesman Wendell Berry.[13] He first alerted me to how popular, beautiful nature calendars usually show no humans in the photographs at all. We then discuss the importance of finding ways to responsibly reclaim humans' place to fulfill that "very good" ideal of the sixth day of creation.

—*Introducing "theocentrism" to religiously motivated environmentalists usually resonates well.* More secular listeners are often intellectually curious about these points, but not at all moved personally, for religious-based teachings simply do not speak to them (for diverse reasons).

Regarding non-humans and animals:

—*Bal Tashchit: the biblical imperative to avoid unnecessary destruction (Deuteronomy 20:19–20).* People are often surprised to learn that this extends beyond humans, even to some trees during wartime. Rabbi Samson Raphael Hirsch framed *bal tashchit* in the context of all of creation.[14] Creation is a divine act. Destroying it violates that initial divine action. When we dispose of things prematurely, we flippantly discard the creative divine energy within them. Our task is to recognize the divine in everything, for "the whole world is filled with God's glory" (Isa. 6:3).

Lest they think such thought is only recent, the twelfth- and thirteenth-century Hebrew work *Sefer Chasidim* (*The Book of the Pious*) states: "Be kind and compassionate to all creatures that the Holy One, blessed be

---

[13] I highly recommend Wendell Berry, *The Gift of Good Land: Further Essays Cultural and Agricultural*, first published in 1981 yet relevant still.
[14] https://www.sefaria.org/sheets/124937

He, created in this world. Never beat nor inflict pain on any animal, beast, or bird, or insect. Do not throw stones at a dog or a cat."[15]

And the sixteenth-century *Code of Jewish Law* (*Shulchan Aruch*) clearly states that "it is forbidden, according to the law of the Torah, to inflict pain upon any living creature. On the contrary, it is our duty to relieve the pain of any creature, even if it is ownerless or belongs to a non-Jew."[16]

Listeners express curiosity about this and related matters, including a growing modern Jewish vegan/vegetarianism movement, all based on ancient texts (e.g., that life in the Garden of Eden was vegetarian). As Arizonans, the ongoing work of Phoenix-area Modern Orthodox Rabbi Shmuley Yanklowitz in the areas of animal rights, Jewish veganism, and synagogue education, and action is receiving more attention, and is of special interest.[17]

—*Other surprises include the Talmudic expansion of Deuteronomy 11:15 to say that animals in our care must be fed before we feed ourselves,*[18] *and that Genesis 1:30 implies a vegetarian diet in the Garden of Eden.* That I am a Jewish vegetarian for fifty years sparks exploration. So does hearing Torah citations about giving work animals rest on Shabbat (Exod. 23:12), not letting animals of different sizes and strength be tied together for work (Deut. 22:10), or helping unload burdens from animals.

—*Pet owners especially appreciate that Balaam's talking donkey (Num. 22:21–39) has been interpreted as showing that animals can be smarter, or more spiritually aware, than people (Rashi).* Balaam's violent response to his donkey's speaking up helped justify *Tza'ar Ba'alei Chayyim*, the commandment to be mindful of the suffering of all living beings. So did the imperative to send away mother birds before taking their young (Deut. 22:9).

—*That some Jewish texts have long stated, or implied, that animals other than humans have some level of what in English is called "soul," and that Jewish references to a "life force" existing in non-humans often expands our conversations.* Before Pope Francis in 1990 declared that pets can go to Heaven, most Christians believed only humans had souls. The Jewish sense of *nefesh* goes beyond pets. But while *nefesh*, *ruach*, and *neshama* are mentioned, we do not go into much depth about their various meanings.

—*While non-Jews almost always know the word "kosher," very few are aware of the ancient concern for animal suffering that underlies much halakhah concerning what and how we eat.* The contemporary "eco-kosher" movement

---

[15] Quoted in Lewis Regenstein, "Commandments of Compassion: Jewish Teachings on Protecting Animals and Nature," The Humane Society of the United States (2008), 4.
[16] Ibid.
[17] See Shamayim: Jewish Animal Advocacy, www.shamayim.us/.
[18] b. *Berakhot* 40a.

with Jews across the spectrum voicing concerns about factory farming is totally new to most. I suggest learning about the transdenominational Jewish Initiative for Animals and other groups basing their position on tradition.[19] Audiences are pleased to learn that while "eco-kashrut" definitely began in more liberal Jewish Reconstructionist and Renewal circles, it now has support from many others on the more traditionalist side of the spectrum, including some Conservative and some Orthodox Jews.

—*The newer Jewish "eco-justice" movement is usually less surprising, given widespread awareness of the Jewish imperative to seek justice in human affairs, such as "Justice, justice you shall pursue" (Deut. 16:20).* However, the newer and enhanced awareness of how environment-related matters often impact human social issues is less familiar.

—*Another sharing about Hebrew that provokes respect is the relationship between Adam's name and adamah (earth).* Our oldest ancestor was described as an "earthling" before being seen as male.

—*Folks are always surprised at the great variety of names and understandings of "God" in Jewish traditions.* That there have been Jewish "panentheists" who sense God both permeating and transcending the universe—and that I usually feel like one—is certainly new to them. Many appreciate hearing of "natural" Jewish names and/or descriptions for the divine including *Tzur* (rock) or *Ruach* (wind).

—*We often brainstorm how different things would be if we really acted from Psalm 24's teaching that the earth belongs to God, not to us.* This can be related to the "theocentric" discussion above.

—*Hearing about the Jewish practice of blessing the Source of Life with gratitude upon seeing large-scale natural wonders (rainbows, rain and dew, mountains, deserts, long rivers, lightning, the sky) and smaller-scale wonders of nature (beautiful animals, trees, people) typically inspires requests for the specific language.* Sometimes I share a handout.

—*Particularly lively conversations arise after folks hear how many nature-awareness connections are built into the Jewish calendar and sense of time.*[20] The list usually includes: the rabbis aligning many holiday observances to coincide with specific seasonal changes; the Hebrew calendar being both lunar and solar; Jews going outside to welcome the moon with *Kiddush Levana*; the Jewish people long identifying with the moon's shrinking but always growing again; *Havdalah* being done after seeing three stars; the many psalmic and other references in prayer services to the Earth being witness

---

[19] JIFA: Jewish Initiative for Animals, https://www.jewishinitiativeforanimals.com.
[20] As a reader-friendly introduction, I often recommend Arthur Waskow's *Seasons of Our Joy: A Modern Guide to the Jewish Holidays* (New York: Summit, 1986).

to the divine and humans singing as part of a larger, joyful "orchestra" of living creatures and elements (and mountains), praising our shared Ultimate Source. Psalm 150—"*Kol ha-neshama tehallel Yah*" ("All that breathes praises God")—is but one example. Whether taken literally, poetically, or metaphorically, these texts demonstrate how Judaism encourages wonder and reinforces sibling-like connectedness with the non-human world. I always share Abraham Joshua Heschel's articulation of this point in *Man is Not Alone*: "The earth is our sister, not our mother."[21]

More General Responses

Hearing that these teachings are ultimately Torah and Tanakh-grounded often leads audiences to inquire about larger, more general Jewish ideas. For example, while "souls" are not restricted to humans, Jews do not require that all species' souls be considered "equal" in order to justify compassionate treatment. In *Genesis Rabbah* 10:7 we learn:

> Our Rabbis said: Even those things which you may regard as completely superfluous to the creation of the world, such as fleas, gnats, and flies, even they too are included in the creation of the world, and the Holy One, blessed be He, carries out His purpose through everything, even through a snake, a scorpion, a gnat, or a frog.

I share how shocked (and dismayed) I was when a student once insisted that if a house was burning, she did not think a human child should necessarily be saved before a pet. She saw this as ecocentrist, wherein all beings are always to be valued ethically as "equal." Jews do vote for saving the child first, albeit with some sadness. It seems natural that as "family" we can identify more with those in our species. With a smile, I often suggest that squirrels are probably more "squirrel-centric," hoping to put their own closer family first. These discussions inevitably lead to more nuanced conversations about when, and to what degree, we should be calling for "equality" in ethics. Different circumstances might yield different answers.

This is one of a few places where conversations turn to the matter of absolutes in ethics, and how Judaism has few "absolutes," being more inclined towards considering specific situations—and towards "both/and" thinking more than "either/or." Many know the Jewish tendency to not be "all-or-nothing" about other ethical issues like abortion and capital pun-

---

[21] Abraham Joshua Heschel, *Man is Not Alone: A Philosophy of Religion* (New York: Farrar, Straus & Young, 1951), 115.

ishment. With this, they often come to better understand its relevancy for environmental thinking.

Responses are predictable. Some see the polyphonic nature of Judaism as only making things more complicated. Some are impressed, finding it more realistic; others are frustrated, calling it "wishy-washiness," a reaction stemming perhaps from their own backgrounds in a more absolutist system. Nevertheless, the canonization of different perspectives, be they different human roles in Genesis 1 and 2 or the acceptance of "two Jews, three opinions," is usually a major takeaway.

We sometimes find ourselves sharing more about the role of "law" and its connection to Jewish ethics and "spirituality." It usually comes as a great surprise to learn that Judaism has what Lewis Regenstein calls "commandments of compassion," and "that Torah and Jewish law teach us to treat animals with kindness and to respect and to protect nature and conserve... are fundamental to Judaism."[22]

Why the surprise? Many non-Jews (and less-informed Jews) think Judaism is overly law-obsessed, and see law as inherently heartless. That "Torah" is often translated only as "law" adds to the problem. Learning that the Hebrew term is also about "instruction" or "teaching," or that God's "law" is often (though not always) about formalizing ethical behavior, and that Jewish practice is in great part about obeying laws in order to help us bring "spirituality" into *this* life by how we live with other humans (or non-humans) always provokes new and engaging conversations.

All are familiar with the Star of David, so I share my favorite teaching about it: one triangle points up to our sense of the divine and our "higher spiritual values." The other triangle points down, to *this* world, how we walk and talk and act. The Jewish punchline is that the "spiritual" is activated here, not totally separate from life.

Part 3: How Interfaith Conversations Have Impacted Me

Early on, I was surprised at how minimal my non-Jewish audiences' knowledge was about Judaism and Jewish thinking. Soon I came to acknowledge my own misunderstanding, or lack of understanding, about others' traditions. Despite years of teaching comparative religions, my understanding of Christianity and Islam was often too simplistic, academic, or abstract.

Engaging with real individuals with whom I share environmental concerns and extended conversations has yielded understandings, including these:

---

[22] Regenstein, "Commandments of Compassion," 1. Regenstein is president of the Interfaith Council for the Protection of Animals and Nature.

- I now acknowledge far more variety in "Christian" views, expressed through different denominations, communities and individuals.
- How Christians' ever-present awareness of Jesus and the power of "love" permeates Christianity, in general and in particular, plays out in their environmental concerns and self-expectations.
- I always thought that for Christians, only humans have souls. As mentioned, some now see some animals as also having souls. Practical implications of this are probably diverse. I am more curious and open now to learning about Christian-based vegan/vegetarianism and animal rights.
- My audiences' sincere curiosity and the conversations that follow their questions have helped us all gain and/or deepen our understanding of each other's religious perspectives. This impacts how we feel about each other as individuals and our respective traditions, as well as about our shared environmental concerns.
- Some discussions have made me more aware of our differences, not only of our similarities. Most of my interfaith environmental conversations have been with Christians. The issue of "love" is probably the biggest example with them. In discussions with new Muslim friends, I have found that while Judaism and Islam certainly are closer in not deifying Jesus, for instance, we see the relationship between the divine and humans quite differently. When I assert Judaism's strong commitment to being God's partner, and that we do more than pray for a better world but must act to contribute to ensuring that it happens, my Muslim friends mostly disagree—often quite strongly.
- In recent times, the "native vs. invasive" debate has become especially high in my consciousness. Many activists I know, especially from the non-Jewish world, are vehemently anti-invasive species, basing their thoughts on what they believe to be hard science. Now more consciously Jewish, I have seriously changed the *degree* to which I automatically question or oppose "non-native" plants and animals—in part because I have learned the science about the matter is more nuanced, but even more so because I have a more Jewishly inspired, nuanced reflex. I now agree more with Arizona State University ecologist Matt Chew and others that many in the environmental movement who are vehemently against non-natives go too far, are too generic, absolutist, etc.[23] This conversation is

---

[23] Matthew Chew and Scott Carol, "The Invasive Ideology," *The Scientist*, September 7, 2011, https://www.the-scientist.com/news-opinion/opinion-the-invasive-ideology-41967.

somewhat new in environmentalist circles, but my inclination now is to agree more with Chew: "Biologists and conservationists are too eager to demonize non-native species." My eco-Jewish identity reminds me that Jews have long been labeled the "outsider"—the "non-native"—and largely because of that, we have been/are too often simplistically perceived as a threat to the "native" culture.

- This relates to another change of reflex. For several years, I team-taught a mini-class entitled "Bioregionalism and Sense of Place." The class was one of my favorites. We created it because, for many environmentalists, cultivating a deep, long-term commitment to a particular "place" is vital to respecting and protecting that place. This involves knowing the area's particular biotic needs and human history. Staying in place was highly prized. I still deeply value long-term commitment to place and appreciate more how Jews—like other ancient tribes—embrace an ancient commitment to home place (Israel). But the larger Jewish experience also moves me to no longer agreeing that "wandering" peoples, or those who live in places other than their ancient homes, are somehow incapable of respecting the places where they are or through which they travel, and so become more responsible for problems that arise in those places. In short, I now include Jews in diaspora, Roma, immigrants, refugees, and the world's many stateless peoples in all my "sense of place" discussions.

While appreciating other traditions more than I did in the past, I am increasingly more appreciative of how Judaism's dialectical, evolving, and "wrestling" approach to all serious matters, including environmental issues, feels more "natural," more "alive," and more organic to me. For these reasons, Jewish environmental ethics seems more workable. My work in interfaith environmental activist circles has deepened my respect for other religiously motivated communities and reinforced how happy I am to still be growing into an ever more committed eco-Jew.

A Difference of Degree: Toward a Post-Anthropocentric Judaism

Jonathan L. Friedmann

In their 1995 book *When Elephants Weep: The Emotional Lives of Animals*, Jeffrey Moussaieff Masson and Susan McCarthy dared to ask, "If humans are subject to evolution but have feelings that are inexplicable in survival terms, if they are prone to emotions that do not seem to confer any advantages, why should we suppose that animals act on genetic investment alone?"[1] At the time, and for many decades earlier, attempts to attribute human-like qualities to non-human animals were widely regarded as "unscientific." Suggestions of emotional or cognitive continuity between humans and non-humans were dismissed as projections or wishful fantasies. Mainstream science favored a dispassionate behaviorism (ethology), which tested stimuli responses and reduced behaviors to evolutionarily adapted traits. Yet, while it is impossible to enter the subjective experiences and perceptions of another species, should this prevent us from recognizing, appreciating, or gaining some insight into the inner lives of non-human animals?

In their own way, scientific objections to "humanizing" non-human species reinforce age-old assertions of humanity's privileged status as intrinsically unique and superior beings—an ideology known as anthropocentrism. Jewish articulations of this viewpoint are emblematic of other Western systems that elevate humans as "apex beings." As my esteemed colleague Rabbi Elijah Schochet summarizes in his comprehensive study, *Animal Life in Jewish Tradition*:

> The following basic conclusion would seem to be warranted: that the world of fauna, although the authentic handiwork of God, is, in reality, far removed from its Maker's hand or concern. Man, on the other hand, emerges as a distinct entity, far superior to the animal, and standing within a special relationship to his Creator. True, man has specific obligations towards animals; he is not to abuse or mistreat them. But these obligations are relatively few, and they bespeak more accurately the relationship of a master toward his servant, or even an artisan toward his tool, than

---

[1] Jeffrey Moussaieff Masson and Susan McCarthy, *When Elephants Weep: The Emotional Lives of Animals* (New York: Delta, 1995), 15.

that of a living being towards his fellow living being, also fashioned by the hand of God.[2]

In recent years, the scientific community has begun to soften its stance. A growing body of literature, from peer-reviewed articles to popular nonfiction books, is coming to terms with the reality of emotions, intelligence, and individuality in non-human animals. Books in my personal library provide a glimpse into this vibrant and diversifying field: Virginia Morrell's *Animal Wise: The Thoughts and Emotions of Our Fellow Creatures*;[3] Frans de Waal's *Are We Smart Enough to Know How Smart Animals Are?*;[4] David Rothenberg's *Bug Music: How Insects Gave Us Rhythm and Noise*;[5] Peter Wohlleben's *The Inner Life of Animals: Love, Grief, and Compassion—Surprising Observations of a Hidden World*;[6] Jennifer Ackerman's *The Genius of Birds*;[7] Greg Berns' *What It's Like to Be a Dog: And Other Adventures in Animal Neuroscience*;[8] John A. Shivik's *Mousy Cats and Sheepish Coyotes: The Science of Animal Personalities*;[9] Rachel Mundy's *Animal Musicalities: Birds, Beasts, and Evolutionary Listening*.[10] While these studies accept that humans are limited by our own bodies and brains, and thus incapable of escaping an anthropocentric *orientation*, they nevertheless reject the ideology that places humans at the center of the world.

Can Judaism similarly overcome—or strive to overcome—anthropocentrism, or its implicitly "theocentric anthropocentrism,"[11] which envisions a God who favors humanity? Can Jewish practitioners champion human rights without marginalizing or subordinating non-humans? Can the belief

---

[2] Elijah Judah Schochet, *Animal Life in Jewish Tradition: Attitudes and Relationships* (New York: KTAV, 1984), 4.
[3] Virginia Morrell, *Animal Wise: The Thoughts and Emotions of Our Fellow Creatures* (New York: Crown, 2013).
[4] Frans de Waal, *Are We Smart Enough to Know How Smart Animals Are?* (New York: W. W. Norton, 2016).
[5] David Rothenberg, *Bug Music: How Insects Gave Us Rhythm and Noise* (New York: Picador, 2013).
[6] Peter Wohlleben, *The Inner Life of Animals: Love, Grief, and Compassion—Surprising Observations of a Hidden World* (Vancouver: Greystone, 2016).
[7] Jennifer Ackerman, *The Genius of Birds* (New York: Penguin, 2017).
[8] Greg Berns, *What It's Like to Be a Dog: And Other Adventures in Animal Neuroscience* (New York: Basic, 2017).
[9] John A. Shivik, *Mousy Cats and Sheepish Coyotes: The Science of Animal Personalities* (Boston: Beacon, 2017).
[10] Rachel Mundy, *Animal Musicalities: Birds, Beasts, and Evolutionary Listening* (Middletown, CT: Wesleyan University Press, 2018).
[11] Pamela Smith, *What are They Saying about Environmental Ethics?* (New York: Paulist Press, 1997), 80.

in humanity's divinely bestowed uniqueness be preserved, even as we learn that humans and other species have far more in common than biblical or rabbinic texts presumed? Is there room to expand Jewish principles devised as *bein adam l'chavero*—between human beings—to non-humans as well? As Jeremy Benstein, co-founder of the Heschel Center for Sustainability in Tel Aviv, puts it: "Why must our fellows [*chaverim*] be limited to members of our own species?"[12]

For animal rights advocates, such reevaluations do not mean that all species are equal in status or performance. Each creature—big, small, and in between—excels and falls short in different capacities and according to different standards. What is argued is that all animals should have an equal right to their own autonomous existence; their basic interests should be afforded the same consideration as like interests of human beings.

Admittedly, my embrace of this outlook owes more to my secular-scientific disposition than to my Jewish identity. I have no problem setting aside the biblical creation myth in Genesis 1—arguably the West's most influential statement of human superiority—and replacing it with an evolutionary model, which requires no divine originator or intervener and views anatomically modern humans as one result of a bottom-up process that has produced the diversity of life on Earth. What makes human beings distinct is the gradual emergence of a particular mixture of physical and cognitive traits, none of which are unique in and of themselves. From this de-mythologized and de-supernaturalized vantage point, even the second creation myth in Genesis 2, which suggests a gentler anthropocentrism through Adam and Eve's tilling of the Garden of Eden and ostensible vegetarianism (Gen. 2:15-16), is problematic since it positions humanity as alpha caretakers—or *tamers*—of the world.

In considering humanity's status *vis-à-vis* other animals, I apply a teaching of Rabbi Sherwin Wine, founder of Humanistic Judaism: It is more important for something to be true than for it to be Jewish.[13] If the extreme gap between humans and other animal species cannot be empirically sustained, then why must we continue enforcing it—regardless of its centrality to Judaism's conception of humanity's place in the world? Yet, while I lead a Humanistic Jewish community indebted to Rabbi Wine's ideas and agree with the core tenets of that movement, I realize that humanism is itself an anthropocentric worldview (as the term implies).[14]

---

[12] Jeremy Benstein, *The Way into Judaism and the Environment* (Woodstock, VT: Jewish Lights, 2006), 107.
[13] Sherwin T. Wine, *Judaism Beyond God* (New York: KTAV, 1995), 133.
[14] See Robert Renehan, "The Greek Anthropocentric View of Man," *Harvard Studies in*

Is "human chauvinism,"[15] as animal ethicist Mary Midgley dubbed it, an inevitable outcome? The short answer is no. When we look at Jainism, an Indian religion that emerged around the time Genesis 1 was being composed (sixth century BCE),[16] we find an articulation of *ahimsa* (nonviolence) that not only counters the decree to "rule the fish of the sea, the birds of the sky, and all the living things that creep on earth" (Gen. 1:28), but also closely resembles contemporary post-humanist and animal liberationist stances: "Nothing which breathes, which exists, which lives, or which has essence or potential of life, should be destroyed or ruled over, or subjugated, or harmed, or denied of its essence or potential."[17]

Some see faint echoes of this view in Hasidic panentheism, which maintains that the divine presence (*Shekhinah*) permeates all things—inanimate objects, plants, non-human animals, and humans—and thus imbues the physical world with holiness. But this holiness is God's, not innate to the object or living things. Furthermore, Hasidic teachings often use non-human animals as metaphors for lower levels of physicality, with the "animal soul" expressing itself in lust and excessive consumption.[18] It is also believed that the souls of wicked people transmigrate into "lower" species after death, "until such time as they become purified of their sins and then begin their ascent to a human level."[19] In contrast to Jainism and some forms of Buddhism and Hinduism, the Hasidic concept of reincarnation did not lead to vegetarianism or veganism, but actually *encouraged* meat consumption: if a person's soul inhabits the body of a kosher animal, then ritual slaughter, requisite blessings, and pious eating would release the soul to a human embodiment.[20]

What should we make of all of this? As noted, my personal views as a non-*halakhically* observant Jew are not dependent on, or even challenged by, Jewish texts or practices. However, there are a number of observant leaders and organizations who "mine the margins"[21] of Jewish texts with the

---

Classical Philology 85 (1981): 239-259.
[15] See Mary Midgley, "On Being an Anthrozoon," *Minding Nature* 5:2 (2012): 11-16.
[16] Zhenshuai Jiang, *Critical Spatiality in Genesis 1–11* (Tübingen: Mohr Siebeck, 2018), 73.
[17] Acharanga Sutra, quoted in Michael Charles Tobias and Jane Gray Morrison, *Anthrozoology: Embracing Co-Existence in the Anthropocene* (Cham, Switzerland: Springer International, 2017), 226.
[18] See Manfred Gerstenfeld and Netanel Lederberg, "Nature and the Environment in Hasidic Sources," *Jewish Environmental Perspectives* 5 (2002), https://www.jcpa.org/art/jep5.htm.
[19] Schochet, *Animal Life in Jewish Tradition*, 238.
[20] Gershon David Hundert, *Jews in Poland-Lithuania in the Eighteenth Century: A Genealogy of Modernity* (Berkeley: University of California Press, 2004), 199.
[21] Brianne Donaldson, "From Ancient Vegetarianism to Contemporary Advocacy: When Religious Folks Decide that Animals are No Longer Edible," *Religious Studies and Theology*

purpose of grounding veganism and animal rights in a *halakhic* framework. They seek to align existing commandments, such as *tza'ar ba'alei chayyim* (suffering of living beings), with values-based food choices, arguing that factory farming—the source of ninety-nine percent of meat consumed in the U.S.—is inherently cruel, thus making animals and animal products, kosher or otherwise, "no longer edible."[22] Their advocacy goes beyond the letter of the commandment against animal cruelty, which does not value the animal's life *per se*, but is primarily concerned that acts of cruelty will tarnish the soul of person committing them. Moreover, classical notions of *tza'ar ba'alei chayyim* only apply to domesticated animals (not wild animals), can be loosened if the cruel act economically benefits humans, and do not include killing animals for food as a form of harm.[23] Even Rav Kook, considered a champion of Jewish vegetarianism, saw plant-based diets as a *future* ideal—a "return to Eden" after all problems of human welfare are resolved. Kook worried that if taking the life of a non-human animal were deemed abhorrent in the same way as killing a person, then the value of human life would be debased.[24]

For these and other reasons, some question whether vegetarianism/veganism is authentically supported in Jewish texts, particularly as the laws of *kashrut* ostensibly promote the selective and "sanctified" eating of meat;[25] but organizations like Jewish Veg, Shamayim: Jewish Animal Advocacy, and JIFA: Jewish Institute for Animals are making a strong case. Academic scholars of rabbinics, such as Beth A. Berkowitz and Mira Beth Wasserman, are re-reading Jewish texts through the lens of animal studies and critical theory, deriving new insights on the value of non-human lives in Jewish thought.[26] David M. Seidenberg has proposed a *kabbalistically* informed

---

35:2 (2016): 38.
[22] Ibid., 43. See Aaron S. Gross, "When Kosher Isn't Kosher," *Tikkun* 20:2 (2005): 52-55.
[23] For a discussion of *tza'ar ba'alei chayyim* and its limitations, see J. David Bleich, "Judaism and Animal Experimentation," in *Judaism and Environmental Ethics: A Reader*, ed. Martin D. Jaffe (Lanham, MD: Lexington, 2001), 333-370.
[24] *Ha-Peles*, 658; *Mishnat ha-Rav*, 212. J. David Bleich, "Vegetarianism and Judaism," in *Judaism and Environmental Ethics: A Reader*, ed. Martin D. Jaffe (Lanham, MD: Lexington, 2001), 376.
[25] Schochet, *Animal Life in Jewish Tradition*, 288-298.
[26] Beth A. Berkowitz, *Animals and Animality in the Babylonian Talmud* (New York: Cambridge University Press, 2018), and Mira Beth Wasserman, *Jews, Gentiles, and Other Animals: The Talmud After the Humanities* (Philadelphia: University of Pennsylvania Press, 2018). See also Jacob Ari Labendz and Shmuly Yanklewitz, ed., *Jewish Veganism and Vegetarianism: Studies and New Directions* (New York: SUNY Press, 2019); Andrea Dara Cooper, "Writing Humanimals: Critical Animal Studies and Jewish Studies," *Religion Compass* 13 (2019): 1-11; Richard A. Schwartz, *Vegan Revolution: Saving Our World, Revitalizing Judaism* (New York:

theology that recognizes "God's image in the more-than-human world."[27] Like these efforts, I do not see inherent contradictions between Judaism and animal rights, but rather opportunities to widen the application of Jewish ethical principles to non-human species. This chapter proposes a shift away from "toxic anthropocentricism"[28] by applying two guiding Jewish principles, creation in the image of God and loving your neighbor as yourself, to non-human animals.

B'tzelem Elohim

From a socio-anthropological perspective, the dogma of human supremacy—in both its religious-theistic and scientific-humanistic variations—is a byproduct of our civilizational separation from the natural world. At the risk of oversimplification, and without implying a universal or one-size-fits-all cultural evolutionary trajectory—or ignoring the many indigenous societies that preserve more symbiotic connections with the natural world—it is generally posited that the first milestone on the path of detachment occurred when human beings transitioned from hunter-gatherers to agriculturalists (Neolithic Revolution, c. 10,000 BCE). With this gradual semi-independence from natural forces, humanity slowly shed its sense of kinship with the surrounding environment. In place of animistic spirituality, which imbues plants, animals, inanimate objects, and natural phenomena with spirits and souls, arose an increasingly human-centered worldview. Russian environmentalists Victor I. Danilov-Danil'yan and Igor E. Reyf outline the process in broad terms:

> Thinking himself a special being, chosen among all others, man delayed little in discarding his zoomorphic gods, who had laid down more than a few commandments against the extermination of living nature. In their place came gods that man had made in his own image and likeness. Likewise, nature itself turned from an object of worship for man into his resource storehouse. This rationalized consumer relationship toward the environment was the norm even in the early civilizations of antiquity. The first civilizations,

---

Lantern, 2020); and Phillip Sherman, "The Hebrew Bible and the 'Animal Turn,'" *Currents in Biblical Research* 19:1 (2020): 36-63; among others.
[27] David M. Seidenberg, *Kabbalah and Ecology: God's Image in the More-Than-Human World* (New York: Cambridge University Press, 2015).
[28] Aaron S. Gross, "Reviewed Work: *Kabbalah and Ecology: God's Image in the More-Than-Human World* by Seidenberg," *Journal of Jewish Ethics* 5:2 (2019): 233.

such as those in Mesopotamia and the Mediterranean, all evolved according to a single, repeated scenario...²⁹

One manifestation of humanity's elevation appears in Genesis 1:26: the creation of man and woman *b'tzelem Elohim*—in the image of God. This principle is foundational to Jewish ethics.³⁰ By virtue of being "little less than divine" (Ps. 8:6), all human beings deserve dignified treatment.

Divine images reflected in humans were not unheard of in the ancient Near East. Regional powers, such as Egypt and Babylonia, maintained that their kings were images of gods on earth who were themselves deified. However, the Torah improved on the idea in two significant ways. First, every human being, not just the king, shared equally in the heightened status of *b'tzelem Elohim*. Second, human beings were not themselves gods, but were created in the image and likeness of God—meaning that we are dependent creatures with the *potential* to actualize qualities associated with God.³¹ The dignity implicit in the Torah's formulation serves as the basis for Jewish approaches to interpersonal and social ethics. But what place do non-human animals have in this equation?

According to Maimonides, the image of God is found in humanity's singular consciousness and ability to make moral choices.³² This is a logical location for the incorporeal God's image to reside: instead of a physical or visual image, *tzelem Elohim* exists in the interior uniqueness of each individual. Yet, this perspective assumes a gap wider than science can support. Gone are the days when non-human animals could be dismissed as merely instinct-driven automata. Contrary to Maimonides' medieval assumptions, there is a spectrum of animal consciousness on our planet, including many species that exhibit episodic memory, future planning, and delayed gratification—characteristics once thought to be exclusively human.³³ Complex communication systems, what we call "language," are likewise present in many species.³⁴ Indeed, if we would simply open our ears and minds, we

---

²⁹ Victor I. Danilov-Danil'yan and Igor E. Reyf, *The Biosphere and Civilization: In the Throes of a Global Crisis*, trans. Steven McGrath (Cham, Switzerland: Springer International, 2018), 97.
³⁰ See, for example, Byron Sherwin, *Jewish Ethics for the Twenty-First Century: Living in the Image of God* (Syracuse: Syracuse University Press, 2000).
³¹ See Lawrence Troster, "Created in the Image of God: Humanity and Divinity in an Age of Environmentalism," in *Judaism and Environmental Ethics: A Reader*, ed. Martin D. Jaffe (Lanham, MD: Lexington, 2001), 172-182.
³² *Mishneh Torah, Hilkhot Yesodei ha-Torah*, 4:8-9.
³³ De Waal, *Are We Smart Enough to Know How Smart Animals Are?*, 157, 229.
³⁴ See, for instance, a series of articles on the topic, "What Can Animal Communication Teach Us about Human Language?," in *Philosophical Transactions of the Royal Society B: Biological Sciences* 375:1789 (2020).

would realize that "animals have been on the planet a lot longer than we have, and have had much longer to evolve sophisticated communication techniques."[35]

Moreover, the fundamentals of morality—distinguishing between right and wrong—are evident in all social animals. Mammals, for instance, have social mechanisms to approve/reward pro-social behaviors and discourage/punish anti-social behaviors (actions contrary or antagonistic to sociable practices).[36] Primatologist Frans de Waal's extensive research on empathy, cooperation, and fairness in non-human primates and other social mammals informs his contention that religion plays a "Johnny-come-lately" role in moral development:

> Morality arose first, and modern religion latched onto it. Instead of giving us the moral law, the large religions were invented to bolster it....It is far from my intention to minimize this role which was vital in the past and may remain so in the foreseeable future, but the wellspring of morality it is not.[37]

Other conventional measurements of our uniqueness have also eroded. Many species use tools, including primates, elephants, ants, wasps, certain birds, and some octopi.[38] Cultural transmission is observed in rats, guppies, ants, bumblebees, and other species.[39] Altruism is seen in insect colonies.[40] Koala fingerprints are almost indistinguishable from human fingerprints.[41] The gene largely responsible for human speech (*FOXP2*) is found in great apes and songbirds.[42] Major parts of our genome look and act like those of

---

[35] Tobias Fischer and Lara Cory, *Animal Music: Sound and Sound* (London: Strange Attractor, 2015), 101.

[36] Patricia S. Churchland, *Braintrust: What Neuroscience Tells Us about Morality* (Princeton: Princeton University Press, 2011), 101.

[37] Frans de Waal, *The Bonobo and the Atheist: In Search of Humanism Among the Primates* (New York: W. W. Norton, 2013), 239. See also Frans de Waal and Stephen A. Sherblom, "Bottom-Up Morality: The Basis of Human Morality in Our Primate Nature," *Journal of Moral Education* 47:2 (2018): 248-258.

[38] See Crickette M. Sanz, Josep Call, and Christophe Boesch, ed., *Tool Use in Animals: Cognition and Ecology* (New York: Cambridge University Press, 2013).

[39] See Kevin N. Laland and Bennet G. Galef, ed., *The Question of Animal Culture* (Cambridge, MA: Harvard University Press, 2009).

[40] See Francis L. W. Ratnieks and Heikki Helantera, "The Evolution of Extreme Altruism and Inequality in Insect Societies," *Philosophical Transactions B: Biological Sciences* 364:1533 (2009): 3169-3179.

[41] David J. Linden, *Touch: The Science of Hand, Heart, and Mind* (New York: Penguin, 2016), 38.

[42] D. M. Webb and J. Zhang, "*FoxP2* in Song-Learning Birds and Vocal-Learning Mam-

bacteria and worms.[43] We share 96% of our genes with chimpanzees, 90% with domestic cats, 85% with mice, 80% with cows, 61% with fruit flies, 60% with chickens, and even 60% with bananas.[44]

To reiterate, none of this diminishes the value of human life or places humans and non-human animals on a level plane. That would not only inaccurately downgrade human beings, but also inappropriately imply that every other animal is the same. With a difference of degree and not of kind as our guiding Darwinian truism,[45] we can begin to see an image of ourselves in other animals and their images in us. And if ours is the image of God, then some of that sanctity should naturally flow to non-human animals as well.

V'ahavta L'reakha Kamokha

Love one's neighbor as oneself—*v'ahavta l'reakha kamokha* (Lev. 19:18)—is another cornerstone of Jewish ethics. Initially, the biblical rule only applied to literal neighbors: Israelites and foreigners living in their midst. The intent was to promote social cohesion: treat other Israelites as you wish to be treated, and treat resident aliens as native-born Israelites. In time, the principle was widened to include all people, and, like *b'tzelem Elohim*, became a reminder of our common humanity.[46] As inclusive as this ideal has come to be, it still operates within an anthropocentric paradigm. If the expansion had continued from Israelite neighbors to all of humanity to non-humans, we would have arrived at the Jain formulation of the "golden rule:" "Just as sorrow or pain is not desirable to you, so it is to all which breathe, exist, live, or have any essence of life. To you and all, it is undesirable, and painful, and repugnant."[47]

There are inconsistencies among Jews who oppose racism, misogyny, ableism, homophobia, transphobia, xenophobia, and other forms of human-directed prejudice—citing a history of oppression and religious precepts affirming the "sanctity of (human) life"—but "do not extend this

---

mals," *Journal of Heredity* 96:3 (2005): 212-216.

[43] Neil Shubin, *Your Inner Fish: A Journey into the 3.5-Billion-Year History of the Human Body* (New York: Vintage, 2009).

[44] Lydia Ramsey Pflanzer and Samantha Lee, "Our DNA is 99.9% the Same as the Person Next to Us—and We're Surprisingly Similar to a Lot of Other Living Things," *Business Insider*, April 3, 2018.

[45] Charles Darwin, *The Descent of Man, and Selection in Relation to Sex* (New York: D. Appleton, 1871), 101.

[46] See John J. Collins, "Love Your Neighbor: How It Became the Golden Rule," *TheTorah.com*, April 27, 2020, https://www.thetorah.com/article/love-your-neighbor-how-it-became-the-golden-rule.

[47] Acharanga Sutra, quoted in Tobias and Morrison, *Anthrozoology: Embracing Co-Existence in the Anthropocene*, 226.

ethical outlook of equality to animals."[48] To paraphrase social psychologist Melanie Joy, our culture—both Jewish and Western writ large—encourages us to eat and wear certain animals and love certain others (e.g., pets and a few wild species, such as pandas and dolphins). This type of prejudice is called speciesism, or the "unjustified disadvantageous consideration or treatment of those who are not classified as belonging to one or more [privileged] species."[49] Why is it, for instance, that we instinctively rephrase the rabbinic adage that sustaining the soul of a single *Jew* is tantamount to sustaining an entire world to "Saving one *person* is like saving an entire world,"[50] but rarely, if ever, look beyond the human? Perhaps "all dogs go to heaven," but what happens to the millions of other species?

Enlarging *v'ahavta l'reakha kamokha* to non-humans might seem like a stretch, especially given the scripturally based and socially enforced chasm between us. However, it is instructive to recall that the Bible abounds with negative and unflattering depictions of dogs as noisy (Ps. 59:7), greedy (Isa. 56:11), filthy (Prov. 26:11), stupid (Isa. 56:10), and more—traits repeated though rabbinic law and lore.[51] Yet dogs are the most popular family pets in the U.S., including in Jewish households, and "*bark mitzvah*" celebrations, commemorating a dog's coming of age, have been celebrated since 1958.[52] If some small shred of "personhood" were similarly granted to cows, chickens, fish, and other culturally determined "edible animals," would it mean the end of carnism: the invisible belief system that conditions us to eat certain animals, not because we need to in order to survive, but because we choose to—typically unthinkingly?[53]

Of course, we cannot be expected to adore all creatures in the same way as we do our domestic companions, whom we think of as family members. But neither can we realistically give all people the same affection as we do our loved ones. At the root of the biblical law is *practice*, not feelings. As one scholar notes, the message is to treat others "in the manner you might

---

[48] Ze'ev Levy, "Ethical Issues of Animal Welfare in Jewish Thought," in *Judaism and Environmental Ethics: A Reader*, ed. Martin D. Jaffe (Lanham, MD: Lexington, 2001), 323.
[49] Oscar Horta, "What is Speciesism?," *Journal of Agriculture and Environment* 23 (2010): 244.
[50] This common rewording of m. *Sanhedrin* 4:5 appears in Ronald H. Isaacs, *Sidrah Reflections: A Guide to Sidrot and Haftarot* (New York: KTAV, 1997), 154.
[51] Schochet, *Animal Life in Jewish Tradition*, 37-38; Natan Slifkin, *Man & Beast: Our Relationship with Animals in Jewish Law and Thought* (New York: Yashar, 2006), 211-228.
[52] Chanel Dubofsky, "Beverly Hills: Home of the Bark Mitzvah since 1958," *Jewish Telegraph Agency*, January 21, 2016.
[53] See Melanie Joy, *Why We Love Dogs, Eat Pigs, and Wear Cows: An Introduction to Carnism* (Newbury Point, MA: Red Wheel, 2020).

treat someone whom you *do* love."[54] Following Benstein's challenge to view all species as *chaverim* (fellows), might we also treat them with the dignity and fairness we wish for ourselves?

Another way to understand the imperative to "love" others is to avoid causing them harm, as in Hillel's rewording: "That which is hateful to you, do not do to your fellow."[55] The general exclusion of non-human species from this moral obligation stems from a Cartesian-esque assessment of non-human animals as little more than stimulus-response machines equipped with useful instincts.[56] Yet, there are inconsistencies here as well. While few are willing to see their pet cat or parakeet as a personality-less "thing," why do we so callously "de-humanize" those mammals and birds whose sole use to us is as food and/or repurposed body parts? The question, as they say, is also the answer. It is a testament to humanity's basic decency that we would rather otherize the source of animal products than deal with the unpleasantness of reflecting on where these products come from or the horrendous processes that give them to us. But there is nothing ethical about willful denial.

Nineteenth-century philosopher Jeremy Bentham was perhaps the first Western philosopher to propose that non-human animals deserve equal moral consideration.[57] However, despite his defense of animal welfare, he condoned the killing and using of animals, so long as needless cruelty could be avoided. In this regard, his position mirrored that of the rabbis. More than a century later, Peter Singer's *Animal Liberation* took a similarly utilitarian view of "lower animals," asserting that only non-human animals that closely correspond to humans (namely mammals) should be given equal moral consideration.[58] The problem is that the more we understand about other animals, the more "human-like" they become. For instance, crows, ravens, and other corvids possess a type and level of intelligence once believed reserved for humans and a few other "higher mammals."[59] Research into cow psychology reveals complex cognitive, emotional, and social characteristics,

---

[54] Collins, "Love Your Neighbor;" emphasis mine. See Jon D. Levenson, *The Love of God: Divine Gift, Human Gratitude, and Mutual Faithfulness in Judaism* (Princeton, NJ: Princeton University Press, 2016), 1-58.
[55] B. *Sanhedrin* 31a.
[56] de Waal, *Are We Smart Enough to Know How Smart Animals Are?*, 4-5.
[57] Johannes Kniess, "Bentham on Animal Welfare," *British Journal for the History of Philosophy* 27:3 (2019): 556-572.
[58] Peter Singer, *Animal Liberation* (New York: Avon, 1975).
[59] See John Marzluff and Tony Angell, *Gifts of the Crow: How Perception, Emotion, and Thought Allow Smart Birds to Behave Like Humans* (New York: Simon and Schuster, 2012).

as well as individual personalities.[60] Fish, it turns out, do feel pain.[61]

None of this should be surprising. The sorts of animals we can confidently "otherize" diminishes daily, and may someday be none. What has changed is not the species themselves—most of which have been around much longer than us—but rather our scientific tools and willingness to bypass inherited assumptions. As such, our default relationship with other beings should be one of humility, respect, compassion, and non-violence. We are neighbors sharing an image.

Conclusion

This reappraisal is not revolutionary. It follows the view that Judaism, in all its kaleidoscopic forms, is not a fixed set of answers to closed questions, but "an ongoing dialogue in which the questions arise, along with various answers from different times and places, and even more generally, a language in which to engage in the dialogue and formulate the questions in the first place."[62] A pressing question for today, which our ancestors rarely asked and could not adequately answer, is whether anthropocentrism is an ethically justified position—let alone an ecologically sustainable one.

Jewish textual interpretation is devoted to "making texts mean what they did not seem to mean."[63] Understanding potential dangers of the biblical mandate to rule over other animals (Gen. 1:28), most commentators through the ages veered away from the surface implications. More common is a stewardship model—akin to Spider-Man's charge, "With great power comes great responsibility"—with some, including Rashi, warning that if we fail in this task, then other species will rule over us.[64] This line of interpretation is particularly important, as even the most traditionalist sources admit that the Genesis story is not a chronicle of history, but "the charter of Man's mission in the universe."[65]

What should our mission be as it pertains to non-humans? While stewardship is clearly preferable to unimpeded dominionism, it remains anthropocentric, imploring humans to behave as benevolent overlords. A

---

[60] Lori Marino and Kristin Allen, "The Psychology of Cows," *Animal Behavior and Cognition* 4:4 (2017): 474-498.
[61] Ferris Jabr, "It's Official: Fish Feel Pain," *Smithsonian Magazine*, January 2018.
[62] Benstein, *The Way into Judaism and the Environment*, 6.
[63] Wine, *Judaism Beyond God*, 20.
[64] Rashi on Genesis 1:26. Yonatan Neril and Leo Dee, *Eco Bible, Volume 1: An Ecological Commentary on Genesis and Exodus* (Jerusalem: Interfaith Center for Sustainable Development, 2020), 7-8.
[65] Menachem Davis, *Interlinear Chumash, vol. 1: Bereishit* (New York: Artscroll/Mesorah, 2006), 2.

perspective that fully embraces humanity's close kinship with other species would go several steps further. Can Judaism adopt this enlightened, post-anthropocentric perspective, or will we continue to repeat the patterns of the past?

Nina Perlmutter responds

Cantor Dr. Jonathan Friedmann's detailed, well-articulated essay touched and stretched me on many levels. My responses come from multiple spaces: as an environmentally concerned human; as a vegetarian Jew committed to applying Jewish teachings about respecting animals and the larger environment; as a public speaker for broad Jewish and interfaith audiences. For his clear presentation of topics about which we agree and differ, and for lingering thought-provoking challenges he poses, I am most grateful.

We agree most strongly on: the importance of challenging both scientific and religious sources long cited to defend extreme anthropocentricism; acknowledging Jewish texts and commentators sometimes contribute to the problem; and the need to promote rational, workable, kinder alternatives to anthropocentric thinking and action.

Our analyses, emphases and responses sometimes differ in degree, sometimes more in substance. Examples:

Friedman seems wary of all forms of anthropocentrism. My reflexes most seriously worry about extreme versions. I find it most feasible to suggest limiting human-centrism by setting us within a larger context. Both his scientific and my theocentric options do this. Interestingly, my sense and application of theocentrism was meant as an *alternative* to anthropocentrism. In contrast, he keeps them together as "theocentric anthropocentrism." I have been contemplating both more, and wondering if Judaism might include both.

He accents the very troubling dimensions of Jewish history, culture, and texts regarding animals, which I cannot deny. But I suggest other sources more supportive of our shared task have long existed, albeit unknown to many American Jews. My first step towards understanding that "dominion" in Genesis 1 is not what it initially appears to mean, and that Judaism has, since pre-urban times, embraced a nature-respecting, nature-aware ethic consistent with our shared vision, came by reading Aloys Huttermann's *The Ecological Message of the Torah*.[1] That history opened me to a very different understanding of Jewish history and texts. Space does not permit expansion here.

Cantor Friedmann's most provocative argument also has me pondering how no culture lives up to its highest ideals. While living in Japan I was horrified watching people eat *living* animals (prohibited in Judaism). Unlike Jains, who do their best regarding animals, not all Buddhists or Hindus are vegetarian. I deeply believe Judaism provides teachings and *mitzvot* for

---

[1] Aloys Huttermann, *The Ecological Message of the Torah: Knowledge, Concepts, and Laws Which Made Survival in a Land of "Milk and Honey" Possible* (Atlanta: Scholars Press, 1999).

ethical engagement with animals. Friedmann appropriately reminds me how many Jews (including both of us) never learned about them, and that those who did do not always live accordingly. This is also true in other cultures.

Friedmann seems to oppose humans ever considering their own species first. I accept their sometimes doing so, but only if others' interests are also made part of decision-making. Thinking of one's own species or family seems natural to me, and I joke about squirrels being squirrel-centric. While preferring theocentrism, I think a "post-*self-only* anthropocentrism" would be an improvement!

Key Lessons

Friedmann's thorough explanation of science taking us beyond anthropocentrism gives me new subjects to think and speak about. As a non-humanist rabbi, I usually emphasize Jewish spiritual teachings. My interfaith audiences often have never heard of "humanist" or "secular" Jews. Some secularists are skeptical—even dismissive—of religious perspectives or language, i.e., "theocentrism." Cantor Friedmann motivates me to include more science talk and references to secular, humanist Jewish thinking.

Because our differing positions are all grounded in Jewish texts, our engagement perfectly illustrates how "wrestling" and "partnering" and "two Jews, three opinions" plays out in the Jewish search for higher understanding (what some call "arguments for the sake of heaven"). Sometimes my students and audiences express confusion (or laugh) about these attitudes. I expect to use our interaction to illustrate the real-world relevance of this Jewish approach.

While acknowledging downsides of Judaism's human-elevating thought, I find it important to share that this *also* has yielded a major positive that many traditions minimize: the widely embraced Jewish commitment to social justice and improving human life. Still, it must be expanded.

Two Questions

Does Friedmann see a science-based "evolving" relationship between humans and the *more*-than-animal world? Extreme anthropocentrism takes a disastrous toll far beyond animals, and I wonder how his scientific call for "post-anthropocentricism" applies to trees, land, water, climate, etc.

More personally, how might his science explain my becoming a vegetarian? My choice was based *neither* on Judaism *nor* the science he describes, but rather on a personal, emotional, spiritual resonance and identification with non-humans large and small, domestic and wild, and seeing each one as a unique individual.

Conclusion

Still pondering much Cantor Friedmann so effectively offers, I am sincerely grateful to be talking and walking with him on the path towards expanding kindness-beyond-humans. While agreeing more on the problem than on approaches for solving it, our essays taken together can hopefully inspire thought and action.

Jonathan L. Friedmann responds

Rabbi Nina Perlmutter opens her astute essay by noting the pervasive misconception that Jewish texts have little or nothing to contribute on ecological issues. Like her, I was ignorant about such teachings before I actively sought them out. During my graduate studies in comparative religion, I was asked by a professor to give a "Jewish take" on the environmental crisis. My mind drew a blank. Years later, when seeking to understand why my Jewish upbringing lacked this crucial piece, I came across an explanatory passage from Rabbi Sherwin Wine's book, *Judaism Beyond God*:

> [T]he Jewish personality, with all its verbal pushy edges, is not a product of peasant lovers of the Torah. It is an urban product, finely tuned to city life and city anxiety....If most Jews adapt easily to the demand and requirements of modern urban living (and are successful out of all proportion to their numbers), it is not the result of their verbal skill in medieval Talmudic argument. Rather, Polish *pilpul* [Talmudic verbal games] was the direct result of an urbanized culture that placed great emphasis on talking and verbal exhibitionism. City communities value verbal skills even more than physical prowess.[1]

In other words, Jewish culture—or at least the Jewish culture that I and most other Jews inhabit—is city-based. As such, ecological awareness largely remains on the margins of Jewish texts or, at best, hiding in plain sight. Affirming these historical circumstances, Steven Schwarzschild, a rabbi-philosopher who escaped Berlin with his family in 1939, proudly called himself an "unnatural Jew" (i.e., a "city Jew"): "Well before the rise of towns and cities, Jews were not supposed to reside where there are no synagogues,

---

[1] Sherwin T. Wine, *Judaism Beyond God* (New York: KTAV, 1995), 113.

physicians, artisans, toilets, water supplies, schoolteachers, scribes, organized charities, or courts."[2]

Yet, as Rabbi Perlmutter rightly asserts, this nature-ambivalent (or nature-averse) Jewish framework—however mainstream it was and still continues to be—is no longer tenable. Humanity's relationship with the natural world is clearly out of balance, as cascading climate catastrophes and the global pandemic remind us. Being able to confront this reality Jewishly, and to engage non-Jews in constructive ecological dialogue, should be a defining feature of Judaism in the twenty-first century. Rabbi Perlmutter is among those leading the charge.

One way her chapter has expanded my own thinking is in its treatment of the "nature vs. invasive" debate. I admit to being among those she describes as "vehemently anti-invasive species," feeling that ecosystems—and especially fragile ones like deserts, wetlands, rain forests, and coastal regions—need all the help they can get to avoid collapse or even extinction. Non-invasion seems to be key to this preservation. However, as Perlmutter states, the degree to which a "purity" approach is possible, sustainable, or even necessary is hotly debated. Throwing humans into the mix further complicates the issue, as opposition to non-native species can easily be conflated with human populations that so-called "natives" view as "invaders:" immigrants, migrants, and minorities whom the dominant group (real or imagined) considers a threat (real or imagined) to the mainstream culture (real or imagined). Because human perspectives are unavoidably human-focused, how we frame our discourse and the rhetoric we use, even when discussing seemingly unrelated topics, can unfortunately be misconstrued or even weaponized. I am grateful to Rabbi Perlmutter for this *chidush* (novel insight).

My views differ from hers on another debate: anthropocentrism vs. theocentrism. While I agree that any shift in thought and action away from excessive anthropocentrism is invariably better for the environment, I am not convinced that Jewish theocentrism, as historically conceived, pushes us far enough. Jewish religious thought is imbued with a theocentric anthropocentrism, wherein humanity is divinely elevated above all other creatures and thus retains its centrality in the world. On its face, there is not much difference between this view and pure anthropocentrism; both place human beings at the apex of creation and are susceptible to the same abuses. Nevertheless, as noted, it is impossible to divorce ourselves completely from a human-centered perspective. Theologies, themselves human constructs,

---

[2] Steven S. Schwarzschild, "The Unnatural Jew," in *Judaism and Environmental Ethics: A Reader*, ed. Martin D. Jaffe (Lanham, MD: Lexington 2001), 227.

inevitably reflect this. That being said, if humbling ourselves before an ethical God helps curtail our worst inclinations *vis-à-vis* nature, then it is unquestionably a noble path. I would love to see Rabbi Perlmutter articulate a Jewishly authentic, textually grounded, environmentally conscious theocentrism that does just that. I know she is more than capable of doing so.

Set Five

The Ethical and Religious Duty for Jewish Clergy: Speak Out, Warn, and Take Action Against All Injustice and Threats to Inclusive American Democracy

Stan Levy

White-Designated Jews Are Obligated to Fight White Supremacy

Robin Podolsky

The Ethical and Religious Duty for Jewish Clergy: Speak Out, Warn, and Take Action Against All Injustice and Threats to Inclusive American Democracy

Stan Levy

Dedicated to the seventeen rabbis who wrote a letter from jail in St. Augustine, Florida, titled "Why We Went," on June 19, 1964 (the ninety-ninth anniversary of the original Juneteenth in Texas in 1865). They were arrested for "assembling in an integrated group as a protest against racial segregation, discrimination, and violence." In their letter from jail, they acknowledged: "the victims of the Holocaust, the millions of faceless people who stood by quietly, watching the smoke rise from Hitler's crematoria, the people with whom we drove, prayed, marched, slept, ate, demonstrated and were arrested." The rabbis had gone to St. Augustine at the request of Rev. Dr. Martin Luther King, Jr.

****

"Do not stand by [in silence] when your neighbors' lives are in danger." – Leviticus 19:16

"In the times and places where no one stands up, you must be the person who stands up." – Pirkei Avot 2:6

"The ultimate measure of a man is not where he stands in moments of comfort and convenience, but where he stands at times of challenge and controversy. The true neighbor will risk his position, his prestige and even his life for the welfare of others." – Rev. Dr. Martin Luther King, Jr., *Strength to Love* (1963)

"In this day and age, said Rabbi Moshe, the greatest devotion—greater than prayer and study—consists in accepting the world exactly as it happens to be." – Hasidic teaching

> *"We must always take sides. Neutrality helps the oppressor, never the victim. Silence encourages the tormentor, not the tormented."*
> – Elie Wiesel, Nobel Prize acceptance speech (1986)

****

My Young Adult Jewish Learning—
The Texts of Judaism and the Texts of Our Lives

When I was a student in Hebrew/religious school, our Hasidic teacher taught us that every name of a person in the Hebrew Bible is actually a dimension of our own personality, every location is a place in our own life, and each person is a symbol and expression of God's presence in our world (Gen. 1:22) and is inherently sacred and precious (Lev. 19:2). We learned that the Torah is the book of the story of all humanity (Gen. 5:1). Adam, Eve, Cain, Abel, Abraham, Hagar, Moses, Miriam, Aaron, Jethro, Joshua, and Deborah are dimensions of my own personality. Eden, Padam-Aram, Sodom, Egypt/Mitzrayim (stranglehold), the swamp of the Sea of Reeds, the wilderness, and the Promised Land are places and times in my own life. We learned to connect the texts of the Torah and prayer books to the script of our own lives.

I was born on December 12, 1941, the day and year Hitler issued the executive order requiring an official German government plan and implementation for extermination of all Jews living in countries and territories under German control. So, the lenses through which I see the world are the Torah and the Holocaust.

My Adult Jewish Learning—Justly Doing Justice

When I studied Martin Buber and read his *On the Bible*, I learned that *mitzvot* in the Torah are addressed and directed to each of us personally to do them.[1] "Don't you know that I, God, need you? How would you exist if I did not need you? That is the meaning of your life." When I studied with Rabbi Abraham Joshua Heschel and read his book *The Prophets*, I learned the meaning of "Justly each of you shall pursue Justice" (Deut. 16:20), meaning both the result must be just and the means must be just.[2] I learned from Heschel that "an act is unjust not because a law has been broken but because a human being has been hurt." I learned from the teachings of Leo Baeck in his book *This People Israel: The Meaning of Jewish Existence*, which he

---

[1] Martin Buber, *On the Bible: Eighteen Studies* (New York: Schocken, 1982).
[2] Abraham Joshua Heschel, *The Prophets* (New York: Harper and Row, 1962). All translations of the Torah are either from *The Living Torah* by Rabbi Aryeh Kaplan or my own.

secretly wrote as a prisoner in the Terezin concentration camp during the Holocaust, that the laws of the Torah protect the most vulnerable members of society: the poor, the elderly, the orphans, the migrants, and not the rich and powerful.[3]

I learned from my studies that there are more *mitzvot* in the Torah commanding each of us to protect the rights, equal treatment, and feelings of migrants (strangers, the ones who are estranged from society) than any other *mitzvot*. I learned that in addition to the 600,000 Israelite men over the age of 20, plus Israelite women and children, there were about 1,000,000 people of mixed nationalities who escaped Egypt with them (Exod. 12:37–38). As a result, there are *mitzvot* in the Torah directing us "Do not oppress a migrant, we know how it feels to be a migrant, we were migrants in Egypt" (Exod. 23:9). "There shall be the same one law for migrants and those born in the country, for I am God of all of you" (Exod. 24:22). "You shall love the people [emotionally and physically] near you [meaning everyone on this small planet]…and the immigrants as you love yourself" (Lev. 19:18, 34). "This is the *mitzvah* of why each of us was created" (High Holy Day liturgy).

This is expressed by Viktor Frankl in his book *Man's Search for Meaning*, about his experiences in the Terezin concentration camp. "To think of ourselves as those who were being questioned by life—daily and hourly. Our answer must consist, not in talk and meditation, but in right action and in right conduct. Life ultimately means taking the responsibility to find the right answer to its problems and to fulfill the tasks which it constantly sets for each individual."[4]

I learned from the writings of Franz Rosenzweig in his *The Star of Redemption* that God needs human love, which is why God asks us to love God and all people with all our heart, our spirit, and our strength (Deut. 6:5).[5] I learned from Buber and Rosenzweig's dialogue about their translation of the Torah into conversational German how to translate the Torah into conversational everyday English, which speaks directly to us.[6]

I learned how Abraham, Moses, and the Prophets stood up, spoke truth and justice to God and to people in power, and opposed social, political, and economic laws, policies, practices, and customs which were unjust.

Abraham Joshua Heschel became my role model as a rabbi because

---

[3] Leo Baeck, *This People Israel: The Meaning of Jewish Existence* (New York: Holt, Reinhart, Winston, 1965).
[4] Viktor Frankl, *Man's Search for Meaning: An Introduction to Logotherapy* (Boston: Beacon, 1959), 73.
[5] Franz Rosenzweig, *The Star of Redemption* (New York: Holt, Rinehart and Winston, 1971).
[6] Martin Buber and Franz Rosenzweig, *Scripture and Translation*, trans. Lawrence Rosenwald with Everett Fox (Bloomington: Indiana University Press, 1994).

he translated his teachings into action in the world in which he lived. He marched in the Civil Rights Movement with his friend and Bible study partner Rev. Dr. Martin Luther King. Jr., and with Dr. King, he spoke out against the American war in Vietnam as an unjust war.

I learned from Rabbi Harold Schulweis, in his book *Conscience: The Duty to Obey and the Duty to Disobey*, that what happened in Germany during the Holocaust could happen under the banner of peace and democracy in America today, unless we speak out for truth and justice.[7] I learned from the writings of Elie Wiesel that we must transform historic events into acts of conscience, and that we humans are co-responsible to bring justice and redeem the world, because we are running out of time.[8]

I learned from Rabbi Donniel Hartman in his book *Putting God Second: How to Save Religion from Itself*, that "justly pursing justice" (Deut. 16:20) is the most important *mitzvah* in Judaism, along with "Doing what is right and doing what is good" (Deut. 6:18).[9] As Abraham forcefully challenged God over the fate of the people of Sodom (a separate tribe from Abraham's), "Will You actually wipe out the innocent along with the guilty? Shall not the judge of the whole world do justly?" (Gen.18.23–25), it is our responsibility and duty as descendants of Abraham to forcefully speak out against any form of injustice or discrimination, prejudice or bias now. Since the "sin" of Sodom was to outlaw poverty and make it a crime punishable by death to anyone who helped a poor person, the Torah has a *mitzvah* to care for poor people: "When in your communities…people are poor, be generous and provide them with the care they need" (Deut. 15:7-8). This is an extension of "Do not stand by [silently] when your neighbors' lives [be they immigrants or citizens] are in danger" (Lev. 19:16).

I learned from the Holocaust scholar, Yehuda Bauer, that three commandments need to be added to the initial ten: "Thou shall not be a perpetrator; thou shall not be a victim; and thou shall never but never be a bystander."[10]

Tzedakah is Economic Justice

Just as I learned in Hebrew/religious school that the word *tzedek* means social, civil, political, and interpersonal justice, *tzedakah* does not mean

---

[7] Harold Schulweis, *Conscience: The Duty to Obey and the Duty to Disobey* (Woodstock, VT: Jewish Lights, 2010).
[8] Elie Wiesel, *The Trial of God* (New York: Schocken, 1995).
[9] Donniel Hartman, *Putting God Second: How to Save Religion from Itself* (Boston: Beacon, 2016).
[10] Yehuda Baer, quoted in Jason Skog, *The Legacy of the Holocaust* (Mankato, MN: Compass Point, 2011), 57.

charity. *Tzedakah* means economic justice that each of us is personally obligated to perform.

Rev. Dr. Martin Luther King, Jr. recognized how essential economic justice is with his March on Washington for Jobs and Freedom on August 28, 1963, and his March for Justice and Jobs in Memphis, Tennessee on March 22, 1968, in solidarity with the sanitation workers strike. (Days later, on April 4, 1968, Rev. King was assassinated in Memphis.)

For Maimonides, the highest form of *tzedakah*/economic justice is to financially sustain a person *before* they become impoverished, by providing them with a substantial enough sum to enable them to have a living wage as a worker, or to open a business so that they become economically self-sufficient and independent.[11]

The Torah has a number of *mitzvot* which direct us to personally and collectively provide this economic justice/*tzedakah*. "When you lend money to My people, poor people among you, do not press them for repayment, nor charge them interest" (Exod. 22:24). "If you take your neighbor's garment [or other property] as security for a loan, you must return the security to them before sunset. With what [or where] shall they sleep?" (Exod. 22:25–26). "When you make any kind of loan to your neighbor, do not go into their house [or take their house] for security. If the person is poor you may not go to sleep holding their security, you must return it to them so they may be able to sleep too" (Deut. 24:10–13). "Do not withhold the [living] wages due to poor workers. Give them their [living] wages the day they are due. Since they are poor, their lives depend on it" (Deut. 24:14–15). "When your brothers [and sisters] become impoverished, and lose the ability to support themselves in the community, you must come to their aid. Help them survive whether they are immigrants or citizens. Do not take any advanced or accrued interest from them. And let them live in your neighborhoods" (Lev. 25:35–37). "Every fifty years is a Jubilee year when you shall declare the emancipation of slaves all over the world" (Lev. 25:10).

My Jewish Living

In the 1960s I was the director of youth education (6th-12th grade) at my synagogue, and then director of The Los Angeles Mitzvah Corps (a summer camp program sponsored by the Union of American Hebrew Congregations for kids going into 12th grade). They also worked in civil rights programs in the so-called Los Angeles barrios and ghettos by day and studied *The Prophets* at night. In the late 60s, I founded and became the rabbi of Congregation B'nai Horin – Children of Freedom, a Jewish community/

---

[11] Maimonides, *Mishneh Torah*, Gifts to the Poor 10:7.

congregation (and I still serve there today, now with my co-rabbi Laura Owens). And I taught courses for a number of years at the Community College of Jewish Studies and the University of Judaism (now American Jewish University).

Additionally, I am one of the founders of Jewish Renewal. I served as one of the Jewish ethicists who developed that movement's clergy ethics standards and procedures, and served as a clergy ethics judge on a couple of their most complicated and difficult cases. Along with serving as rabbi of Congregation B'nai Horin, I was also the first rabbi of Congregation Beth Chayim Chadashim, Los Angeles' pioneer LGBTQ+ synagogue; I was among the first rabbis of the residential addiction treatment center, Beit T'Shuvah; and I was a special guest rabbi at Temple Beth Solomon of the Deaf, "speaking" on "The 'sign' language of God," including the rainbow, Shabbat, and the *V'ahavta*.

Also by the late 1960s, I had translated my being a rabbi by praying with my actions, as Heschel had done, integrating my rabbinate with my law career as a civil and human rights attorney. I litigated many voting, civil, and human rights cases in federal and state courts. As a teacher at a major Los Angeles law school, I developed curricula in voting rights, anti-poverty, anti-systemic racism and discrimination, and civil and human rights law.

Growing up on the southwest side of Chicago, and as an undergraduate university student in Los Angeles, I personally experienced antisemitism from white "Christians." When I was rejected from attending Harvard Law School because the "Jewish quota was filled," I learned about institutional antisemitism. But as a civil rights lawyer, I never experienced any personal antisemitism from any of the Black or Hispanic organizations or individuals with whom I worked.

By the early 1970s, I also helped found three major public interest law firms: Western Center on Law and Poverty, Public Counsel, and Bet Tzedek, all of which are still vibrant today, providing free legal services to tens of thousands of poor people in Los Angeles each year.

In 2009, I became the founding national director of Bet Tzedek's Holocaust Survivors Justice Network, which has recovered about 30 million dollars in reparations payments from Germany for thousands of Holocaust survivors in the United States and Canada.

I have presented programs in law schools and to community organizations on *Nuremberg: Its Lesson for Today* and the difference between free speech and hate speech.[12] I have been an attorney on several "friend of

---

[12] *Nuremberg: Its Lesson for Today*, The Schulberg/Waletsky Restoration, Schulberg Productions, 2009, http://www.nurembergfilm.org/.

the court" briefs to the U.S. Supreme Court on Nazi confiscated art cases, which are really about institutional antisemitism.

My Duty to Warn

Under my "duty to warn," I have spoken out on the antisemitism, white nationalism, neo-Nazi Jewish conspiracy lies identical to *Der Stürmer* in Nazi Germany, and threats of totalitarianism and white supremacy in America today. As a lawyer and student of history, I know that the "rule of law" is not enough to protect people from injustice and oppression. Every action by Germany during the Holocaust, including stripping Jews, homosexuals, and Roma of their liberty, property, dignity, and finally annihilating them, was done according to specific German laws which enabled those actions, ordered them, and made them legal. During the Holocaust, Germany was a country where the "rule of law" prevailed. "We can never forget that everything Hitler did in Germany was 'legal,'" wrote Rev. Dr. Martin Luther King, Jr. in his "Letter from a Birmingham Jail" on April 16, 1963. America is also a country where the "rule of law" prevails, but "equal justice under law" does not (yet). Indeed, as James Q. Whitman, professor at Yale Law School, confirms in his book, *Hitler's American Model: The United States and the Making of Nazi Race Law*, the notorious Nazi Germany Nuremberg Race Laws in the 1930s were based on American white supremacy race laws, anti-immigration laws, and anti-miscegenation laws of the same period, thus linking the Holocaust, the worst sins of Germany's past, to slavery and racism, the worst sins of America's past.[13]

Our Duty as Jewish Clergy

Our survival as the human species depends on our speaking out. Therefore, it is our Jewish clergy's "duty to warn" that white nationalists in the U.S. are out to strip Blacks, Hispanics, Asians, indigenous Americans, Jews, and LGBTQ+ people of their dignity, rights, freedoms, justice, and equality; to destroy our democracy and replace it with a tyrannical government to protect white supremacy; and have white supremacists rule our country and, by extension, the world.

The Duty to Not Remain Silent or Ignore the Threat

This duty to warn and not remain silent, and the danger of turning a blind eye, brings to mind a quotation from a Jewish newspaper in Berlin in 1933, which is found in both Jonathan Weisman's *(((Semitism))): Being Jewish in*

---

[13] James Q. Whitman, *Hitler's American Model: The United States and the Making of Nazi Race Law* (Princeton, NJ: Princeton University Press, 2017).

America in the Age of Trump and Timothy Snyder's *On Tyranny*:

> We do not subscribe to the view that Mr. Hitler and his friends, now firmly in possession of the power they have so longed desired, will implement the proposals circulating in [Nazi newspapers]; they will not suddenly deprive German Jews of their constitutional rights, nor enclose them in ghettos, nor subject them to jealous and murderous impulses of the mob. They cannot do this because a number of crucial factors hold powers in check...and they clearly do not want to go down that road. When one acts as a European power, the whole atmosphere tends towards ethical reflection on one's betterself and away from revisiting one's earlier oppositional posture.[14]

Our Duty to Speak Out Against Injustice

I believe rabbis and other Jewish clergy have the religious and ethical obligation and duty to speak out, including from the pulpit, against injustice in any form, whether economic or workers' rights, racial, social, or gender rights, political or voting rights, educational rights, environmental rights, or interpersonal rights—whenever and wherever people, animals, and/or the environment are being unjustly hurt. It is *Tikkun Olam*—repairing a broken world.

Speaking Out on Injustice Internationally—
Injustice by the Israeli Government Against Palestinians

I believe Jewish clergy have an obligation to hold all countries, including the U.S. and Israel, to international standards of human rights and against genocide. And with respect to the government of the State of Israel, to hold the government to the words expressed in the Declaration of the Establishment of the State of Israel, May 14, 1948, specifically as follows:

> The State of Israel will be open for Jewish immigration and for the ingathering of the exiles; it will foster the development of the country for the benefit of all inhabitants; it will be based on freedom, justice and peace as envisaged by the Prophets of Israel; it will ensure complete equality

---

[14] Jonathan Weisman, *(((Semitism))): Being Jewish in America in the Age of Trump* (New York: St. Martin's, 2018), 218; Timothy Snyder, *On Tyranny: Twenty Lessons from the Twentieth Century* (New York: Crown, 2017), 23.

of social and political rights to all its inhabitants irrespective of religion, race or sex; it will guarantee freedom of religion, conscience, language, education and culture; it will safeguard the Holy Places of all religions; and it will be faithful to the principles of the charter of the United Nations. We appeal—in the very midst of the onslaught launched against us now for months—to the Arab inhabitants of the State of Israel, to preserve peace and participate in the upbuilding of the State on the basis of full and equal citizenship and due representation in all its provisional and permanent institutions. We extend our hand to all neighboring states and their people in an offer of peace and good neighborliness and appeal to them to establish bonds of cooperation and mutual help with the sovereign Jewish people settled in its own land. The State of Israel is prepared to do its share in common efforts for the advancement of the entire Middle East.

Our Obligation to Not Just Teach but to Do

I believe that we, as Jewish clergy, have the religious obligation to see and explain Torah through the lens of our communities, cities, states, nation, world, and universe today, not just some ancient yesterday, and to teach what we, as Jewish humans, are religiously obligated to do in our current situations and conditions in our world. It is the *mitzvah* of our creation and lives as human beings: "To love and treat one another fairly, whether they are our neighbors or migrants, as we love and treat ourselves" (Lev. 19:18, 35). As we are taught in the Torah and the Haggadah: "We were Syrian migrants and refugees, and we became slaves in Egypt" (Deut. 26:5). We should know what it feels like to be immigrants and live in slave-like conditions, and "to do what is right and what is good" (Deut. 6:18). "It is not too complicated or complex, it is very close to us, in our actions, our thoughts and heart… to make wise life choices and do them" (Deut. 30:11–19).

I learned to always ask myself the basic questions God is asking all of us at every moment: "Where are you?" (Adam). "What have you done (with your life)?" (Eve). "Are you angry, are you depressed, where is your brother/sister? Aren't you your brother's/sister's safe keeper?" (Cain). "Why are you crying out to me? Tell people to move forward" (Moses). "What are you doing (with your life) here?" (Elijah).

As was made clear in the Holocaust, and stated in the Torah, "Destruction of life is God's children's fault, not God's own, you warped and twisted generation" (Deut. 32:5). God does not intervene in human affairs, but prays to me, you, and all of us, that we will intervene and prevent injustice and suffering. As Erich Fromm teaches us in his book *You Shall Be as God*: Does God intervene in the historical process? No. Humans are left to themselves, and no one can do for them what they are unable to do for and by themselves.[15]

We are the ones (to whom God prays). We will stand up to and speak out and act against injustice, and warn people what the dangers are when we do not. The Holocaust and so many Jewish and human tragedies before and since have taught us that God is not going to intervene and do it for us. We have to intervene and redeem and repair a broken world (*Tikkun Olam*).

God, Humanity, and the Jewish People on Trial

It is not just God who is on trial in our world at this time, it is religion, clergy, and humanity on trial—and we are running out of time. This is not a time for deafening silence and therefore complicity. It is a time to speak out and warn. If we do not, we are betraying our religion, betraying the most important *mitzvot* in the Torah, betraying our own ancestry and history as migrants from Syria and slaves in Egypt. We are betraying our families, our parents and grandparents who were immigrants to America from Russia, Eastern Europe, the Sephardic world, and elsewhere, and we are betraying the victims and survivors of the Holocaust. We are betraying our children and our children's children by not protecting our democracy and fighting for "equal justice under law." And we are betraying God by not fulfilling our responsibility as Jewish clergy to our part of the Covenant.

We are Running Out of Time

To paraphrase the German Lutheran clergyperson Martin Niemoeller's famous teaching about not speaking out and warning about the Holocaust, because he was not Jewish, Catholic, etc., until it was too late:

> As the White Nationalists and neo-Nazis came after the migrants and refugees, the LGBTQ+, the Blacks, Hispanics, Asians, Muslims, and indigenous Americans, under their racist lies, including their replacement theory lies (the same lies used during the Holocaust), I did not speak out and warn, because I was not (identifying with any) of those communities, or I was afraid to offend the government or other Jews. As they are now coming after the Jews, ("Jews

---

[15] Erich Fromm, *You Shall Be as God: A Radical Interpretation of the Old Testament and Its Tradition (New York:* New York, Holt, Rinehart and Winston, 1966).

will not replace us") many of us will continue to remain silent. Some of us will stand up, speak out, protest, and warn. But will it be too late?

The question before each of us today from *Pirkei Avot* is "If not now, when?"[16] As Joan Chittister, OSB, a Benedictine nun writes in her recent book *The Time is Now: A Call to Uncommon Courage*:

> One thing has stood out and convinced me of the certain triumph of the great gamble on equality and justice. Everywhere there are people who…refuse to give up the thought of a better future….They never lose hope that the values they learned in the best of times or the courage it takes to reclaim their world from the worst of times are worth the commitment of their lives….They are the prophets of each era who prod the rest of the world into seeing newly what it means to be fully alive, personally, nationally, and spiritually…these average but courageous people who forever seek the truth, defend the weak, bring the peace, and always, always, always stand up to protest injustice.[17]

---

[16] *Pirkei Avot* 1:14.
[17] Joan Chittister, *The Time Is Now: A Call to Uncommon Courage* (New York: Crown, 2019), 5.

White-Designated Jews Are Obligated to Fight White Supremacy

Robin Podolsky

Like all Americans, American Jews have been tried and tested in recent years. A pandemic has laid bare the vulnerabilities of our bodies and the webs of relationships that compose our social, public, and communal life, forcing irrevocable changes. We who have survived the worldwide plague re-learned what, as Jews, we were supposed to know already: the exposure of creatureliness, the impermanence of our lives. We have been invited to pray more slowly, learn more deeply, and meditate more profoundly on what is vital to the Torah we live.

We have not all had the same pandemic. In 2020, the CDC reported that Black Americans contracted COVID-19 in numbers disproportionate to their share of the population.[1] People of color with COVID died at higher rates than whites.[2] Centuries of inequality in housing, employment, and healthcare access have rendered the bodies of people of color and poor people more likely to be weakened by environmental pollution or inadequate health care and, therefore, to be more affected by COVID-19.

During this reckoning has come another. Thanks to technology that allows people to record events which, before, went undocumented, everyone in the U.S. with access to media is faced with mounting evidence of how casually too many law enforcement agencies and self-appointed white vigilantes treat the lives of Black people. Of course, the situation is not new—Black Lives Matter had been founded years earlier, after the deaths of Philando Castile, Trayvon Martin, and many others. White violence against Black bodies has characterized our country since its founding. But the killings of George Floyd, Breonna Taylor, Ahmaud Arbery, Elijah McClain, and those who followed became catalysts for a new kind of focused national action. Despite the pandemic, the streets filled with outraged mourners, the life-force reasserting itself in the face of so much death. Longstanding institutions and practices were, and continue to be, interrogated, challenged and, sometimes, changed. The focus of protest widened from the issue of

---

[1] Erin K. Stokes et al., "Coronavirus Disease 2019 Case Surveillance – United States, January 22-May 30, 2020," *Weekly Report* (CDC) 69:24 (June 19, 2020): 759-765.
[2] CDC, "Risk for COVID-19 Infection, Hospitalization, and Death by Race/Ethnicity," updated daily, https://www.cdc.gov/coronavirus/2019-ncov/covid-data/investigations-discovery/hospitalization-death-by-race-ethnicity.html.

police brutality to the matrix of systemic racism that contours the lives of all Americans. Such initiatives as the *New York Times* series The 1619 Project pushed the public conversation of how the very notions of "Black" and "white" people, which many now take for granted, emerged along with American national identity, shaped by the particular form that American capitalism took.

Jewish communities and agencies in the U.S. were part of that uprising. Many Jews joined and led marches and other protests. The short film *40 Days of Teshuvah*, by Hannah Roodman and Yehudah Webster, documents the example of Webster's leadership as a Black Jew who created a ritual of mourning and confession that lasted for forty days in advance of Tisha B'Av.[3] In the country's Jewish spheres, the national uprising in defense of Black lives launched a wave of introspection and study under the rubric of diversity and equity training. Jews of Color, such as Webster and Rabbis Sandra Lawson and Angela Buchdahl, have risen to leadership in their Jewish communities, articulating a vision of peoplehood that goes beyond "acceptance" to solidarity and family. Rabbi Buchdahl's powerful Yom Kippur sermon challenged Jews to reject the paradigm of race in understanding Jewish peoplehood,[4] calling for us to identify instead as a family that takes attacks on our siblings of color very personally.[5]

The events of 2020 also prompted analysis of the relationship between racism and antisemitism. Such books as *The Price of Whiteness* by Eric L. Goldstein and *How Jews Became White Folks and What That Says About Race in America* by Karen Brodkin gained renewed attention, because they expand the growing conversation about the particularities of how race is constructed in the U.S. and how those groups (like Jews) that do not fit easily into the white/Black binary are tangled up in the system.[6]

We are forced to engage with the question of our particularly Jewish obligations in this moment of potential transformation. We are forced to recognize systematized white supremacy and how it is threaded through American life, including the lives of all American Jews. We are forced to

---

[3] Hannah Roodman and Yehudah Webster, *40 Days of Teshuva*, https://www.insideoutwisdomandaction.org/40days.
[4] Angela Buchdahl, "We Are Family: Rethinking Race in the Jewish Community," Central Synagogue, Yom Kippur 5781/2020, https://youtu.be/FNhG8aW6gbI.
[5] Angela Buchdahl, "'We Are Not a Race': A Rabbi of Color Speaks Personally on Yom Kippur," *The Forward*, September 28, 2020, https://forward.com/life/455275/for-this-korean-american-rabbi-jewish-peoplehood-is-powerful-and-real-and/.
[6] Eric L. Goldstein, *The Price of Whiteness: Jews, Race, and American Identity* (Princeton, NJ: Princeton University Press, 2008); and Karen Brodkin, *How Jews Became White Folks and What That Says About Race in America* (New Brunswick, NJ: Rutgers University Press, 1998).

articulate and act upon our particular obligations as American Jews in the public square. What are our Jewish ethical imperatives at this time and in this place?

The Guidance of Narrative Theology

We are a tradition of praxis; of learning and doing. Our ethics, those principles meant to govern our behavior, come from Torah, written and oral, from generations of commentary and rulings, and from our teaching stories. Rabbi Rachel Adler instructs, "A *halakhah* is a communal praxis grounded in Jewish stories. Ethicists, theologians, and lawyers who stress the centrality of narrative would argue that all normative systems rest upon stories....A praxis is more than the sum of the various practices that constitute it. *A praxis is a holistic embodiment in action at a particular time of the values and commitments inherent to a particular story*" (italics in original).[7]

Rabbi Gordon Tucker's example of applied narrative is especially useful for us now, as we consider situations specific to our time and place which our *halakhah* did not anticipate.[8] Tucker teaches:

> We would do well to speak of Halakhah....when we wish to denote not only collections of rules and precedents, but... include the accretions over time of theological and moral underpinnings of the community of faith. And a vision of a Halakhic methodology would then be one that would include the more conventional halakhic methods but would also appeal to aggadic (narrative) texts that have withstood the tests of time to become normative Jewish theology and ethics.[9]

Let us turn, then, to our foundational story as a people, that of *yetziat Mitzrayim*, the liberation from slavery that brought us to Sinai and our *brit* (covenant). That story begins with Moshe leaving the comforts of Pharaoh's palace, where he had been raised as the adopted son of Pharaoh's daughter, to see his Hebrew "kin" (Exod. 2:11). Having struck down and killed an overseer who was brutalizing a Hebrew slave, Moshe found himself existen-

---

[7] Rachel Adler, *Engendering Judaism: An Inclusive Theology of Ethics* (Boston: Beacon, 1999), 25-26.
[8] As a Conservative rabbi, Tucker is working within a halakhic framework as a vehicle for ethical imperatives. Not all Jews take this step.
[9] Gordon Tucker, "Halakhic and Metahalakhic Arguments Concerning Judaism and Homosexuality," Rabbinical Assembly, 2006, https://www.rabbinicalassembly.org/sites/default/files/public/halakhah/teshuvot/20052010/tucker_homosexuality.pdf.

tially bound up with the other Hebrews. He did not react to the overseer's death like a prince of Egypt who could certainly have murdered a commoner with impunity. He reacted like an abjected other, hiding the corpse, aligning himself irretrievably with his enslaved people, leaving his liminal palace life forever. (Of course, the next day, when he attempted to assert leadership over the slaves, he was challenged: "Who made you judge and ruler over us?" (Exod. 2:14). So has many a budding liberal activist been made to pay their dues before earning respect.) Moshe responds to this challenge when he escapes to Midian. There, he finds a group of male shepherds attempting to bully a group of women. Moshe responds, even though these women are not his kin, when he sees an imbalance of power threatening innocents. He finds a way to defend the women without killing anyone. Moshe is learning who he is, who he is meant to be. As Nechama Leibowitz teaches:

> Moshe intervened on three occasions to save the victim from the aggressor. Each of these represents an archetype. He first intervenes in a clash between a Jew and a non-Jew. Second, between two Jews, and the third between two non-Jews. In all three cases Moses championed the just cause.
>
> Any further clash belongs to one of these three categories. Had we been told of the first clash, we might have doubted the unselfishness of his motives. Perhaps he had been activated by the sense of solidarity with his own people, hatred for the stronger oppressing his brethren rather than pure justice. Had we been faced with the second example we might still have had our doubts. Perhaps he was revolted by the disgrace of witnessing internal strife amongst his own folk, activated by national pride rather than the objective facts. Then came the third clash (between the shepherds and the daughters of Yitro at the well) where both parties were outsiders, neither brothers, friends nor neighbors. His sense of justice and fair play was exclusively involved. He instinctively championed the just cause.[10]

From Moshe, then, we learn that his identification with his oppressed kindred led seamlessly to an identification with an oppressed other whom he did not know. This paradigmatic prophet began his journey with an alliance,

---

[10] Nechama Leibowitz, *New Studies in Exodus*, trans. Aryeh Newman (Jerusalem: Maor Wallach, 1996), 40-41.

first with his own oppressed people, and then with solidarity toward all who are persecuted.

The climax of our Exodus story happens at Sinai. We arrive at the mountain an *erev rav*, a mixed multitude—not a single ethnos. We become *am echad*, one people, by accepting our *brit*, our covenant with Hashem, binding us to the Divine, to the law and to one another.

As Emmanuel Levinas reminds us, only a free people can take on the honor of an obligation. Levinas, whose guiding idea of ethics as first philosophy brought a generation of assimilated Jews back to Talmud Torah, teaches:

> The trauma I experienced in the land of Egypt constitutes my humanity itself. This immediately brings me closer to all the problems of the damned on earth, of all those who are persecuted as if in my suffering as a slave I prayed in a prayer that was not yet oration, and as if this love of the stranger were already the reply given to me through my heart of flesh. My very uniqueness lies in the responsibility for the other man [sic]; I could never pass it off on to another person, just as I could never have anyone take my place in death: obedience to the Most-High means precisely this impossibility of shying away; through it, my "self" is unique. To be free is to do only what no one else can do in my place. To obey the Most-High is to be free.[11]

This responsibility, this *brit*, is what unites the Jewish people, irrespective of whatever race any of them have been assigned wherever the paradigm of race takes hold. As Daniel and Jonathan Boyarin remind us in their foundational article, "Diaspora: Generation and the Ground of Jewish Identity," the majority of rabbinic Jewish identity formation took place under conditions of diaspora. The Boyarins state, "Jewishness disrupts the very categories of identity because it is not national, not genealogical, not religious, but all of these in dialectical tension with one another."[12]

Jews constitute a community of praxis based in discourses of textual inquiry, prayer, food practices, common stories, and common values. Jews speak many vernacular languages and, most pertinently for this discussion, are born with skin that ranges from the palest possible to the darkest.

---

[11] Emmanuel Levinas, "Revelation in the Jewish Tradition," from *Beyond the Verse: Talmudic Readings and Lectures* (Bloomington: Indiana University Press, 1994), 127-147.
[12] Daniel Boyarin and Jonathan Boyarin, "Diaspora: Generation and the Ground of Jewish Identity," *Critical Inquiry* 19:4 (1993): 721.

Therefore, while the category of race is not native to Jewish thought, Jews have been assigned disparate racial identities according to the prevailing constructions of their places of residence.

In the U.S., the majority of Jews at this time are considered to be white, although, as we shall see, this remains a precarious and vexed status. There is nothing in our tradition that commands our allegiance to this whiteness, but our tradition of relentless inquiry into the truths of our condition demands that we acknowledge and come to terms with it. What follows, then, is a necessarily brief and truncated historical account of the construction of race in the United States and the shifting positions of Jews within that structure of meaning.

Expulsion and "Discovery"

Two world-changing events took place in 1492 CE: Columbus sailed the ocean blue and the Jews were expelled from Spain. The age of racialized colonialism had begun.

As the era of European conquest began—a time in which colonization would be justified through the imposition of Christian hegemony—Spain produced a new kind of racialized antisemitism, enacted through the *limpieza de sangre*, cleansing of the blood. This term refers to a range of practices whereby Jewish and Muslim converts to Christianity and their descendants were made into permanent objects of suspicion. It was these Jews who were targets of the Inquisition. No longer was the convert welcomed into the body of Christ—such persons were suspected of infecting that body with an inherited contagion. Doctrinal purity could be compromised by unclean blood.

This policy, which combined Christian supremacy with dehumanization of non-European peoples, was crystallized in the Doctrine of Discovery, based on a bull issued by Pope Alexander VI on May 4, 1493. The bull declared that any land "discovered" to be inhabited by people who were not Christian was fair game for the taking, that such land could be colonized by violence, if need be, "and that barbarous nations be overthrown and brought to the faith itself."[13]

As the inhabitants of such lands often looked different from Europeans in various ways, including the color of their skin, theories of "race" began slowly (over centuries) to emerge in order to justify what had become a commitment to the enrichment of empires through colonization. At first, it was simply a matter of contingency. The people whom the Portuguese, Spanish,

---

[13] Pope Alexander VI, "Inter Caetera," in *Religion, Postcolonialism, and Globalization: A Sourcebook*, ed. Jennifer Reid (New York: Bloomsbury, 2014), 15-18.

and other European colonizers began to enslave and displace through colonization had darker skin and different features than had most Europeans. In the colonialist mind, these features became conflated with "heathenism:" that state which entitled the European to subjugate, usurp and, when possible, Christianize the indigenous peoples of the lands they wish to colonize and exploit. That this coincided with the increasingly violent abjection of Jews in those Christian lands where colonialism was ascendant is hardly accidental.

Patricia Seed documents the extent to which Spanish colonizers actually debated the question of whether the indigenous inhabitants of what would become the Americas were ensouled human beings.[14] The debate centered on whether such people possessed a "rational soul," as evidenced by their willingness to convert to Catholicism. The marked disinterest in conversion on the part of many native peoples precipitated the discussion.

Some Jews, faced with the demand that they choose expulsion, conversion to Christianity, or death, turned to the Muslim world where they could live openly as Jews. Others joined the colonial enterprise as hidden Jews, participating in the displacement and enslavement of indigenous peoples, hoping, perhaps, that in a new place, they would be free to practice their tradition unimpeded or, at least, to pass as Christians. Such hopes would have been in vain, because the Inquisition followed them. An emblematic example of such a person is Don Luis de Carvajal, a colonial governor in what is now Mexico. Carvajal had risen to prominence as both a slave trader and Indian fighter, but that did not save him when his background was discovered and he and his family were accused of "Judaizing." Perhaps finding something like dignity, he "confessed" before he died, "I was Jewish. I was holding Shabbat services, Friday night services."[15] Some historians say that Carvajal, shrinking from the flames at the final hour, expressed a willingness to become a true Catholic and that, in exchange, he was granted the mercy of a quick death by broken neck before his body was burnt. There is no record that Carvajal ever expressed remorse for his role in establishing the racialized colonial system that eventually killed him.

The United States: Why 1619?

In 1619, a year that has recently become the focus of much attention, the Dutch vessel *White Lion* docked in Jamestown, then an English colony, with a cargo of slaves. This event would prove to be paradigmatic in the

---

[14] Patricia Seed, "'Are These Not Also Men?': The Indians' Humanity and Capacity for Spanish Civilisation," *Journal of Latin American Studies* 25:3 (1993): 629-652.
[15] Ronnie Perelis, "The Manuscripts of Luis de Carvajal," *Smart History: The Center for Public Art History*, October 23, 2017, https://smarthistory.org/luis-de-carvajal-2/.

establishment of race as a reality in what would become the United States of America. The slaves were African, their enslavers were European. Nikole Hannah-Jones, the Pulitzer Prize winning author of The 1619 Project, which began as a series of essays in the *New York Times* and is now a book, writes, "I wanted people to know the date 1619 and to contemplate what it means that slavery predates nearly every other institution in the United States."[16]

It is imperative to understand that The 1619 Project, like other such scholarship, is not an exercise in tracing the development of a prejudice. Rather, such thinkers as Hannah-Jones are tracing the establishment of systems of power which governed such concrete matters as who may marry and to whom, who may legally learn to read, who may carry weapons, who has at least nominal freedom of movement and, of course, who may own whom. Our country, founded with such systems threaded through it, continues to be shaped by how those institutions develop and also by the titanic struggles of resistance that such institutions necessarily provoke.

Certainly, such systems of power generate, maintain, and are reinforced by ideologies that embrace prejudices about everything from physical attractiveness to mental capacity. But when we talk about systemic racism, we are talking about a self-perpetuating material reality. Within a century of their arrival in North America, the differences between those people who were assigned blackness and those assigned whiteness appeared to be self-evident. While all Black people were not enslaved, a great many of them were. Where white people could be indentured into servitude, they could earn their freedom. Very often Black people could not. This state of affairs was consolidated following Bacon's Rebellion of 1676 in Virginia, an armed action by a coalition of white and Black bond-slaves. Slave owners realized the danger in a situation where Black and white enslaved people had common interests. Soon, "slave codes" were passed into law in the Southern colonies, through which the very meanings of "Black" and "white" were constructed. White bond-slavery (indentured servitude) dwindled away; Black chattel slavery became an inherited condition. Thus, enslavement or vulnerability to enslavement became a marker of assigned Black "racial" identity. By the time the United States became a country, its economic life depended on the implications of that identity and the labor which could be extracted from those designated by it.

When we step back and examine critically the Black/White binary, we see that it is a contingent artifice. Of course, people are born with differing amounts of melanin in their skin, different textures of hair, different eye

---

[16] Nikole Hannah-Jones, *The 1619 Project: A New Origin Story* (New York: Random House, 2021), xxii.

colors, and so forth. But the meanings and categorizations that people assign to these traits are what we mean by social constructs. Even the words "white" and "black" are, when considered, metaphors that centuries of use have literalized. Few human beings have skin that could be called true white or true black. The use of these extreme opposite colors to categorize people whose skin actually runs to various hues of beige or brown has become normalized, but it is precisely not natural; it is a linguistic naturalization of social categories. That a person could "pass" indicates how artificial those categories are.

Further, that binary, also called the "color line," has functioned as a kind of distorting prism, shaping the possibilities available to people who do not easily fit into either category: indigenous people, people of Asian descent, mestizo people—and Jews.

The racialized capitalism on which the United States was founded was intertwined with the settler colonialism. Native peoples were displaced, often killed and, eventually, forced onto reservations where, far too often, children would be forced into boarding schools designed to make them discard their languages, cultures, and religious traditions. The United States was constituted on the appropriation of Native land and Black labor. The Black/White binary was a system for defining the condition of those people who would be essential to building the new country; that the binary tends to erase the existence of Indigenous Americans is a feature, not a bug. The Doctrine of Discovery would become the basis of European colonial claims in the Americas and, later, the warrant for the United States' continental expansion. In the U.S. Supreme Court in the 1823 case *Johnson v. M'Intosh*, Chief Justice John Marshall's opinion in the unanimous decision held "that the principle of discovery gave European nations an absolute right to New World lands."

By the time the United States was established, Jews, not all of whom would today be categorized as white,[17] had begun to live openly in the "New World." Most Jews of European descent were included in white society. George Washington's famous "Letter to the Jews of Newport" of 1790 states:

> All possess alike liberty of conscience and immunities of citizenship. It is now no more that toleration is spoken of as if it were the indulgence of one class of people that another enjoyed the exercise of their inherent natural rights,

---

[17] For example, if one looks at the Gilbert Stuart portrait of Anna Lopez, wife of Aaron Lopez, a former hidden Jew who had returned to Judaism in New England, and her son, Joshua Lopez, their African heritage is obvious.

for, happily, the Government of the United States, which gives to bigotry no sanction, to persecution no assistance, requires only that they who live under its protection should demean themselves as good citizens in giving it on all occasions their effectual support.[18]

To people who had come to this country seeking freedom from persecution, this could only be a welcome gesture. However, one may wonder if this letter, written in the context of the effort to pass the Bill of Rights and secure freedom of religion, did not spark some questions. The letter was composed at a time when Washington was touring the states, seeking ratification of those first ten amendments, accompanied by his secretary of state, Thomas Jefferson, who was, like Washington himself, a slave owner. Did any of those Jews, relieved and gratified to be included in the new country's bright future, wonder about the "all" who possess liberty of conscience; wonder if it might include those people who were classed legally as property? Effectively, by this letter and similar gestures, European-descended Jews were placed on the "white" side of the divide and, in the main, did not protest.

In *The Price of Whiteness*, Eric L. Goldstein records the centuries-long negotiation of American Jews with their assigned racial status. Each succeeding generation of Jewish immigrants had to discern and maneuver their place in an alien hierarchy while finding ways to maintain their particular heritage. For the West, the nineteenth and early twentieth centuries were periods in which race "science," with its mania for classifying, naming, and assigning characteristics to various races (the Caucasian, the Nordic, the Asiatic, and, of course, the Negroid) had intellectual respectability. Note that some of these "races" were subgroups of whiteness. Goldstein documents the extent to which many nineteenth-century Jews of Western European extraction embraced the idea of racial or ethnic identity as a strategy for maintaining their difference along with their social whiteness; and, further, how Jews were held in a kind of racial suspension by many of their compatriots:

> Jews, however, presented a mix of qualities that was unusual among American "racial" groups and proved particularly resistant to categorization within the black-white system. In the minds of white Americans, Jews were clearly racial outsiders in many ways, demonstrating distinctive social patterns, clustering in urban neighborhoods, concentrat-

---

[18] George Washington, "Letter to the Jews of Newport," August 18, 1790, Washington Papers, 6:284-85.

ing in certain trades and professions, and largely marrying within their own group. At the same time...Jews appeared to be thoroughly implicated in the urban, industrial, capitalist order that characterized the modern "civilized" world. Because white Americans saw Jews as racially different and yet similar to themselves in many ways, the image they attached to them tended to be much more ambivalent than the one fastened on African Americans....While the black-white discourse of race bolstered white Americans' sense of confidence and superiority, their image of the Jew reflected the doubts and anxieties they harbored about their own society.[19]

Like all putative white Americans, such Jews were tested in the years leading up to and during the Civil War, when the question of racialized slavery demanded attention. Most Jews, northern and southern, tended to fall on the side of their neighbors, although there were some outstanding Jews like August Bondi, who fought pro-slavery militias alongside of John Brown, served with distinction during the Civil War, and went on to a career of service as a postmaster.

Notably, two rabbis stood out for relying on the guidance of our foundational narrative. Rabbi Sabato Morais, an Orthodox rabbi, and Rabbi David Einhorn, a Reform rabbi, issued unusually fervent denunciations of slavery, and each of them did so by referencing our liberation story.

During his Thanksgiving sermon in 1864, Rabbi Morais thundered, "Not the victories of the Union, but those of freedom [of] my friends, we do celebrate. What is Union with human degradation? Who would again affix his seal to the bond that consigned millions to [enslavement]? Not I, the enfranchised slave of Mizraim."[20]

In that same year, Rabbi Einhorn asked his Philadelphia congregation: "Is it anything else but a deed of Amalek, rebellion against God, to enslave beings created in His image, and to degrade them to a state of beasts having no will of their own? Is it anything else but an act of ruthless and wicked violence, to reduce defenseless human beings to a condition of merchandise and relentlessly tear them away from the hearts of husbands, wives, parents and children?"[21]

---

[19] Goldstein, *The Price of Whiteness*, ii.
[20] David M. Cobin, Earl Schwartz, and Dorothy Roberts, "The Encrypted Sermons of Sabato Morais," *Journal of Law and Religion* 23:1 (2007/2008): 147.
[21] Robert R. Mathison, ed., *The Routledge Sourcebook of Religion and the American Civil War:*

It could not have been easy for the Orthodox Rabbi Morais to *paskin*, render a rabbinic ruling, directly from the written Torah, bypassing the mitigations and reformations of slavery found in rabbinic *halakhah*. He was attacked by pro-slavery rabbi Jacob Morris Raphall, who said in 1861, "How dare you denounce slaveholding as a sin? When you remember that Abraham, Isaac, Jacob, Job…were slaveholders, does it not strike you that you are guilty of something very little short of blasphemy?"[22]

Actually, as Raphall had to eventually admit, American slavery was so brutal and dehumanizing that it fell far short of Talmudic-rabbinic standards which had attempted to regulate what was a ubiquitous institution in their ancient world. But both the Orthodox Morais and Reform Einhorn moved beyond the existing *halakhah* to an *aggadic chidush* (new insight), condemning as evil that institution which made one person the property of another. Their model leads us to a robust conception of the Talmudic principle *kavod ha-briot*, human dignity, and they remain examples of how Jews can embrace the challenges of modernity while staying true to our Torah as our center of gravity and accountability.

Toward the end of the nineteenth century and the beginning of the twentieth, a new wave of Jewish immigrants, mostly from Eastern Europe, came to the U.S. Many had migrated from the Pale of Settlement, that area within the Russian Empire where Jews were allowed to live. As Karen Brodkin documents in *How Jews Became White Folks and What That Says About Race in America*, many of those Jews were either religious or socialist or both and, therefore, had a firm grip on their Jewish identity, a strong identification with the oppressed, and a disinclination to assimilate into American whiteness.

This group of immigrants included those storied Jews who led the creation of unions in the 1910s and fought for the Scottsboro Boys in the 1930s, who created mutual aid organizations and American Conservative Judaism. Of course, as Brodkin reminds us, the majority were not on the front lines (although if those were picket lines, they would probably have refused to cross them). Many were happy to simply partake of the jobs or businesses offered to them in their new country and to enjoy communal life in Jewish neighborhoods. Many were willing, eventually, to move into those suburbs where they were allowed to live (where there were no restrictive covenants to keep them out, housing discrimination being quite legal then), whether or not Black people were allowed to live there also (they usually were not). Politically, they tended toward the left, but it was

---

A History in Documents (New York: Routledge, 2017), 336
[22] "Rev. Dr. Raphall's Discourse," *New York Times*, January 5, 1861.

standout leaders who really carried that water. As Brodkin reports about her own upbringing, "In a sense, then, being a Jew meant being part of a multigenerational community, not really political, but Democrat, pro-union, anti-management and secular in the way one saw the world. It also meant standing somewhat apart from the white world, being bi-cultural in a way Jews shared with other upwardly mobile European ethnics."[23]

As indicated earlier, the social phenomenon called "race" in the global West, and in the United States in particular, was formed through the construction of categories that are not native to Jewish thought or Jewish peoplehood. In the U.S., successive generations of Jews have found themselves caught between social dimensions; to see themselves through a Jewish lens and the dominant culture's lens was to live with a kind of distorted double vision. It would be disingenuous for Jews of European descent to pretend that we have not been coopted into the project of whiteness or that we have not benefited from economic and social systems of racism—whether we wanted to benefit or not, whether or not we actually find such hierarchies to be, based on our own values, repugnant.

To acknowledge this situation is to take nothing away from those Jewish immigrants who came to the United States with little money and big dreams; people who built congregations and organizations and businesses, some of which survive today. We are, however, compelled to wonder if, for instance, the Jews confined by Russian Czars to the Pale of Settlement, many of whom stagnated in poverty, were any less industrious or creative in Eastern Europe than their descendants were in the U.S. Were there not conditions in the U.S. that allowed these Jewish immigrants to prosper in ways that were impossible when it was they who were an abjected group? Materially, the situation of European-descended Jews improves to the extent that each generation is further cathected into whiteness.

One can read the stories of the later Yiddishist writers, such as Sholem Asch, Lamed Shapiro, and Isaac Bashevis Singer, and encounter stories of Eastern European ghetto life that could have been written by Iceberg Slim, an African-American writer whose experiences as a pimp in the 1950s informed his fiction. These Yiddishists portrayed grinding poverty, daily violence, unemployed fathers, dejected mothers, disrespectful children seeking solace in alcohol or joyless sex. Early twentieth-century accounts of first-generation New York City Jewish life, such as *Bronx Primitive* by Kate Simon or *Jews Without Money* by Michael Gold, offer a harrowing picture of that transitional time.[24] (Budd Schulberg's *What Makes Sammy Run?*

---

[23] Brodkin, *How Jews Became White Folks*, 9.
[24] Kate Simon, *Bronx Primitive: Portraits in a Childhood* (New York: Penguin, 1982); and Michael Gold, *Jews Without Money* (New York: Horace Liveright, 1930).

portrays an extreme example of a flight into assimilation and the abyss of a consciousness stripped of positive identity and obligation.[25]) As squalid and challenging as urban life was for those first immigrant generations, it offered new possibilities for them and their children, because the bottom rungs of the social ladder were already filled by Black people and others who were deemed different racially from whites.

Even the New Deal, which did much to restore the U.S. economy in the Great Depression, contributed to racist systems and the maintenance of racial categories within which white-designated Jews fit uneasily. As Richard Rothstein documents in his book, *The Color of Law: A Forgotten History of How Our Government Segregated America*,[26] the Federal Housing Authority, established in 1934 to provide working people with loans so that they could build wealth by buying homes, refused to lend to buyers in neighborhoods where predominantly people of color lived, a practice known as redlining. It is not as though the residents of those neighborhoods could buy elsewhere. Housing discrimination was legal, and often white homeowners were bound by "restrictive covenants," which they signed as a condition of buying a house, contracting them to refuse to sell their property to people of color—and, often, to Jews. The film *East L.A. Interchange* by Jewish filmmaker Betsy Kalin documents the example of Boyle Heights, a neighborhood in Los Angeles County where, for a time, Jews, African Americans, Asian-Americans, and Latinos lived together. After World War II, Jews were permitted to buy homes in West Los Angeles and the San Fernando Valley—they discovered, in fact, that because of redlining, it would be cheaper to buy into new housing developments than to buy the Boyle Heights homes in which they already lived. Once again, white Jews found themselves in a sort of middle category: they could get home loans which people of color could not obtain, but they were confined to particular neighborhoods until the Supreme Court case *Shelley v. Kraemer* in 1948 struck down housing covenants.

Of course, World War II and the Shoah changed many things. For one, American Jewish men, like American Black men, learned that, stereotypes aside, they were quite capable to wield weapons of war and observe military discipline—that they could fight fascism and win. They also observed that they were fighting a racist regime with a segregated army, and perhaps that fact pointed them to unfinished work on the home front. And they witnessed the horrific endpoint of dehumanizing racial narratives (a lesson

---

[25] Budd Schulberg, *What Makes Sammy Run?* (New York: Random House, 1941).
[26] Richard Rothstein, *The Color of Law: A Forgotten History of How Our Government Segregated America* (New York: W. W. Norton, 2017).

that, perhaps, the white Jewish soldiers experienced as a greater disruption to their view of the world).

The shock of the Shoah, along with that of the atom bomb and the general uprising of colonized nations in Africa, South America, and Asia, precipitated the postmodern revolution in Western thought. Master narratives fell under suspicion, along with the kind of universalizing assumptions that undergirded the pressure on Jews and other Western minorities to suppress their particularities and assimilate. The 1947 film *Gentlemen's Agreement* portrays the increasing impatience of American Jews with antisemitic discrimination and with those Jews who sought to blend in to the point of self-obliteration.[27]

It was the younger siblings and children of the World War II generation who would begin a long transformation of American consciousness. In the mid-1950s, Black southern students and clergy started the work with sit-ins, voter registration drives, and marches. Soon, young white people volunteered to join them, and Jewish youth participated in numbers beyond their percentage of the American population. Many of these activists rejected the assimilation into American whiteness that their parents had begun to take for granted as a positive goal. Eventually, however, they were also obliged by their Black comrades to take stock of the privileges that categorical whiteness afforded them, even when they no longer sought such advantages.[28] For example, the Student Nonviolent Coordinating Committee expelled its white members in 1967, hoping that such people would take leadership within their home communities and combat white racism at the source. In his important article, "Negroes Are Anti-Semitic Because They're Anti-White," written in 1967, James Baldwin records the antagonism he and his family felt toward their Jewish landowners and employers, not because those Jews behaved differently from the majority of whites he encountered, but because they did not. Baldwin writes:

> In the American context, the most ironical thing about Negro anti-Semitism is that the Negro is really condemning the Jew for having become an American white man—for having become, in effect, a Christian. The Jew profits from his status in America, and he must expect Negroes to distrust him for it. The Jew does not realize that the credential he offers, the fact that he has been despised and

[27] Elia Kazan, dir., *Gentleman's Agreement*, 20th Century Fox, 1947.
[28] For a thorough treatment of this topic, see Marc Dollinger, *Black Power, Jewish Politics: Reinventing the Alliance in the 1960s* (Waltham, MA: Brandeis University Press, 2018).

> slaughtered, does not increase the Negro's understanding. It increases the Negro's rage.
>
> For it is not here, and not now, that the Jew is being slaughtered, and he is never despised, here, as the Negro is, because he is an American. The Jewish travail occurred across the sea and America rescued him from the house of bondage. But America is the house of bondage for the Negro, and no country can rescue him. What happens to the Negro here happens to him because he is an American.[29]

Baldwin, a gay Black man who became more radical, not less, as he matured as a writer, represents a certain quickening of his generation's social conscience. A long social upheaval had begun, in which power imbalances on the basis of race, gender and sexual orientation were met with organized opposition, culturally and legally.

Where We are Now

The United States is now at a crossroads with regard to race and the entire structure of racialized capitalism is being called into question. We are in the midst of two national debates: do we continue to draw out the conversation about race into the public square and into our educational systems or do we suppress it; and, assuming that we wish to extend the conversation, what are we actually going to do in order to transform?

American Jews are obliged to be part of this national conversation. As we learn in Talmud Bavli, *Shabbat* 54b:

> Anyone who is able to protest against [the transgressions of] one's household and does not, is liable for the actions of the members of the household; anyone who is able to protest against [the transgressions of] one's townspeople and does not, is liable for the transgressions of the townspeople; anyone who is able to protest against [the transgressions of] the entire world and does not is liable for the transgressions of the entire world.

We must believe that, in a presumed representative democracy, all of us are those who are able to protest and, therefore, liable for the misdeeds of our communities and country. It is not enough to "work on our racism" as

---

[29] James Baldwin, "Negroes Are Anti-Semitic Because They're Anti-White," *New York Times,* April 9, 1967.

an aspect of our personalities and conduct. It is necessary that we engage with those aspects of the social relations in which we participate that are oppressive to others. It is necessary that we oppose systemic racism where we find it.

The effects of centuries of systemic racism remain with us. As noted above, the course of the COVID pandemic has provided a clear demonstration of that phenomenon, as do patterns of police abuse and incarceration. The wealth gap, maintained by such policies as redlining, continues. As Rothstein documents:

> Median white family income is now about $60,000, while median black family income is about $37,000—about 60 percent as much. You might expect that the ratio of black to white household wealth would be similar. But median white household wealth (assets minus liabilities) is about $134,000, while median black household wealth is about $11,000—less than 10 percent as much. Not all of this enormous difference is attributable to the government's racial housing policy, but a good portion of it certainly is.[30]

It is a matter of *ahavat Yisrael*—love between Jews—to acknowledge that the situation of Jews of color in the U.S. is different from that of white-assigned Jews, and that is because of systemic racism. According to "Counting Inconsistencies: An Analysis of American Jewish Population Studies with an Emphasis on Jews of Color," produced by the Jews of Color Initiative (JCI), such Jews compose twelve to fifteen percent of American Jews.[31] That number was derived by including only those self-identified Jews of color who affirm Judaism as their "religion." This population, then, does not identify with other Jews "ethnically" or "racially" but on the basis of our religious culture, peoplehood (which is not, in their view, racially constituted), and our *brit*. We learn from "Beyond the Count: Perspectives and Lived Experiences of Jews of Color," another JCI study, that a vast majority of these Jews report not only experiencing racism outside the Jewish world in the course of their daily lives, but also within Jewish settings.[32] For these Jews, working to

---

[30] Rothstein, *The Color of Law*, 184.
[31] Ari Kelman, Aaron Hahn Tapper, Izabel Fonseca, and Aliyah Saperstein, "Counting Inconsistencies: An Analysis of American Jewish Population Studies with an Emphasis on Jews of Color," Jews of Color Initiative, May 2019.
[32] Tobin Belzer, Tory Brundage, Vincent Calvetti, Gage Gorsky, Ari Y. Kelman, and Dalya Perez, "Beyond the Count: Perspectives and Lived Experiences of Jews of Color," Jews of Color Initiative, August 2021, https://jewsofcolorinitiative.org/wp-content/uploads/2021/08/

undo systemic racism and all injustice in the world at large, as well as within Jewish spaces, is a key element in how they manifest their Judaism—and it is what they would like to see from their Jewish communities.

Furthermore, American Jews cannot afford to forget that we have consolidated enemies in white nationalists. In his foundational article, "Skin in the Game," Eric K. Ward documents the centrality of the Great Replacement narrative in today's white supremacist movement.[33] According to this narrative, a variant of the sort of conspiracy theory that can be traced back to the *Protocols of the Elders of Zion*[34] and beyond, Jews support immigrant justice because we seek to "replace" white Christian workers and voters with immigrants of color who, these racists believe, Jews could manipulate. For those white nationalists, Jews are not white at all.

We dare not forget who actually murders us. The Pittsburgh massacre of October 27, 2018 at the Tree of Life synagogue, in which eleven Jews were murdered, and the Poway Chabad shooting of April 27, 2019, in which a Jewish woman was killed and a rabbi injured, were perpetrated by white supremacists. As long ago as 1999, a white supremacist invaded a San Fernando Valley Jewish Community Center with the intention to "kill Jews," shooting five people and murdering a postal worker of Filipino descent.[35]

Conclusion

Yehudah Webster, in *40 Days of Teshuvah*, links the lack of clarity within the Jewish world regarding systemic racism with the condition of exile itself: "It started with us turning away from Hashem, turning away from Torah, turning away from justice, and embracing baseless hatred instead."[36] Rabbi Aryeh Cohen teaches:

> Denying and destroying the image of God is exactly what Pharaoh did, it is what American enslavement of African people did, it is what Jim Crow did, it is what all racism does. The first step in overcoming racism and white su-

---

BEYONDTHECOUNT.FINAL_.8.12.21.pdf.

[33] Eric W. Ward, "Skin in the Game," Political Research Associates, June 29, 2017, https://politicalresearch.org/2017/06/29/skin-in-the-game-how-antisemitism-animates-white-nationalism.

[34] A hoax promulgated by Czarist political operatives, *The Protocols of the Elders of Zion* purports to be a manifesto of a gathering of Jewish elders planning world domination through the undermining of Western society.

[35] Rene Sanchez and Cassandra Stern, "Gunman Wounds 5 at Summer Camp," *The Washington Post*, August 11, 1999.

[36] Roodman and Webster, *40 Days of Teshuva*.

premacy and the possibility of oppression is recognizing that no people has a right to enslave another people. That is the Exodus that allows for hearing the word of God....Last year George Floyd was killed several days before Shavuot. On Shavuot there were mass demonstrations around the country and here in Los Angeles. They were mostly nonviolent until the police turned on the demonstrators. When some property was damaged, many in our community complained more about the damage and less about the brutal police killing of a Black man....We were not ready to hear "you shall have no other gods before me."[37]

Jews can be a counterculture within the United States, participating in the public square with good faith as Americans, yet reserving our ultimate allegiance to the ethical demands of our Torah. Those Jews who are designated white can withhold allegiance from whiteness while acknowledging the benefits it thrusts upon us. It is not enough, or even entirely possible, to "refuse" those benefits as individuals—our tradition demands that we undo the system which produces them. We arrive at Sinai an *erev rav*, a mixed multitude. We become one people by accepting our *brit*, our covenant with Hashem, binding us to the Divine, to the law and to one another.

At the end of the day, there is no contradiction between doing the right thing and doing the politically smart thing. No Jew will ever be safe as long as institutional racism persists along with all its ideological and functional props, including antisemitism. And we will not be true to ourselves and our covenant if we do not devote ourselves to overcoming this idolatrous construct, which we should not be embarrassed to call evil.

---

[37] Aryeh Cohen, "Slouching Toward Sinai," *Jewish Journal*, May 13, 2021, https://jewish-journal.com/commentary/opinion/336572/slouching-toward-sinai/.

Stan Levy responds

Rabbi Robin Podolsky's chapter, titled "White-Designated Jews Are Obligated to Fight White Supremacy," is a thorough discussion and analysis of the historical and current state of conflict and confusion in both "white" Americans and Jewish Americans/American Jewish communities about whether Jews are minorities (meaning non-white) or white. In fact, all Jews are minorities and Jews of Color. Rabbi Podolsky's essay is also an articulation of the depth and breadth of systemic anti-Black American racism in every aspect of our society. Another fact that is clear in the essay is that race is not a scientific term; it is a cultural and social term used to "define" social and political classism in the United States.

This is analogous to the Nazi German government In the 1930s and 40s that defined German Jews as non-Aryans, non-German nationals, and defined all Jews in the world as "subhuman." And the solution for the Jewish problem in Germany and the world was to annihilate the Jews.

So, what will white American supremacists do in the United States of America to solve the Black American, Hispanic American, Asian American, LGBTQ+, immigrant American, and Jewish American problem? And where will American Jews be in this white supremacists' problem? What will we, as American Jews or Jewish Americans, do? And how did and do Jews define and identify ourselves, both historically and currently, in America?

Will we Jews in the United States resist white supremacy and align ourselves with other minorities, or will Jews attempt to "pass" ourselves off as "white" and take advantage of "white privilege"? The choice is for each of us to decide. As I quoted Elie Wiesel in my essay on the duty of Jewish clergy: "We must always take sides. Neutrality helps the oppressor, never the victim."

Robin Podolsky responds

In his chapter, "The Ethical and Religious Duty for Jewish Clergy," Rabbi Stan Levy reminds us of the *duty to warn*. In these days of crises, he calls us to confront growing income disparity, systemic racism, climate catastrophe heightened by policies that put profit before the common good, and other injustices and global threats. Rabbi Levy highlights a teaching from Shoah scholar Yehuda Baur, suggesting that we add three new mitzvot to our store of commandments: "Thou shall not be a perpetrator; thou shall not be a victim; and thou shall never be a bystander."

Rabbi Levy brings teachings from both traditional and contemporary Jewish sources, demonstrating that what we now tend to call "social justice activism" is threaded through our Jewish tradition. He shows how this imperative was baked into our tradition before it was called Judaism, that is, from our written Torah and our prophets.

Interestingly, Levy translates Leviticus 19:16, *lo ta'amod al dam rei'echa*, which is usually translated literally as "Do not stand over your neighbor's blood," or more commonly as "Do not stand idly while your neighbor bleeds," more generally, that is: "Do not stand by [in silence] when your neighbors' lives are in danger." In this, his interpretation is in line with that of our rabbis in b. *Sanhedrin* 73a, who teach, "...one who sees another drowning in a river, or being dragged away by a wild animal, or being attacked by bandits, is obligated to save him," and with Maimonides, who comments that this obligation includes one who is able to hire help to save the endangered person.[1] This implies that it is not only in moments of immediate danger that one is obligated, but also in times of ongoing crisis, protracted enough that a person might either act or contribute monetarily to help the ones in danger.

This sort of Talmudic reasoning is more or less absent from Rabbi Levy's piece. He relies mostly on the Tanakh and twentieth and twenty-first-century thinkers for prooftexts. Yet, there is so much in our Talmudic tradition to support the important points he makes.

Without doubt, Rabbi Levy relies so heavily on great modern thinkers, such as Rabbi Abraham Joshua Heschel, Eli Wiesel, and Dr. Martin Luther King Jr., because their teachings and examples of conduct influenced his life profoundly. The autobiographical sections of his essay, recounting the ways he has put his beliefs into practice, have a great deal to teach us.

For instance, Rabbi Levy chose to become, in addition to a spiritual leader, a practicing attorney. He writes, "...by the late 1960s, I had translated my being a rabbi by praying with my actions, as Heschel had done, integrating my rabbinate with my law career as a civil and human rights attorney. I litigated many voting, civil, and human rights cases in federal and state courts. As a teacher at a major Los Angeles law school, I developed curricula in voting rights, anti-poverty, anti-systemic racism and discrimination, and civil and human rights law." In this way, he brings to mind our rabbis and sages who not only studied, taught, and interpreted Torah, but also earned their living among the people they served as physicians, shepherds, and entrepreneurs.

Rabbi Levy reminds us as well that American Jews have not always had

---

[1] Maimonides, *Mishneh Torah, Hilchot Rotze'ach* 1:14.

access to every professional choice. He was rejected from Harvard Law School because "the Jewish quota was filled." It is important that such records of this generational experience be preserved.

It is also not amiss for us to remember how fertile the twentieth century was in the profusion of Jewish thought that it birthed. The crises of the time brought forth a generation of leaders such as Rabbi Leo Baeck, Martin Buber, and Franz Rosenzweig—people who received the best education that the West had to offer and placed the tools and ideas they acquired at the disposal of the Jewish people. They drew from the dominant culture but remained accountable to Torah with its religious and ethical demands.

This essay alerts us that, in these pivotal times, we all have neighbors who are bleeding. Rabbi Levy cites economic inequality, attacks on immigrants, systemic racism, and the growing threat of an emboldened white supremacist movement—as well as the inequities which Palestinian people endure. He insists that, as dedicated Jews, it is imperative that we draw on our tradition to speak out and oppose injustice even when—or especially when—it is committed by our own.

Rabbi Levy writes with great urgency. He reminds us, "We are running out of time." There is no guarantee that freedom won is freedom preserved. We are in a period in which anti-democratic forces are gaining in confidence, numbers and economic support for their efforts. There is a movement to actively push back against the teaching, in public schools, of the history of systemic racism and the vast gulf between those in our country who have resources and those who do not.

Rabbi Levy draws on Jewish sources, but he turns to another inspiration as well: to American Christians who have fought consistently and at personal risk for the promise of our democracy. He reminds us that we have a *movement lineage* of people who have turned spiritual inspiration into lifelong commitments of action.

In his personal example and great range of learning, Rabbi Levy offers uplift and spiritual nourishment to new generations of Jewish activists. May his writing inspire us to delve deeper into the sources he provides and to emulate his courage with our deeds.

Set Six

The 13 Principles of Ethics at the Academy for Jewish Religion California

Mel Gottlieb

Spiritual Ethics: Rachamim

Susan Goldberg

Part Six

The Lilli Hornig Endowed Fund,
Academic for Jewish Religion, California

Dedication

Spiritual Ethics: Reclaiming
Susan Goldberg

The 13 Principles of Ethics at the Academy for Jewish Religion California

Mel Gottlieb

When we established the Academy for Jewish Religion California over two decades ago, we committed ourselves to creating an institution that would not only be a place of rigorous text study, but also an environment where ethical behavior and personal spiritual growth would be a primary emphasis. The following thirteen ethical/spiritual principles found in our ancient literature were utilized as a guide to implement the values of our transdenominational school.

1. Listening – *Sh'mia*

The first three principles are found in the *midrash* recorded in the introduction to *Ein Yaakov*, a sixteenth-century compilation of classical *aggadic* (story) material with commentaries.

> Ben Zoma says: The verse that is the most encompassing in the Torah is the verse of the *Sh'ma* (Deut. 6:4). Ben Nanas says, we have found a verse that is even more inclusive, the verse "And you shall love your neighbor as yourself" (Lev. 19:18). Shimon Ben Pazi surprisingly says: We have found a verse even more important than these and that is the twice daily sacrifice, "And you shall offer the one sheep (*keves*) every morning, and the second sheep shall you offer in the afternoon" (Exod. 29:39). R. Ploni stood up on his feet and said the ruling is as Ben Pazi says.

In this *midrash*, we have gathered three principles that we have incorporated in our school. The first value, inherent in the *Sh'ma*, is the emphasis on prayer in our daily curriculum. The intent is to develop a sense of connection to the Almighty through concentrated daily prayer in a *minyan*, partaking from the energy of the whole community in communal prayer. Through the value of *Sh'ma*, we also emphasize the spiritual dimension, and the utmost importance of listening. This implies listening to others respectfully and carefully, listening to the whispers of the Infinite in the universe, and listening to the voice of the soul within.

Our Sages teach that while, in the physical world, the highest of the senses is seeing, the highest of the senses in the spiritual world is hearing.[1] This is based on the verse in Exodus 20:15, which described the revelation of Torah at Mt. Sinai: "All the people witnessed the thunder and lightning, the blare of the horn and the mountain smoking; and when the people saw it, they fell back and stood at a distance." The rabbis recognize that it should have logically said that they "heard" the sounds of the shofar, but our rabbis point out that they were on such a high spiritual level of unity at Mt. Sinai, it was as if they saw God through their *hearing*. (Their hearing was like seeing, and their seeing was like hearing.)

2. Lovingkindness – *Chesed*

The second value, inherent in the verse "Love your neighbor as yourself" (Lev. 19:18), is to promote the supreme value of connecting and honoring our fellow community members, each of whom is created in the image of God. We emphasize that although it is easy to feel close, empathize with, and find intimacy with those who are "like us" (those who have similar temperaments and proclivities), it is important to reach out to others who may be "different" than us in their habits, lifestyles, and attitudes. We stress that not only *rachamim* (empathy and compassion are virtuous traits) but *chesed* (giving to others) is an essential character trait to be developed, so that we can reach out to even those whom we are not innately drawn to.

3. Consistency – *T'midut*

The third value that Ben Pazi teaches us—the twice daily sacrifice—is the fundamental necessity and importance of daily "consistency." This leads us to impart our expectation that daily *mitzvot*, including prayer, learning, and good deeds, are expectations for success in our school. The Mishnah is perhaps surprising in its elevation of this value above all others, but it is a prudent teaching, as our tradition foregrounds *na'aseh v'nishmah*: through the "doing will come the understanding." Consistent doing is the indispensable requisite value that creates a community of holiness that can be an example for our world. The maintaining and sustaining of consistent ethical behavior, in particular, is the catalyst to spreading the light of holiness and bringing about the messianic ideal. "How goodly are thy tents O Jacob, your dwelling places, O Israel" (Num. 24:5).

---

[1] Rabbi Akiva in *Mechilta D'Rabbi Yishmael* 20:15:1.

4. Concentrated Study – *Talmud Torah*

The fourth value is the emphasis on disciplined, concentrated study: *talmud Torah k'neged kulam*—"Torah study is equal to all other *mitzvot*."[2] We have instituted a hearty curriculum that covers *tefillah* (prayer); biblical studies (Torah, Ketuvim, and Nevi'im with traditional and modern commentaries); rabbinics (Talmud, Mishnah, *midrash*, codes); Jewish history; Jewish thought; professional skills; and Hebrew. We expect our students to progress to the level of being able to read texts in their original language, to lead services with competence, and to apply wisdom to current events constantly evolving in our Jewish community and beyond. Their studies also include introspective growth to develop the tools and consciousness to relate maturely to their communities and to be an ethical exemplar to the congregations and communal settings that they serve. To this end, part of our curriculum includes study in Mussar groups (spiritual development workshops) and spiritual direction seminars.

Students in our Mussar groups meet on Sunday evenings for one hour to acquire and develop ethical skills necessary for professional leadership. The groups are made up of six to eight students and a leader trained in Mussar and group process. In the past, the groups have used Alan Morinis' *Everyday Holiness* and studied selected character traits from the book for two-week periods.[3] They kept nightly journals related to the character trait, worked to recognize the traits in their everyday interactions and deliberations, and how they were progressing or struggling with each of the traits.

This ethical training is reinforced in our required annual three-day retreats and are part of the ethos of each class. During monthly faculty meetings and the annual faculty retreat, the faculty has also participated in discussions to strengthen and support the ethical dimension of our programs. Throughout the school, our staff, administration, faculty, and board likewise have opportunities to cultivate, carry out, and model the expectation of dignified ethical behavior.

5. Humility – *Anivut*

We aspire to impart our fifth value, taken from the Book of Micah 6:8: "What does God require of you, but to do justly, act with lovingkindness, and to walk humbly with your God." To strive for humility is a prioritized goal

---

[2] b. *Shabbat* 127a.
[3] Alan Morinis, *Everyday Holiness: The Jewish Spiritual Path of Mussar* (Boston: Trumpeter, 2007). Eighteen character traits are explored in the book: humility; patience; gratitude; compassion; order; equanimity; honor; simplicity; enthusiasm; silence; generosity; truth; moderation; loving-kindness; responsibility; trust; faith; and *yirah* (fear/awe).

in our school because of the innate tendency to feel "superior" as scholarly and practical skills competence increases. Sometimes, competitiveness and the need for recognition interfere with the core value of humility that is the basis of a healthy, interconnected community that acknowledges and shares the talents and insights of all its members.

Part of our Mussar exercises involves examining what is potentially blocking our humility. We believe that this recognition is a requisite to make progress with this virtue. Through journaling and sharing with others in Mussar group meetings at our school, students identify certain patterns in themselves and in each other. They become aware and grow through greater consciousness and the support of classmates in the group, who provide encouragement and help mark progress along this challenging journey. With patience, persistence, and prayer, they come to a deeper and more mature understanding of themselves, which is grounded in and further increases humility.

6. Pursuit of Justice – *Tzedek Tirdof*

In our courses, we emphasize the pillar of justice that is so central throughout our tradition. We introduce the laws of property damage found in Talmudic tractates of *Bava Kamma* and *Bava Metzia*, and how the Talmud defines a human being as one who has a proclivity to be a "damager." Therefore, we must be very conscientious, careful, regardful, and take precautions in our behavior towards others, so as not to cause harm. Students learn of the intricate, special attention to detail with which our rabbinic tradition pursues in enacting just behavior in all aspects of life. They are awed by the proclamations of the prophets to act justly, and examine the ethical dictums in Proverbs and Ethics of the Fathers (*Pirkei Avot*). Their souls are touched when they learn that the commandment mentioned thirty-six times—more than any other in the Torah—is fair and compassionate treatment of the stranger (even the estranged within the self) and all who have the least protection (e.g., Exod. 23:9). This awakens them to the conditions of our contemporary world, and how the values of Judaism must be implemented in order to create the world of justice and peace that our tradition proclaims will emerge through our elevated deeds. *Tzedek, tzedek tirdof*—"Justice, justice you shall pursue" (Deut.16:20) is a resounding theme in the Academy.

7. Universal Love – *Ahavat ha-Briot*

The prophetic plea for justice leads to a seventh principle proclaimed by Ben Azai, who posited the following as the most important verse in the Torah: "This is the book of all humanity, every human being is created in the image of God" (Gen. 5:1). This verse instructs us to work for justice for *all* humanity, including and especially those of other faiths and folkways, to create a more just and living world. We have joined with Loyola Marymount University, a Jesuit institution where our campus is now located, to implement the corresponding charges in both of our traditions to confront injustice and bestow love on all of humanity. We join in gratitude to form a strengthened voice to promote a robust climate change policy to repair the planet, equal opportunity for all, affordable housing, fulfilling work, and finding connections to God through our encounters with nature. We raise our voices to eliminate racism, sexism, and isolation of any and every less empowered group, and to work for greater economic justice to reduce poverty for those with fewer resources.

8. Individual Uniqueness – *Gadlut ha-Adam*

We strive to eliminate judgmental opinions of others' behaviors and virtues or lack thereof. We follow the dictum of Rav Yisrael Salanter who taught that, "Rather than worrying about another person's spiritual level and your own physical needs, worry about another's physical needs and your own spiritual level." He continued: "The Torah came to create a *mensch*, the more human you are, the more Jewish you are."[4] We are careful to correct behaviors that are not ethical, while still holding respect for the person as one created in God's image, always holding out the possibility for growth and *teshuva* (lit., "return"). Thus, moving toward greater "wholeness" and consciousness leading to ethical behavior is our goal, not "perfection."

Along these lines, our school comprises small classes where we are able to focus on the dynamics of each individual. The Mishnah states that God created each individual singularly. Each human being is unique and has absolute value, thus it is stated, "If you destroy one human being it is as if you have destroyed the whole world and if you save one human being it is as if you have saved the whole world."[5] Each instructor is asked to recognize and evaluate the students they are responsible for, and help them reach their potential. This feeling of care and concern by each of our faculty members and administrators is felt by our students, and this promotes a very warm, supportive environment and a strong feeling of community. The spirit is palpable and stems from the value that acting with love and care helps to strengthen bonds between students and elevate their self-esteem.

---

[4] Dov Katz, *Tenuat Hamusar*, vol.1 (Tel Aviv: Avraham Tzioni, 1963), 296.
[5] m. *Sanhedrin* 4:5.

9. Joy of Acceptance – *Sameach b'Chelko*

The following four principles are culled from ethical teachings in *Pirkei Avot* 4:1, which asks, "Who is happy? One who is satisfied with one's lot. Who is wise? One who learns from all people. Who is strong? One who can control his impulses. And who is honored? One who honors others."

"Who is Happy?" In our advanced curriculum, we know that some individuals will at times feel distressed and discouraged at their inability to reach their goals. As such, we try to promote a realistic assessment of what is possible and an acceptance of all the positives that they have achieved, as well as an encouraging and accepting atmosphere that leads to happiness. Knowing that the spread of a disgruntled energy is counterproductive to learning, we aim to be alert to students who may be struggling and help them find satisfaction in that which they have already achieved in their "lot."

10. Learning from Others – *Lomeid mi-Kol Adam*

"Who is wise?" We attempt to cultivate the value of learning from each other—from the different experiences and perspectives—thereby promoting a healthy learning environment. We have a wide range of ages in our student body. Some have succeeded in other careers, some have the experience of years of service, and some are fresh out of college. Thus, there is a sharing of youthful energy, sharing of the wisdom of years, and an eagerness to learn from and feel gratitude for this wide range of backgrounds in our student body. *Lomeid mi-kol adam*—learning from everyone.

11. Strength in Discipline – *Gevurah*

"Who is Strong?" Discipline and commitment to study, especially at the graduate level, is an arduous task. There must be a sacrifice of previous distractions and comforts in order to prioritize their studies. This takes great discipline and discernment in order to plan properly and say "no" to too many competing interests and to postpone short-term interests. *Koveish et yitzro*—conquering inclinations.

12. Honoring Others – *Kibbud ha-Briot*

"Who is honored?" We expect a modicum of respect to be manifest in all our actions and attitudes toward others. The appreciation of the faculty's knowledge and experience, the honoring of teachers as Torah scholars and ethical humans whose best interest is for the welfare of the students is extremely important. The honoring of students by faculty and classmates is a strength in our culture. *Kibbud ha-briot*—respect for (human) creatures.

13. Interconnection of All Jews – *Kol Yisrael Arevim Zeh l'Zeh*
Finally, the thirteenth principle in our transdenominational school is to respect other denominations and unaffiliated Jews. *Kol yisrael arevim zeh l'zeh*—All of Israel is responsible for each other.[6] We honor the strengths of Orthodox Judaism and its commitment to expansive Torah study, and the close bonding and loyalty to their community and continuing education; the Conservative Movement and its development of *responsa* to contemporary issues, commitment to maintaining tensions between tradition and new conditions that develop in modern society, and its strong Camp Ramah movement which educates their youth and teenagers; the Reform movement with its strong commitment to social justice and social action, and its vibrant interfaith programming to confront the ills of our society; the Reconstructionist movement with its sophisticated appreciation of the historical development of the communal aspects of "Jewish Civilization" and its understanding of God as a natural rather than supernatural being; the Renewal movement, with celebration of joyful prayer, new creative rituals emphasizing spirituality and acceptance, and its honoring of a plethora of lifestyles; the Humanist movement, with its emphasis on ethics and free formulation of beliefs that do not require a traditional concept of God. We also honor the new, independent, creative, non-affiliated synagogues that have emerged over the past years, bringing in Jews who do not have membership in denominational synagogues.

Our intent in creating a transdenominational school was to imbibe from the strengths of each movement and attempt to develop a greater sense of unity within the Jewish community rather than a "worship" of a specific denomination. The fragmentation and divisiveness within the broader Jewish community discouraged students who were looking for a spiritually based program that taught from all strands of Judaism, and emphasized a common experience of a Jewish peoplehood as a whole. They possessed a deep appreciation of the depths of Jewish spirituality and its powerful potential contribution to our contemporary society, and wanted to drink from its deep wells. There was a hunger to taste the depths of Torah and tradition in an atmosphere that allowed free inquiry and honored individuality and creative expression. We felt each of these souls would make distinct and important contributions to a revival of Judaism, and bring relevance to the diverse population of Jewish people yearning to discover or return to their roots.

We are very proud of our nearly 200 graduates, who are each bestowing ethical and spiritual leadership throughout the United States. We are confident that now, more than two decades after the Academy's founding, this

---
[6] b. *Shavuot* 39a.

transdenominational model is gaining momentum in Jewish educational institutions throughout the country, offering ever-widening opportunities to experience the broad spectrum of Jewish wisdom, scholarship, history, and contributions to the larger world. We hope that this creative educational endeavor continues to attract talented students of all ages who wish to dedicate themselves and their talents to sharing the wellsprings of Jewish knowledge and uplifting our world with their special passions and gifts.

Spiritual Ethics: Rachamim

Susan Goldberg

Judaism is a conversation through the generations. Our ancients speak to us through the presence and the absence of texts and through their lived experiences. We create from them and, through our own lives, continue the conversation for those to come. Our cup overflows with wisdom texts, poetry and prayers, stories, melodies, movements, spiritual disciplines, folktales, arts, rituals, cultural traditions, biographies, and more, which extend a conversation back and forward in time. I am held lovingly by Jewish traditions and want to give lovingly to those who come after me. Yet, I have also been unseen and missed in traditions that are also filled with assumptions, paradigms, laws, and cultural norms about women, queer folk, foreigners, and the "other" that have created jagged cliffs in our history and in our present. The teachings in this chapter are for everyone, and especially for those of us who have not always felt seen and held and known. There is wide-open creative space on the margins, and great beauty and truth for everyone when the margin is centered.

In an exploration of spiritual ethics, we find in the deep middle of Jewish life the *middot*—our most important values—such as faith (*emunah*), justice (*tzedek*), kindness (*chesed*), and compassion (*rachamim*). These values are also held by many other ancient and modern traditions. They are cherished and pursued by people of other faiths and cultures, each bringing their own unique wisdom and practices. The Jewish centering of the *middot* is part of a wisdom tradition and spiritual discipline known as Mussar, developed by Rabbi Israel Salanter in nineteenth-century Lithuania and drawing on teachings reaching back centuries.

I claim these values, these *middot*, and I am claimed by them: evocative, challenging, embodied, profound spiritual values that hold us even as we hold them. They are a compass in the wilderness of the unknown that stretches all around us. They give us direction, but they are not directions. There is no turn-by-turn playbook for the adventure of living. But these *middot* point us in the direction we should head. When I was a kid, my dad would sometimes ask us to orient in direction and point to the mountains in the north, now to the west towards the ocean, now to the east towards the desert. He asked us so many times that we knew in our bodies, no matter where we were standing in our city, where we were and which direction we were headed. Many times, in this vast metropolis, I have needed to stand solid on the ground and orient to the mountains and ocean and desert to find my way.

There are times in our lives when we have a choice—either this way or that way—when a clear ethical or life choice is in front of us that requires a clear definitive yes or no decision. These are rare. Most of life is navigating the unknown, the wilderness, *ha-midbar*, with many choices. We are big enough, expansive enough, not to have to make an overly simplistic split into this/that, either/or thinking. Spiritual ethics and spiritual growth hold fluidity, continuum, and space on all sides of where we might get stuck in a binary; it invites us to see that there is more. We are big enough to hold it all.

In Hebrew, the word *middah* means a "measurement," a measure in balance; we are dancing in the fulcrum of balance inside of each *middah*. Sometimes it can be fruitful to name the binary we think we are limited to, so that we can find wisdom in each and then expand beyond the edges. Some of the *middot* have a duality within them that we can excavate. In diving into both, we get to know them better, to draw near, and to find the possibilities opened in moving beyond dualistic thinking and into a nonbinary spirituality.

In learning more about each *middah*, we open our ancient texts for wisdom, we open our lives to learn from our experiences, and we commit to a discipline of spiritual practice. It is wonderful to contemplate the ideas of love (*ahavah*), courage (*ometz lev*), and compassion (*rachamim*), and to deepen our understanding. But understanding alone does not make these values the compass in our lives. There is a challenge and discipline to spiritual practice. Our growth in understanding is connected to our growth in the daily living of our values. Our ancients are nudging us to talk our talk *and* walk our walk. Our values need to be in our mouths as we speak or refrain from speaking, in our work spaces as we make business and professional decisions, in our families and friendships as we care for those we love, in our own minds as we shift cruel inner speech to tender speech, in our legs as we stand for justice and healing and repair in our communities and nation. There are many *middot* to center in all of these realms. For the purpose of this chapter, I will explore *rachamim*—compassion. In so doing, I hope to also open a pathway of possibility in centering a liberated Mussar for spiritual ethics, growth, and transformation of our lives.

When we pick up a *middah* and hold it close, we see that it lives in many realms of our lives at once. This is true of *rachamim* and each of the *middot*. We learn about, practice, and develop each *middah* in our inner selves, our interpersonal relationships with those we are close to, with those we are in community with, and in the world all around us. Rav Kook, an important early twentieth-century rabbi, wrote poetically of a fourfold song:

> There is one who sings the song of her own life, and in herself she finds everything, her full spiritual satisfaction. There is another who sings the song of her people. She leaves the circle of her own individual self, because she finds it without sufficient breadth, without an idealistic basis.... There is another who reaches toward more distant realms, and goes beyond the boundary of the people of Israel to sing the song of humanity.... Then there is one who rises toward wider horizons, until she links herself with all existence, with all God's creatures, with all worlds, and she sings her song with all of them.... And then there is one who rises with all these songs in one ensemble, and they all join their voices. Together they sing their songs with beauty, each one lends vitality and life to the other. They are sounds of joy and gladness, sounds of jubilation and celebration, sounds of ecstasy and holiness. The song of the self, the song of the people, the song of humanity, the song of the world all merge in her at all times, in every hour.[1]

We sing this fourfold song in each of the *middot*. Each realm has its own beauty and importance and our goal is to join the voices together. It is helpful to draw out and focus on one realm at a time, always knowing that all four are singing at once. As we move with compassion, the songs are loud and strong, each contributing to the other. Interpersonal compassion, compassion for others in our community, society, and world, and self-compassion all live inside *rachamim* as breathing, repeating compassions.

Rachamim: Compassion

In the Hebrew language we begin with a *shoresh*, typically a three-letter root, and from there the word changes form but always retains a connection to its root. Branches grow in different shapes of grammatical forms, but the root tells us the core meaning. It is the ground we stand on. In our prayers, this happens repeatedly with the root of compassion, *rachamim*: *reish*, *chet*, *mem*. We noun compassion; we verb compassion; we adjective compassion. In our daily prayer *Ahavah Rabbah* (Abundant Love) we chant this verse: *Ha-Rachaman ham'racheim racheim aleinu*, "The Compassionate One who acts compassionately please have compassion on us."

Compassion lives in ongoing and continuous emphasis and repetition

---

[1] Abraham Isaac Kook, *Orot Hakodesh*, vol. II; translation from James McGinnis, *Educating for Peace and Justice*, 8th ed. (Washington, D.C.: U.S. Department of Education, 1981), 16.

in our lives. We have compassion for those we know and care about, compassion for those we do not know, compassion for ourselves—it is a daily, repeated spiritual commitment. Compassion needs to be given, acted on, and affirmed repeatedly. God as Compassionate One; we as compassionate ones. Our society, families, and communities are places where compassion lives, can live, needs to live. *Rachamim* spreads in all directions around us.

Rachamim is concern and care that moves to action. It is caring expressed in doing. There is movement in *rachamim*. Dr. Kelly McGonigal shares: "Compassion is not 'I feel bad for you.' Compassion is 'I believe it is possible to relieve suffering or to find joy, meaning, connection, hope in the midst of suffering.' Compassion is a process that begins with the recognition of suffering, moves to a sense of care and connection, that moves into a desire to relieve suffering."[2] Compassion begins with awareness, moves to care and concern, and then moves into action. I see you are struggling and I move to action to relieve your suffering.

In the Jewish mystical tradition of Kabbalah, *rachamim* is centered between *chesed* and *gevurah*. *Chesed* is overflowing kindness and *gevurah* is strength that can provide boundaries and solid ground. When we are in the flow of lovingkindness, we can float in our empathy and concern for others. *Gevurah*, strength, comes to remind us that to be compassionate, we need the boundaries that move us to action and care for ourselves and those around us. It is beautiful to float, but *gevurah* allows us to move. However, too much *gevurah* and our approach to ourselves and others, though often well intentioned, will not feel kind. Too much *chesed* and we may be spinning in circles. Compassion balances kindness with strength. It is the care and concern that moves to action.

You and Me: Interpersonal Compassion

Imagine you are seeing your dear ones, those who are closest to you in this life, surrounding you. Imagine your compassion enveloping them with ease, with words that connect, with little and big gestures of care, with a baseline of compassion that they feel from us and in us. We want this for them, especially for them, but it does not always go like this. We find blocks and frustrations and a need for skills and support to make our daily interactions a possible home base for compassion. "Possible" because it is not going to be at all times and all moments, but we do want to pursue with intent the

---

[2] Kelly McGonigal, "The Practical Science of Compassion," Compassion in Therapy Summit, February 2021. See also Kelly McGonigal, *The Science of Compassion: A Modern Approach for Cultivating Empathy, Love, and Connection* (Newark, NJ: Audible Audiobook, 2016).

possibility of a baseline of *rachamim*. Indeed, it is with the ones we are closest to that this is so vital and yet so challenging.

In the realm of interpersonal compassion with our children, parents, partners, friends, lovers, our dear ones, the first move is into empathy. Empathy is often confused with compassion, but empathy and compassion are not the same. Empathy can help us connect with another and, from there, move to action. In our interpersonal relationships, empathy that moves to action is compassion. Sometimes we might need to stay with empathy for a while. But we need to be cautious of an empathy that stays in its own deep well for too long. We can become so deeply underwater that it is difficult to move and almost impossible to take in the whole around us. In our intimate relationships, the practice of compassion creates a groove of empathy that we can find again and again. Relationship agility with empathy makes it possible for the person right here with us to be heard, seen, acknowledged, and held. Not just near us but with us, in us. As e. e. cummings penned, "i carry your heart with me(i carry it in my heart)."[3]

In the motion of *rachamim* we move into empathy. Empathy steps into the interior experience of another (or ourselves) without judgment, critique, advice, minimizing, exaggerating, catastrophizing, or pity. The feelings and experience of the other person simply are what they are. It is simple—simple yet sometimes profoundly challenging to enter into a state that is curious and receptive, without judgement, without an agenda. A gentle move towards you, to look around with curiosity and wonder. In empathy, I wonder what it is like for you. I wonder about the landscape, its texture, its logic, its flow. I am not changing it, I am inhabiting it. What is it calling out for?

One of the many names we use for the divine in Judaism is *Ha-Makom*, The Place. In cultivating a spiritual state of empathy, we enter into an expansive *makom*. Time changes; we are unhurried and able to open into a limitless expanse. Even if it is only for a moment or two, the willingness and the ability to do so creates the grounded genuine reality of connection.

In the field of somatic studies, we learn that the way a movement begins, its initiation, decides the course of action (Laban Movement Analysis).[4] When someone is in pain or needing to find new patterns of movement, we look carefully at how they initiate everyday movement to see where a new point of initiation can begin in order to transform what comes next.

---

[3] e.e. cummings, *Complete Poems: 1904–1962*, ed. George J. Firmage (New York: Liveright, 1991), 776.
[4] See Peggy Hackney, *Making Connections: Total Body Integration Through Bartenieff Fundamentals* (New York: Routledge, 2003); and Carol-Lynne Moore, *Meaning in Motion: Introducing Laban Movement Analysis* (Denver, CO: MoveScape Center, 2014).

Sequence is crucial. So it is with compassion for those we are close to: how we begin, how we initiate, is integral to *rachamim*. Empathy is step one. And, oh so often, it is the step that is missed. Missing empathy shapes what unfolds next. We need empathy to grow and develop as humans. For many of us, the lack of empathy in childhood becomes a theme that colors our lives. Humans need the experience of what Dr. Daniel Siegel calls "feeling felt" by another.[5] The powerful sense that you "get" me, that what I am experiencing is grasped and felt by you. Not just an outline of understanding but a deeper knowing. We want and need to experience that we are held inside of another, on a fundamental level, without corrections, criticism, or hiding of our true self.

When a young child falls down, an adult invariably comes over and says, "You're fine. You're alright." The child might be fine, but there is no space before they are being told what and how they are to feel. No space to wonder or give compassion. If the child is crying, the tears will often elicit an even more forceful assertion that they are fine. What if, rather than telling them what they feel, a moment of connecting and asking: "You fell down. Are you okay? How does it feel?" It is just a moment, but it creates a profound difference in what is possible after this moment.

This state of curiosity and empathy inside of *rachamim*, or the painful lack of it, continues as children become adults: When they are twenty-six and going through a heartbreak, being told, "You're fine, you're fine;" or losing a job at fifty-two; or being diagnosed with a rare form of cancer at forty-one. "You're okay, you're brave, you're a fighter." Where is the curiosity and empathy? How about asking the person, rather than deciding for them, how they feel, especially during hard experiences? We can say: "Wow. Cancer. How are you doing with everything going on? What is this like for you?" "You lost your job. How are you managing?" "I heard about your father. I can imagine. How are you doing with the grief today?"

There are so many missed opportunities to connect with people we genuinely want to be compassionate toward. Ask someone how they are and then be open to hearing their real answer. Telling people what they feel lacks humility; even though it is an attempt at compassion, it often wildly misses the mark. This kind of communication generally comes from fear. The prevailing culture we live in is profoundly emotion phobic. When people are trying to tell you what to feel, especially to steer you away from the difficult feelings of fear or grief or anger, it is because they are uncomfortable with their own feelings. What is happening to you is likely freaking them out. So,

---

[5] Daniel Siegel, *Mindsight: The New Science of Personal Transformation* (New York: Bantam, 2010), 10-11.

they tell you to reassure *themselves*. There is kindness in this, but it is hard to see because it is masked in a lack of curiosity and empathy. Thinking about how you want to express your concern and care is a practice of compassion. If you know that you are actually unable to hear what is real for the other person, it is also a practice of compassion to not ask until you are ready to hear and take in what they have to say.

Our feelings are incredible signals of our values, of what is important to us, of what we need to live meaningful lives. When we ignore them, push them down, battle against them, we lose the depth and beauty of living. Learning how to give empathy to another person is one way we deepen our connection to life. Our ease and fluency with feelings and our ability to cultivate curiosity and empathy are skills we can develop. Unfortunately, these skills are often left out of our educational curriculum (both in general and religious education), but they are skills we can intentionally develop.

I purposefully use the term "skills" in relation to interpersonal empathy. Judaism emphasizes ritual and ethical actions as the foundation of our spiritual lives. These practices are worked on and deepened over time. When we develop our skills of *rachamim*, we are deepening our connection to our spiritual path: the cultivation of a state of curiosity and empathy, the ability to communicate that empathy (the idea of "giving empathy"), and identifying actions to apply that empathy.

There are many tools and programs that can assist in honing these skills. The interpersonal compassion work developed by Marshall Rosenberg greatly supports the growth of interpersonal empathy, the emotional literacy required, and the communication support that moves empathy from a concept to fully realized, everyday words and actions.[6] Dr. Kathy Simon, whose work is based on Rosenberg's, created lists of feelings and needs to help facilitate the doing of compassionate communication, both with those with whom we want to connect and those with whom we are in conflict. Compassionate communication begins with curiosity and wonder and naming the feelings that are present. This is followed by a recognition of needs that are either being met or unmet. From there, one moves into requests that bring about positive action. These lists of feelings and needs are helpful in bringing clarity and deeper connection into hazy, difficult, or overwhelming moments.

---

[6] See Marshall Rosenberg, *Nonviolent Communication: A Language of Life* (Encinitas, CA: PuddleDancer, 2003).

Feelings – precious aspects of our humanity

AFFECTIONATE
compassionate
friendly
loving
openhearted
sympathetic
tender
warm

CONFIDENT
empowered
open
proud
safe
secure

ENGAGED
absorbed
alert
curious
engrossed
entranced
fascinated
interested
intrigued
involved
stimulated

EXCITED
amazed
animated
ardent
aroused
dazzled
eager
energetic
enthusiastic
giddy
invigorated
lively

EXHILARATED
blissful
elated
enthralled
exuberant
radiant
rapturous
thrilled

GRATEFUL
appreciative
moved
thankful
touched

HOPEFUL
expectant
encouraged
optimistic

JOYFUL
amused
delighted
glad
happy
jubilant
pleased
tickled

INSPIRED
amazed
awed
wonder

REFRESHED
enlivened
rejuvenated
renewed
rested
restored
revived

PEACEFUL
calm
clearheaded
comfortable
centered
content
equanimous
fulfilled
quiet
relaxed
relieved
satisfied
serene
still
tranquil
trusting

AFRAID
apprehensive
dread
foreboding
frightened
mistrustful
panicked
petrified
scared
suspicious
terrified
wary
worried

ANNOYED
aggravated
dismayed
disgruntled
displeased
exasperated
frustrated
impatient
irritated

AVERSE
appalled
disgusted
dislike
hate
horrified
hostile
repulsed

CONFUSED
ambivalent
baffled
bewildered
dazed
hesitant
lost
perplexed
puzzled
torn

EMBARRASSED
ashamed
chagrined
flustered
self-conscious

FATIGUED
depleted
exhausted
lethargic
listless
sleepy
tired
weary

YEARNING
envious
jealous
longing
nostalgic
wistful

DISCONNECTED
alienated
apathetic
bored
detached
distant
distracted
indifferent
numb
withdrawn

DISQUIETED
agitated
alarmed
disturbed
rattled
restless
shocked
startled
surprised
troubled
uncomfortable
uneasy
unsettled
upset

TENSE
anxious
cranky
distressed
distraught
edgy
fidgety
frazzled
irritable
jittery
nervous
overwhelmed
restless
stressed

SAD
depressed
dejected
desperate
despondent
disappointed
discouraged
disheartened
forlorn
gloomy
heavy hearted
hopeless
melancholy
unhappy
wretched

PAIN
anguished
bereaved
devastated
grief
heartbroken
hurt
lonely
regretful
remorseful

VULNERABLE
fragile
guarded
helpless
insecure
leery
reserved
sensitive
shaky

Based on Marshall Rosenberg's Nonviolent Communication, adapted by Kathy Simon, 2019
kathysimon@icloud.com
www.kathysimonphd.com

HUMAN NEEDS for THRIVING

CONNECTION
acceptance
affection
appreciation
belonging
caring
communication
community
companionship
compassion
consideration
cooperation
empathy
familiarity
inclusion
interdependence
intimacy
love
mutuality
nurturing
partnership
respect

CONNECTION, cont.
support
to know and be known
to see and be seen
to understand
to be understood
trust
warmth

AUTHENTICITY
honesty
integrity
presence
self-expression
truth
wholeness

AUTONOMY
choice
confidence
freedom
independence
privacy
self-respect
space

MEANING
awareness
awe, wonder
celebration
challenge
clarity
competence
contribution
creativity
discovery
effectiveness
growth
inspiration
learning
mourning
power
purpose
self-actualization
understanding

WELL-BEING OF OTHERS
We have all of these needs in relation to people we care about

PEACE
beauty
ease
equanimity
harmony
tranquility

PHYSICAL WELL-BEING
air, food, water, shelter
balance
comfort
movement, exercise
rest, sleep
relaxation
sexual expression
safety
touch

PLAY
adventure
fun, joy, laughter
spontaneity

Based on Marshall Rosenberg's Nonviolent Communication, adapted by Kathy Simon, 2019
kathysimon@icloud.com
www.kathysimonphd.com

Charts by Kathy Simon. Used by permission.

Guiding questions while doing this work include: How many of these feelings do you feel at ease in recognizing in yourself or others? Are there some that you know very well and others that seem less familiar? When you think about your beloveds, your close relationships, how often are you curious about the range of feelings they may be experiencing? At my home, we have this list of needs posted on our refrigerator for easy access. I highly recommend keeping it close. We grab it when there is conflict, when there is something happening that seems deeper than what is being talked about, or when things just feel difficult and someone needs support.

When we step into compassionate communication, we do so with curiosity, wonder, and the intent to name the feelings present and the needs that are either being met or unmet. If we are not in a state of curiosity and openness, it is good not to enter in. One of the keys to interpersonal compassion is recognizing when we are not able to do it, so that we are not faking it when we are agitated, annoyed, frustrated, or maybe running late for something else. It is very important to know when we are simply not in the proper emotional or mental state, and to be able to say, "I know you are wanting me to hear you and connect but I can't right now. Can we set aside some time later when I get back?" Or, "I can tell this is not going to go well. I am too angry. I need to go for a walk." Pushing into *rachamim* when we are distracted or overwhelmed will not turn out well.

Only when we are in a state of curiosity and empathy can we enter the practice of interpersonal compassion. To be sure, this is not always achievable. Not only do we need to reach this open state, but so too does the other person. If we do not have the room to be curious about the other person, or if there is someone in our lives who is not able to do so for us, that is important to know so that we can shift our expectations and not be continuously trying to connect in a way that is not possible.

When we are able to, we begin by listening to the experience of the one sharing with us and wondering aloud about the feelings and needs that might be present for them. They can and should tell us if they feel we are hearing them and to identify for us feelings and needs that are present but were not initially heard. It is a dynamic process and one that often uncovers new aspects of the landscape we did not know about or had passed over too quickly.

The Torah tells us that Jacob, after leaving his family home in Beer-Sheba, heads to Haran. Along the way, he stops for the night and in that sleep has an incredible dream with angels going up and down a stairway and God appearing to speak to Jacob about his destiny and that of his people. When Jacob wakes from his dream he says, "Surely God is in this place (*makom*) and I did not know" (Gen. 28:16). There is the potential of opening to the divine presence in every place; Jacob realizes that this ostensibly random place where he slept, a one-night stopover, was enlivened by the divine. This is precisely the process that occurs when we are open to curiosity and wonder about others, about ourselves, and about our world. Judaism nudges us to explore everything around us more deeply, from all sides and all angles. When we do so, we enter into a *makom*, a sacred space of exploration, wonder, and awe about ideas, principles, and the multifaceted and multi-sided human being right here in front of us. This space yields a far greater depth and consciousness than we were aware of before we began. The exploration can connect us with the unending possibilities of the divine in each place, in each moment, in each person, in all things. This is the beauty of reflexive consciousness.

It can be a highly supportive, potentially sacred, process to explore feelings and needs. However, it is not yet fully realized compassion until and unless we move from ideas to actions, from requests for help to meeting their needs. Compassionate actions can take on many forms in our interpersonal relationships. They are unique to the people we are close to and what they want and need. The creative possibilities for compassionate actions are endless; there are always many more creative actions than we at first imagined. And the more specific we can be as to what we or the other person needs, the more deeply compassion and care land in us. One of the biggest misconceptions of close relationships is that we are supposed to magically always know what someone wants us to do for them. Hearing what someone needs and coming up with specific actions we can take for them is invaluable, both for the giver and the receiver. We can ask: "Please say hello to me and the kids when you come in from work before checking your phone or doing any other task. I want to connect after not seeing you all day." "Could you please wake me up three times each morning because I'm a teenager and I'm not able to get up the first time you come in? And it helps if you know that and are not surprised and frustrated with me every morning."

Of course, other things are not as simple and require more work. For example, "I am wanting more connection with you in the evenings and that is hard when you are drinking every night. My request is that you drink less." Or, "My request is that you look into why you have been drinking so much more." Or, "My request is that you get some help." The process still begins with coming to an understanding about what we are needing in our lives, signaled by our emotions, and the necessary action may or may not be something that the other person can do. If we only stayed in empathy, the person may say, "Yes, I see that is hard for you," but no change is made.

It is when the empathy and concern move to action that it becomes compassion, *rachamim*.

Relationship compassion begins with empathy and moves from there. We cannot skip over empathy, but we also cannot stay in it as a continuous state. We dip in and out of it as needed—the agility of empathy. Without empathy, what follows lacks depth and fortitude; but if we stay there forever we are swimming in a stagnant pond. Empathy and understanding can signal to us the path we need to take, and then we must get up and go there.

Me to Me: Self Compassion

When we develop our skills in interpersonal *rachamim*, we also learn more about how we want others to connect and relate to us and how we relate to ourselves. For some of us, it is much easier to be empathetic to others than to ask that others interact with us that way, or to actively give ourselves self-empathy. Developing skills in empathy nudges us to also include ourselves in the kindness and compassion that we righteously believe all people deserve, but sometimes exclude ourselves from.

There is a beautiful phrase repeated in Jewish prayer, *chein v'chesed v'rachamim*—"Grace, lovingkindness, and compassion." We pray that grace, kindness, and compassion surround us and all the people around us. We repeat these three together. It is how we want to be held by God; it is how we want to hold each other.

I often wonder how we would collectively walk, talk, and act in the world were we to feel grace, lovingkindness, and compassion surrounding us. What is possible when we feel that? What is possible when we act *as if* we feel that? When we offer ourselves self-compassion, we are tapping into the continuous *shefa*, the divine flow, of grace, kindness, compassion.

Verses in prayer or chanting are repetitive for a reason. Many ancient cultures have practices of repeated phrases or mantras. The intention is to develop a spiritual premise—a spiritual baseline that we return to again and again, which shapes how we move through the world. Many of the people who come to me for spiritual counseling do not have a baseline of compassion in relation to themselves. If you were to write down the most often repeated phrases you tell yourself about yourself, what would they be? Would they be filled with kindness and grace?

Rachamim has a plural ending form, literally "compassions." This points us even further in the direction of the plural, of the repetition inside of compassion. There is spiritual wisdom in repetition, both in the repeated phrases we tell ourselves and in the repeated spiritual lessons we seem to circle around, again and again, throughout our lives. And these two, the messages and the repeated lessons, are related to each other. Humans repeat, repeat, and repeat. We learn and then return to the same lesson, and need to learn and grow again. Our development is a spiral. When children are little, they often circle back to tap into what is needed for the next round of spiraling growth. Unfortunately, this is often labeled as "regression" when it is actually a time for support and preparation for more growth. Adults do this too. As it turns out, adults continue to grow—or have the potential to grow—all throughout our lives.

The goal is not to learn everything all at once; that is an unrealistic expectation that can leave us judging ourselves harshly. We develop throughout our lives, circling back at different times to learn a new layer of the same lesson. Sometimes this is frustrating. This again? Yes, this again. A practice of self-compassion embraces our repeated learning and integrates the new pieces of insight that come in each spiral of learning and re-learning.

Each of us have our unique, specific learnings that we circle back to. They are our accompanists in our lives. Their music is familiar, their presence is consistent; we grow in their directions. They are our unique spiritual curriculum. Often, our repeated patterns, the repeated lessons we circle around, come with a story we tell ourselves about ourselves. The story encapsulates who we think we are, what we can and cannot do, and why things happen to us. The stories are often born from a painful or diminished place, and when they repeat constantly inside of us, as they do, they shape how we see ourselves and what we are able to offer others and the world. Most often, they are not internal stories filled with compassion and kindness.

A practice of self-compassion is to draw these stories into the light and see if they are true to who we are and who we can be. As we come to know our repeated internal stories we tell ourselves about ourselves, we can begin to suffuse them with kindness and grace. Their continued presence can become not a frustration, but an invitation to their ongoing and continuous teaching. We can hold them lighter and lighter as our acknowledgement and connection to their teachings grows.

In the Book of Exodus, *Shemot*, when Moses comes to the burning bush and hears the presence of the Divine telling him that he needs to go back to Egypt—to *Mitzrayim*, the Narrow Place—and lead a movement for freedom, he immediately responds, "No, I don't think I am the right person for this. It's not me. I am not able to do that." God says, "Oh yes, it is you" (Exod. 3:11-12). And it truly does seem that it is him. Moses was a child raised in two worlds: the home of his people, and the adopted home of Pharaoh's daughter and the rest of the household. He has access to power, he speaks their language, and he has also witnessed the injustice. Moses continues resisting, "No it's not me. They won't listen to me." And God continues to respond: "Yes, it is you." Moses: "I have a speech impediment, they really won't listen to me" (Exod. 4:10). God: "Yes, it is you." This continues back and forth. Finally, God tells Moses that he does not have to do it alone. Moses' brother Aaron can help with his speaking (Exod. 4:14-18).

Moses goes to Pharaoh and says, "Let my people go" (Exod. 5:1). After Moses' attempt, Pharaoh makes it harder on the people. Now no straw is provided for the bricks. The Hebrew slaves must make the same number of bricks and also gather the straw as well. Forced to work harder, they say to Moses and Aaron, "What are you doing to us? May God punish you for this!" (Exod. 5:21). Moses goes back to God and says, "I told you that I cannot do this. The Israelites will not listen to me. Pharaoh will not listen to me. It is my speech impediment—*Ani aral sh'fatyaim.*" (Exod. 6:12). Moses blames his lack of success on his speech, rather than, say, the Pharaoh's use of the Hebrews as a source of labor, his desire to keep power, his avoidance of appearing weak, his fear of inspiring others to rebel, or many other warranted reasons. It is an inaccurate and self-defeating story Moses is telling himself about himself.

Our formative narratives have such power in us; they can take hold over our lives. Sometimes they are true and sometimes they are not true. Dr. Susan David discusses how we get hooked into these stories, like the hook of a song that we cannot get out of our heads.

> The human mind is a meaning-making machine, and a big part of being human is laboring to make sense of all of the input around us...our way of making sense is to organize all the sights and sounds and experiences and relationships around us into a coherent narrative....The narratives serve a purpose: We tell ourselves these stories to organize our experiences and keep ourselves sane...The trouble is we all get things wrong...we accept the pervasive self-accounts without question as if it's the whole truth....We crawl into these fables and let a sentence or a paragraph which may have originated (many years ago) and never been tested and verified, represent the totality of our lives.[7]

---

[7] Susan David, *Emotional Agility: Get Unstuck, Embrace Change, and Thrive in Work and Life*

We tell ourselves these words as our continuous inner messages. Usually, they do not sing out with *chein, chesed, v'rachamim*—grace, kindness and compassion.

A self-compassion practice begins with embracing the lessons and messages that repeat inside of us so that we can hear them clearly. We notice them and draw them out. Often, we need to cultivate an intentional practice of quiet to hear these messages and other times they are so loud that we know immediately what they are. It can be helpful to write them down: these are the messages that I repeat to myself, the story that I tell about myself, and about why my life is this way, and these are the patterns that I repeat, repeat, repeat.

In a compassion practice, alongside drawing out these internal, always-present messages, we create new phrases to repeat: phrases that are kindly tailored to our own growth in compassion. In Jewish practice, we look through our prayers, psalms, or passages of scripture to find verses that we can repeat. We can select from verses found in prayer or scripture or in other spiritual sources. Poetry and song lyrics are other places to look. You might also write a short phrase that you create yourself. You can then set an intentional time to repeat the verse or mantra, such as a morning practice or an evening prayer or when you stop at a red light or every time you drink water. You can hear the phrase in your mind or recite it out loud. One practice is to whisper chant the verse while rocking back and forth, allowing the phrase and the repetitive motion to help integrate the words into your being.

Once you begin the regular recitation of the phrase, you will likely find that it is ready to come out when it is needed: in moments of stress or heightened moments of negative or judgmental self-talk. The first step is to interrupt and *shavat*, cease, the old patterned message and let the new phrase enter. The more we carry the new phrase, the more it is at the ready to enter in. In a practice of self-compassion, we actively interrupt and refrain from the unkind patterned response. This step is essential because it means that we are hearing it and not just letting it be part of the continuous background music that is present with us. We are aware of it, draw it out, intentionally refrain from its continuous repetition, and offer a new phrase, a new repetition. Sometimes, the affirming verses, phrases, or mantras are ongoing and help to shape our baseline. At other times, they are there to support us through a particularly difficult moment, a crisis time.

I had a teenaged congregant who was dealing with an unexplained digestive condition that became so painful and taxing that she was unable to

---

(New York: Avery, 2016), 18.

attend school. She ended up spending most of her time in bed. Struggling to figure out what was ailing her, the doctors began telling her that it was likely caused by anxiety and stress. She knew this was not true, and their dismissiveness only added to the pain and exhaustion brought on by the condition. Finally, a nutritionist made a link between her symptoms and those of a former client. She suggested that the girl ask her doctor about a rare condition, which turned out to be what she had. A specific surgical procedure could mend the condition. She was relieved but also very scared. She wanted a comforting verse for when she was preparing for the day of surgery, entering the surgical room, and during the time she was separated from her parents. Together, we looked through the *Birkat ha-Shachar*, the morning blessings, and she chose the blessing, *Baruch atah Adonai Eloheinu Melech ha-olam matir asurim*: "Blessed are you Sacred Name, our God, sovereign of the world, for releasing the captive." She felt she had been captive of this condition for so long and now was finally going to be released. Repeating this phrase was a way she comforted and strengthened herself—an act of self-compassion during a scary and important time.

There is an incident in Torah, in the Book of Numbers, *Bamidbar*, where the people are journeying in the *midbar* (wilderness) and are bitten by snakes (Num. 21:6-9). In order to help the people, God tells Moses to make a sculpture of a snake out of copper on the top of his staff. Each person who was bitten must stare into the eyes of the copper snake in order to be healed. Likewise, we can take the struggle points that are biting us, reshape them, and stare into them to find healing and transformation. This is true of our repeated life patterns and of our ongoing internal messages. Pull them out into the light, see the snake that is biting us, change their shape and message, and stare directly into them. Self-compassion requires a commitment to truth telling and a willingness to work with what is always present inside of us to transform it with and for grace, kindness, and compassion.

We: Collective Compassion

When we open our sacred scripture, the Torah, there is a commandment that we find over and over. It tells us in clear and unambiguous language to care for the stranger, the widow, and the orphan (e.g., Exod. 22:20-21). It is the commandment most repeated in the Torah: Pay special attention to and care for the most vulnerable in society. This is collective *rachamim*. Similar teachings are found in sacred texts of other ancient traditions, stressing the importance of concern and care for those who need help and support. Compassion is a value shared the world over. It is an integral part of who we are as humans.

There are many avenues to move from concern into action on behalf of those who are most vulnerable, and there is no lack of need. We hear from friends and family, from our own experiences, and from seeing the world all around us. Some of us are acutely aware of the countless manifestations of vulnerability and oppression in our society and in the world. Some of us learn from listening to others or from media. There are so many articles, podcasts, news programs, books, songs, expressions of the pain and suffering in the world. Sometimes, I feel that when I open the morning paper it shapes into an open, gaping mouth and swallows me whole. In this learning, we are growing our understanding; but learning alone—empathy alone—is not sufficient. We must *act*.

How about doing an inventory? Take out a sheet of paper and write down two numbers. The first number: How much time each week do you spend learning, hearing, reading about what is happening in the world from friends and family and media? The second number: How much time are you spending taking actions to change, transform, bring compassion to areas of need in the world? How much difference do you find in the two numbers? The two might never be in a full, equal balance, but it is possible for them to come pretty close. And, if you miss watching the news, or hearing a report, or reading a piece about something that is happening in the world because you are spending that time in the service of making it better, know that there will always be more to read and learn. Moving from understanding and concern into action is the movement of compassion, *rachamim*.

Compassion can be brought into the world in numerous ways. Some people feel angst and genuine concern for the world around them, yet are immobilized by the belief that they must do something big—something that will eliminate a problem altogether—before they feel they can take a step toward do something, anything, to help. However, according to Judaism and many ancient traditions, we *must* be of service to others. We can focus on our own community and help a neighbor in need. We can form a group of ten neighbors and set up mutual aid. We can reach out to local organizations and volunteer to give food or help to find shelter for our unhoused neighbors. We can learn more about why people are unhoused and begin to advocate for new policies on a citywide, countywide, statewide, or national level. Social service is helping find someone food or shelter; social justice is asking why people are hungry and without homes and working to change the conditions. There are many ways to bring compassion into the world.

The Ayni Institute shares that there are three main ways people chose to engage in making the world better: personal transformation, changing dominant institutions, and creating alternative models.[8] They use the

---

[8] Ayni Institute, https://ayni.institute/.

example of a schoolteacher who has worked in a well-funded, privileged school and then transfers to a new school in a neighborhood with a legacy of racism and poverty. She immediately observes the inequity and injustice. She decides to focus on helping individual kids in her classroom. She raises funds to help the kids with tutoring, field trips, and extra curriculars. She continues to do so through their high school years and sets up college funds for her students. She believes in the power of personal transformation and the idea that helping even one individual can have a tremendous impact.

Another teacher in this same situation decides that to make it better for her students, she needs to get involved in changing the unfair educational system as a whole. She believes that systemic change is fundamental to improving conditions, not just for her students but for many others. She gets involved in organizing with other teachers, students, and parents, and is active in campaigns for changes in the educational system in her city and state. She is committed to changing dominant institutions.

A third teacher in this same scenario decides that she wants her students to have a new way to experience education. Together with a couple of her colleagues, she starts a new school with different priorities and approaches to education. She believes that we do not need to wait to create the schools that students deserve now. She is committed to creating alternative institutions.

All three of the teachers care about their students and want to make positive changes. They have learned about and have empathy for the challenges that an unfair educational system brings to students. And they all take actions in the world to make it better. They are embodying *rachamim* in different ways. Each of these educators embodies deep compassion for their students and each expresses that compassion in their own way.

There is no lack of possibilities to be involved in expressing compassion in the world. You begin with the harm, injustices, and vulnerabilities that need to be addressed, your own skills and talents, and where your passion and energy lead you. You can also see what friends and family and neighbors are involved in and join them. Getting involved together with family, friends, and community helps to support your commitment and long-term involvement. It also greatly encourages the participation of additional family and friends who witness your collective action.

Rachamim is expressed in action. Sometimes the actions are small and sometimes the actions are on behalf of largescale change. Compassion is present when we listen deeply to those we love and care for in specific, kind, and supportive ways. It is present when we hear an old, harsh storyline we tell ourselves and interrupt it with a new baseline. It is alive when we move to make the world a better place for one person, and when we join together to make systemic, lasting change. *Rachamim* moves and breathes in ongoing and continuous acts that hold us as we hold others.

May you move with compassion towards those you love.

May it dwell in your insides with grace and kindness.

May it guide and inspire your continuous actions of care for the most vulnerable in our society and world.

Mel Gottlieb responds

Rabbi Susan Goldberg's rich essay articulating the dynamics of *rachamim* is filled with creative, astute insights into the dynamic of this important *middah*. Rabbi Goldberg describes this trait as a movement beginning with the requisite energy of awareness, then moving to a feeling of care and concern for another, and then actualizing this energy into concrete action. One sees another struggling, and moves actively to understand and "stand with" the other in holy relationship. One cannot take away another's suffering, but the act of active listening and understanding leads to a reduction of pain and potential resilient recovery to a state of balance.

I resonated with her use of *rachamim* as defined by Danny Siegel: feeling felt by another. She elaborates that this means being felt by another without correction, criticism, or hiding of one's true self. This is congruent with the Torah's description of an ameliorative relationship in chapter 19:17-18 of Leviticus: "Thou shalt surely correct your neighbor....Love your neighbor as yourself." I think these verses mean that if you are to directly communicate with your neighbor, it must not only be done honestly, but you must treat the other as your neighbor with love and respect.

Rabbi Goldberg draws out a very important skill in developing a relationship that is filled with *rachamim* by pointing out the importance of *asking* a person what they are feeling, rather than describing what you think they may be feeling, as the latter habit deprives the other of being accurately understood. She advises that it is important to be patient, to slow down, and respect the other's capacity to communicate. She gives examples of how this empowers the other to confidently share what they are feeling. Thus, self-awareness and some psychological insight are also requisite in the ability to convey *rachamim*. It takes great sensitivity, intuition, and experience with children to learn the importance of waiting a bit before reacting, in order for the reality of the other person to be brought forth.

Therefore, Rabbi Goldberg also suggests honest curiosity as a necessary skill to bring forth the depth of another's soul. This insight can only be possessed by someone who has a true understanding of *rachamim*, and her instruction is an important learning tool for anyone who wants to increase their expertise in becoming a healer, or a spiritual counselor helping to enable another's growth. Rather than "advice giving" or "reassurance," the most valuable and effective skill to enter the space of *rachamim* is the ability to learn about another through the other's confident expression, brought forth by the trait of *rachamim*.

Rabbi Goldberg defines "relationship compassion/*rachamim*" as containing the components of 1) empathy, 2) understanding (concern), and 3) action. The dynamic of action is crucial to her view of the embodiment of this trait. If the trait is to contribute to the healing of another, it must be utilized practically in the real world of relationship with others. Modeling this trait, and acting from a place of *rachamim*, is a very high spiritual level—a trait that is identified with the center of God's being. It is one of the thirteen traits that describes God's relationship to the world, and we are urged to work to embody these traits to actualize God's presence in our world.

Rabbi Goldberg astutely points out that the trait of compassion must also apply to the way we view and treat ourselves. If we are critical or overly judgmental to ourselves, we are unlikely to be capable of sharing *rachamim* with others. She points out that the word *rachamim* is expressed in the plural form, and she extracts from that the insight that we often repeat our judgments toward ourselves. We repeat stories about ourselves from childhood embedded in our psyches, often without consciousness of this inner process. As we move along in the life process, the stories may shift but retain the initial negative perceptions acquired from our early family life or outer environments. Thus, there is work to be done in examining our inner attitudes toward ourselves, and becoming more conscious of the repetitions that control us and inhibit our capacity for self-compassion.

Rabbi Goldberg suggests that some of the practices of the Mussar movement may aid our ability to ameliorate our proclivity toward self-judgment, and move to the realm of self-compassion. One suggestion that she presents is utilizing a conscious "interruptive phrase" as an antidote and counter-force to the habitual repetitive self-critical chatter that goes one within our psyches without our self-awareness. When we begin to notice our negative messages through heightened consciousness and commitment to grow, we can then interrupt this "old record" with a substitute "mantra" such as *Shiviti* ("I place God in front of me at all times"), or *Sh'ma*, or a pleasant memory or scene in nature that brings balance and the potential to own the loving part of our soul, along with God's love for us even with all our imperfections. This active practice is essential to develop the important self-compassion that is necessary in developing "relational *rachamim*."

A final important contribution in her essay is the recognition that one must bring the trait of *rachamim* as a powerful force to change institutional, systemic forms of anti-*rachamim*. It is not only on a personal and interpersonal level that the benefits of *rachamim* can be beneficial, but in the larger systems in which we live. How can we bring *rachamim* into our workplaces, by identifying how these systems may be oppressive, anti-humanistic, and filled with judgments that obviate the possibility of *rachamim* to heal and elevate the spirit of an institution? One way is to first notice these institutional power structures and observe whether they are consonant with the importance of the *rachamim* that we so highly value. The observation, the analysis, and the respectful feedback given to those who create and sustain these systems may be a first step in creating more humane work environments, and a variety of relational systems, and indeed this is a great blessing.

Susan Goldberg responds

It was a delight to read Rabbi Mel Gottlieb's essay for this collection. It captured the soulful ethics he brings to all of his endeavors and, importantly, has brought to the Academy for Jewish Religion California during his tenure of leadership. As an alumna of the Academy and a student of Rabbi Gottlieb, I have had the opportunity to experience the fruits of the intentional commitment he describes: "we committed ourselves to creating an institution that would not only be a place of rigorous text study, but also an environment where ethical behavior and personal spiritual growth would be a primary emphasis."

It was this very sentiment that led me to choose the Academy as the yeshiva/seminary for my rabbinical training. I was hoping for an environment that cultivated rigorous intellectual and spiritual development, rather than prioritizing one over the other, and that was indeed what I found.

The Mussar learning at the Academy in both classes and in our weekly spiritual development groups created an environment where students were invited and challenged to develop spiritually in a profound relationship with the *middot*. Beyond the curriculum, the environment of the school itself— guided by the principles Rabbi Gottlieb elucidates—created a home for learning where everyone was engaged in meaningful growth. In particular I want to highlight the *middah* of *anavah*, humility, which Rabbi Gottlieb includes as one of his 13 ethical principles of the Academy. The faculty and, in particular, the administrators were centered in humility. There was confidence in their own knowledge but also a willingness to grow, acknowledge assumptions, and to meet each person and each situation with an openness to what they uniquely had to offer. This humility and generosity of spirit spurred on our growth as students. Alan Morinis describes *anavah* as the ability of each person to "Occupy a rightful space, neither too much nor too little."[1] At the Academy, we were encouraged to grow into our full selves and to leave room for others to occupy their space fully. This *anavah* was

---

[1] Alan Morinis, *Everyday Holiness: The Jewish Spiritual Path of Mussar* (Boston: Trumpeter, 2007), 45.

modeled by the administration repeatedly. This foundation in humility also connects with the principle of "Individual Uniqueness – *Gadlut ha-Adam*" as shared by Rabbi Gottlieb. Each student was viewed and treated as a unique soul with unique gifts and challenges. We did not feel there was only one way to grow in our learning and in our leadership. Rabbi Gottlieb would often remind us: "Any way can be a way as long as you make it a way."

As Rabbi Gottlieb comes to the end of the tenure of his leadership at the Academy, I am curious what he feels now as he reflects on the school and these guiding principles. I wonder if it would be a meaningful endeavor to reflect with students on these principles and gather stories on how these ideals became reality in the everyday working of the Academy. I imagine he would be uplifted by the concrete examples of these aspirational principles. I imagine, too, that there would be areas that have fallen short of the ideals, since perfection is unattainable and in fact not the goal. A commitment to spiritual ethics means a continuous commitment to growth, including and perhaps especially when we miss the mark in a particular instance or arena. I am honored to be an alumna of the Academy and a student of Rabbi Gottlieb precisely for the ideals expressed in his essay, and in the incredible work he is engaged in to make these principles a reality.

About the Contributors

Rabbi Corinne Copnick, M.R.S. (AJRCA), M.A. (McGill University), C.M. (Canada Medal) is the author of several books, including *A Rabbi at Sea: A Uniquely Spiritual Journey* (2020) and *Cryokid: Drawing a New Map* (2008). She served as Guest Staff Rabbi on select cruises to many parts of the world for five years and as a virtual touring author for the Jewish Book Council Network. In Los Angeles, she currently serves as a *Dayan* and Governor of the Sandra Caplan Community Bet Din and as the founding rabbi (2015) of Beit Kulam, a study group that explores Judaism in terms of contemporary challenges.

Cantor Jonathan L. Friedmann, Ph.D., is Professor of Jewish Music History and Academic Dean of the Master of Jewish Studies Program and Rabbinical School at the Academy for Jewish Religion California, President of the Western States Jewish History Association, Director of the Jewish Museum of the American West, and the author or editor of over two dozen books on Judaism, music, and religion. He also leads Adat Chaverim-Congregation for Humanistic Judaism in Los Angeles.

Joel Gereboff, Ph.D., is Associate Professor of Religious Studies at Arizona State University and Professor of Bible and Jewish History at the Academy for Jewish Religion California. His research and publications focus on early rabbinic Judaism, American Judaism, Jewish ethics, and Judaism and the emotions.

Rabbi Susan Goldberg is Founding Rabbi of Nefesh, a vibrant, *middot*-driven Jewish spiritual community in Los Angeles's multicultural east side. She has a special focus on revitalizing LA's east side Jewish community, and helped to lead the renewal of the historic Wilshire Boulevard Temple in Koreatown, Temple Beth Israel of Highland Park, and served as rabbi-in-residence for East Side Jews, a project of the Silverlake Independent JCC. Previously, she was a dancer, choreographer, and movement analyst, and continues to work as a consultant for art, television, and media projects.

Rabbi Mel Gottlieb, Ph.D., is President Emeritus and former Dean of the Rabbinical School of the Academy for Jewish Religion California, where he also teaches courses in mysticism, biblical commentaries, and Hasidism. He has taught in various academic settings, including Columbia University School of Social Work, Yeshiva University, USC School of Social Work, and Pacifica Graduate Institute, and has served as Hillel Director at MIT and Princeton University, and as rabbi of several congregations in Los Angeles. Rabbi Gottlieb is involved in numerous interfaith and social action initiatives, and has published widely on topics ranging from spiritual psychology to ethical eating.

Rabbi Art Levine, Ph.D., J.D., z"l, divided his time between Jerusalem and Southern California. An attorney and expert witness with a doctorate in history focusing on the insurance industry, Art specialized in workers compensation insurance premium disputes. Teaching the depth and beauty of Jewish traditions and values was his passion and avocation. His writings can be found at www.rabbiartlevine.com.

Rabbi Stan Levy, J.D., is Co-Founder of the Academy for Jewish Religion California, where he is Professor of Spiritual Development, and Founding Rabbi of Congregation B'nai Horin–Children of Freedom. He is also general counsel of a nonprofit organization. Stan and his wife Lynda, a psychotherapist, have three grown sons, three daughters-in-law and seven grandchildren.

Rabbi Nina Perlmutter served Congregation Lev Shalom in Flagstaff, Arizona and teaches as Faculty Emerita at Yavapai Community College, where she headed the Philosophy and Religious Studies Program. She is President of the Chevra Kadisha of Northern Arizona. At Grand Canyon National Park, she is the designated Jewish contact and enjoys leading Jewish programs and performing life-cycle events. Interfaith learning and environmental activism are two of her special priorities.

Rabbi Robin Podolsky serves on the Board of Governors of the Sandra Caplan Community Bet Din, writes at TribeHerald and jewishjournal.com, advises the Jewish Student Union at Occidental College, and serves as writing facilitator and script editor for Queerwise, a spoken word and writing group.

Rabbi Stephen Robbins, Psy.D., a graduate of Hebrew Union College, is Co-Founder and Past-President of Academy for Jewish Religion California, where he teaches mysticism, liturgy, and practical rabbinics. He is also Co-Founder and Co-Spiritual Leader of Congregation N'vay Shalom. Rabbi Robbins holds a Psy.D. from Ryokan College, has a Kabbalistic psycho-spiritual healing practice, and is a member of International Association for Near-Death Studies.

Rabbi Rochelle Robins, ACPE Certified Educator, is Vice President and Academic Dean of the Chaplaincy and Rabbinical Schools at the Academy for Jewish Religion California. She is the Co-Founder and President of Ezzree.com, an online platform for chaplaincy and social services. As a lifelong learner, Rabbi Robins is a Ph.D. candidate in Biblical Studies at Greenwich School of Theology in the United Kingdom. She is exploring reflective and reflexive practices as intrinsic to biblical literature.

Shaiya Rothberg, Ph.D., is a teacher and human rights activist in Jerusalem. He holds a Ph.D. from Hebrew University in Jewish Thought and a B.A. in Jewish Philosophy and Talmud from Bar-Ilan University.

Revital Somekh-Goldreich, M.J.S., is Professor of Biblical Studies and Jewish History at the Academy for Jewish Religion California and the Hebrew University of Jerusalem's Melton School for Adult Jewish Learning. She is also a stained-glass, faith-based artist for public and private sanctuaries, and the author of books describing the shared process of communities and artists to co-create meaning and visual arts installations.

www.ingramcontent.com/pod-product-compliance
Lightning Source LLC
Chambersburg PA
CBHW070548160426
43199CB00014B/2421